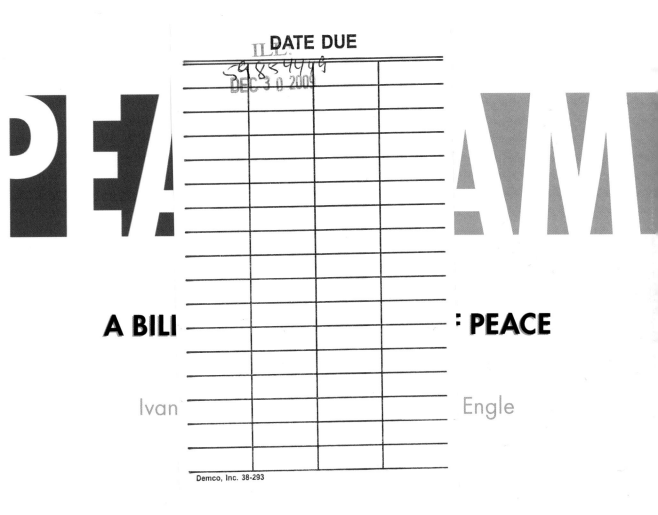

DATE DUE

ILL
39859499
DEC 3 0 2009

PEA   AM

A BILI   PEACE

Ivan   Engle

Demco, Inc. 38-293

PUFFIN BOOKS

Published by the Penguin Group

Penguin Young Readers Group, 345 Hudson Street, New York, New York 10014, U.S.A.

Penguin Group (Canada), 90 Eglinton Avenue East, Suite 700,
Toronto, Ontario, Canada M4P 2Y3 (a division of Pearson Penguin Canada Inc.)

Penguin Books Ltd, 80 Strand, London WC2R 0RL, England

Penguin Ireland, 25 St Stephen's Green, Dublin 2, Ireland
(a division of Penguin Books Ltd)

Penguin Group (Australia), 250 Camberwell Road, Camberwell, Victoria 3124, Australia
(a division of Pearson Australia Group Pty Ltd)

Penguin Books India Pvt Ltd, 11 Community Centre,
Panchsheel Park, New Delhi - 110 017, India

Penguin Group (NZ), 67 Apollo Drive, Rosedale, North Shore 0632,
New Zealand (a division of Pearson New Zealand Ltd.)

Penguin Books (South Africa) (Pty) Ltd, 24 Sturdee Avenue,
Rosebank, Johannesburg 2196, South Africa

Registered Offices: Penguin Books Ltd, 80 Strand, London WC2R 0RL, England

Published by Puffin Books, a division of Penguin Young Readers Group, 2008

1 3 5 7 9 10 8 6 4 2

LIBRARY OF CONGRESS CATALOGING-IN-PUBLICATION DATA
Engle, Dawn Gifford.
PeaceJam : a billion simple acts of peace / by Dawn Gifford Engle
and Ivan Suvanjieff.
p. cm.
ISBN 978-0-14-241234-3
1. Youth and peace. 2. PeaceJam (Organization) I. Suvanjieff, Ivan. II. Title.
JZ5579.E64 2008   303.6'6—dc22   2008024865

Puffin Books ISBN 978-0-14-241234-3

Printed in the United States of America

Book design by Natalie C. Sousa

This book is dedicated to the countless millions of young people around the world who recognize suffering and injustice and who are willing to take action. Their faith is greater than their fear, and it will be through their simple yet compassionate acts of peace that our world will be transformed.

TABLE OF CONTENTS

INTRODUCTION

A Nobel Call to Action

What vision of heartbreaking misery, what manner of dire poverty, what degradation of the human spirit must we all see before we stand up and actually commit to doing something about it?

This book is your personal invitation to become part of one of the most exciting youth movements of our time: **PeaceJam's Global Call to Action**. PeaceJam is bringing young

people together with Nobel Peace Laureates to tackle the toughest issues facing our planet—issues ranging from basic needs, such as access to water, to basic rights, such as social justice and human security. Change starts here, and we are inviting you to become a part of it. How will you answer the call?

For the two of us, it took a very long time to realize that some kind of "call to action" was even possible. We are the children of Detroit factory workers, average and flawed people from very ordinary American backgrounds. There is absolutely nothing fancy or outstanding about either one of us. Dawn financed her college education by waiting tables and applying for scholarships; Ivan worked on the line at Ford Motor Company and played in a rock and roll band. Dawn worked her way up the ladder as a policy maker in Washington, D.C.; Ivan became a writer and an artist and a very accomplished busboy. Somehow we both ended up living in Colorado in the summer of 1993 (call it fate).

The Genesis of PeaceJam

That summer, in the rough-and-tumble barrios of Northwest Denver, gang activity hit a record high. There were so many drive-by shootings, so many young people dying, so many tragic cases of innocents caught in the cross-fire, that the media dubbed it "The Summer of

Violence." Anything can become normal, and, sadly, drive-by shootings were becoming normal in Denver's everyday life.

One day, as he was leaving his apartment to go to work, Ivan saw four young boys carrying guns. "These guys were my neighbors," Ivan explains. "These guys had lived across the street from me for years. I said, 'Hey, come on over here. I want to talk to you for a second.' They came over and said, 'What's up?,' and I said, 'What are you doing with a gun?' They said, 'We have a business.' And then I said, 'Well, what do you need the gun for?' And they said, 'To protect our turf.' 'To have a business, you've gotta be pretty smart,' I said, adding, 'I haven't seen you guys go to school in three years.' I asked them the question, 'Who's the president of the United States?' They said, 'We don't know and we don't care, because the president of the United States doesn't represent our interests.' I said, 'You know, many of us at times don't think the government represents us,' and they seemed shocked to hear this.

"We kept talking. Somehow we tripped over the subject of South Africa. They lit up at this, saying, 'Yeah, Desmond Tutu stood up to the Man, got thrown in jail, never carried a gun and he's this little guy! He's dope! He stared down all the guns and gathered his people, he freed his country!' Now it was my turn to be stunned. I asked, 'You think this man who used non-violent techniques to change his country is really cool?' And they said, 'Yeah, man!' So I said, 'Why don't you be a little more like Desmond Tutu and not carry a gun?'"

That urban encounter proved to be the genesis of PeaceJam. Ivan was on fire—if these guys could get excited about the idea of non-violent change, he thought, anyone could. He had a huge brainstorm—maybe what Denver needed was to put young people together with Nobel Peace Laureates like Tutu, to inspire young people to use their energy to work for positive change. Maybe this was what the world needed. He had never been more excited about an idea in his entire life, but he didn't know where to start. He had no one to turn to until he remembered Dawn Gifford Engle, a new colleague at work. So every day, day after day, Ivan kept talking and talking to Dawn about his great big

idea, driving her crazy, saying, "Nobel Peace Laureates and youth, kids and Nobel Peace Prize winners. It really could work, I know it could!"

"He would not stop talking about it—this went on for *weeks*," Dawn says. "He was so excited about the idea that finally I said, 'You know what, yes, I'll help and actually I kind of *do* know a Nobel Peace Prize winner from my days in Washington, D.C.' So we put in a lot of effort and created a plan for a peace education program based on service learning, then we contacted the chief of staff for the Dalai Lama. And in an amazing turn of events, the chief of staff said yes; come to India and you may present your idea to the Dalai Lama. We had to borrow money from friends to fly to India, but somehow we made it, and the Dalai Lama liked the idea and he said, 'Yes, I will do this.' But he also told us to involve some of his other Nobel Peace Laureate friends so young people could study these friends' lives and get many different perspectives on the world. So we ended up back in Ivan's unheated loft in Denver, cold-calling Nobel Peace Prize Laureates, so incredibly fired up about the idea that we didn't realize just how impossible it really was."

Before long, the PeaceJam program was launched, and to date more than six hundred thousand young people have participated in the United States and in countries around the world. PeaceJammers have created almost 1 million service projects designed to address problems in their own schools and communities. Archbishop Tutu recently commented on the creation of PeaceJam, saying, "It seemed like a crazy idea at the time, but it has gained an incredible kind of momentum, and it has made a huge, huge difference in the lives of many young people by giving them hope and direction." One person really can make a difference, and PeaceJam has proven it repeatedly by empowering young people to become agents of change, all over the world. We have never worked so hard, and we have never been so inspired. There was absolutely nothing that could have prepared us for the incredible global journey we embarked on when we created PeaceJam.

Ten Years Later

Then another amazing thing happened. In September 2006, ten leading Nobel Peace Laureates and more than three thousand young people traveled from all over the world to Denver, Colorado, to celebrate the Tenth Anniversary of the PeaceJam Foundation. The Dalai Lama, Desmond Tutu, Jody Williams, Rigoberta Menchú Tum, President Oscar Arias Sánchez, Máiread Corrigan Maguire, Adolfo Pérez Esquivel, Shirin Ebadi, Betty Williams, and President José Ramos-Horta came together in the largest gathering of Nobel Peace Laureates ever held in US history. Working together, they launched a ten-year Global Call to Action campaign, designed to tackle what they saw as the ten greatest challenges to the survival and well-being of our planet today. Here is what they said:

Today we ask the young leaders of PeaceJam, and the youth of the entire world, to join us in a Global Call to Action. For the next ten years, we invite you to work side by side with us as we address ten fundamental issues. These ten core problems are at the root of much of the suffering in our world, and we believe that young people can mobilize to make a difference in these ten key areas:

Equal Access to Water and Other Natural Resources

The lack of access to clean water and arable land is an increasing problem for many people around the world, and the struggle over these limited resources provides fuel for war and conflict, especially in those parts of the world where the population is exploding. We must work to ensure access to at least the most basic of natural resources—safe drinking water—for all.

Ending Racism and Hate

Racism and the growing divide between rich and poor are endemic, and they are problems that affect all of us. In many countries there are two societies—one that is a reflection of the media image of prosperity, and one that is hidden and full of suffering. This divide is creating a tremendous time bomb, ready to go off at any moment, and making it easier for demagogues to fuel hate and to rule by fear.

Halting the Spread of Global Disease

One of the effects of globalization is the spread of disease. National boundaries no longer mean what they once did. The rapid movement of people and goods means that many "third world" diseases are now threatening the developed world, and have now become the problem of everyone. We must address these diseases together, as one human family.

Eliminating Extreme Poverty

Our world cannot be secure when hundreds of millions of people are forced to exist on less than $1 per day, without access to even the most basic levels of shelter, sustenance, or education. Extreme poverty can be eliminated in our lifetimes, and doing so must remain a fundamental goal.

Social Justice and Human Rights for All

The lack of basic human rights and civil liberties, and the persistence of social injustice over long periods of time with no hope or plan for progress or change, always creates a backlash. To

try to impose a military solution without addressing the fundamental issues at the core of a broken society feeds the growth of paramilitary groups, violence, and lack of security in that society.

Rights for Women and Children, and Their Role as Leaders

It is essential to bring an end to the exploitation of children, and to defend the basic human rights of women around the world. This includes the right to a decent education. The role of women and youth as leaders in local communities, in developing creative solutions to problems, must be fostered and encouraged.

Restoring Earth's Environment

The earth is our mother, and it is wounded. It is out of balance and needs to be healed. Global warming is a reality, and only by a concentrated effort involving individual citizens, civil society, and our government leaders can we address the many causes for the precarious situation we have created for ourselves here on earth.

Controlling the Proliferation of Weapons

It is incomprehensible that the world spends nearly a trillion dollars each year on the weapons of war. We must change our values and our priorities as we enter the twenty-first century. We must end the ever-increasing spiral of expenditures on arms, both nuclear and conventional, which increases the likelihood of violent conflict.

Investing in Human Security

In order to create increased security in this new world in which we live, we must focus on the issue of human security. When we ensure that basic human needs are met, we are creating a more secure world. When we work to establish

social justice, or to stop global warming, or to provide decent education, or to end racism, we are creating a more secure world. The time has come to shift our energy and our resources from military security to a long-term investment in human security.

Breaking the Cycle of Violence

One of the first things we must do is dismantle our own armed consciousness—we are children of a culture of violence, and our minds have been armed. Peace is the grand revolution for which humanity has been waiting. What is required is a profound understanding of the new realities created by our increasingly interconnected and interdependent world.

By the year 2018, with your help, these Nobel Peace Laureates are hoping to inspire One Billion Global Call to Action projects, so that together—the Nobel Peace Laureates, the youth of the world, and everyone else who joins the campaign—we will begin to transform the future of humankind.

This audacious campaign of hope has already begun. In each of the chapters of this book, you will read the incredible story of young people who heard the Global Call to Action in Denver, Colorado, and decided to do something about it.

In Chapter One, The Dalai Lama guides Loden, an eighteen-year-old refugee from Tibet, as he wrestles with the growing water crisis in India, and tries to provide equal access to safe drinking water by building a water pipeline for 144 destitute families who live at the edge of town.

In Chapter Two, Archbishop Desmond Tutu inspires and mentors Scrooge, a twenty-four-year-old spoken-word poet and musician from the township of Khayelitsha, as he works to help his community overcome the stigma of HIV/AIDS by creating a townshipwide Get Tested for HIV/AIDS Now campaign.

In Chapter Three, Máiread Corrigan Maguire counsels fourteen-year-old Libby from England, who is trying to overcome her own fears as she reaches out to Muslim people in her community and attempts to understand the injustices they have faced since 9/11, and to work for greater protection of civil liberties for everyone.

In Chapter Four, José Ramos-Horta works side by side with twenty-one-year-old Vidal, who is attempting to lift the income of his people to more than $1 per day by cultivating the forests that were clear-cut during the thirty-year Indonesian military occupation of East Timor, and is starting a Youth Conservation Corps to begin planting trees both for firewood and for export.

In Chapter Five, Oscar Arias Sánchez meets with sixteen-year-old Maria, who is frightened by the rush of gangs and small arms into her home town of San José, Costa Rica, and who wants to start a campaign to reduce the violence by getting people to sign a pledge disavowing the use of weapons, both on a local and international level.

In **Chapter Six**, Rigoberta Menchú Tum works to educate seventeen-year-old Fernando about five hundred years of discrimination against the Mayan people in Guatemala. Fernando will then use what he's learned as he stands up to the widespread racism expressed on a daily basis by his friends and neighbors in his own hometown, as Rigoberta Menchú Tum launches a historic race for the presidency of Guatemala.

In **Chapter Seven**, Betty Williams encourages twelve-year-old Sonny Ray, a Mexican American student in Colorado, as he mobilizes his school and lobbies the politicians of his state, encouraging them to deal with global warming on a local level by legislating compliance with the Kyoto Protocols throughout the state of Colorado.

In **Chapter Eight**, Shirin Ebadi mentors nineteen-year-old Mymoena, a young Muslim who wants to teach girls throughout her country to stand up for their own rights; Mymoena also wants to mobilize international support for a petition drive for the rights of the women of Iran.

In **Chapter Nine**, Adolfo Pérez Esquivel coaches eighteen-year-old Fito, a former Argentine street kid, who intends to use the training and the skills he's learned as a student at Adolfo's Peace Village to break the cycle of violence and improve the lives of the families in his shantytown on the outskirts of Buenos Aires.

In **Chapter Ten**, Jody Williams coaches twenty-two-year-old Jessica as she struggles to get her state—Missouri—to disinvest from Sudan, and to redirect that money into the bankrupt Missouri education system, where a series of struggling schools face takeover by the federal government under the Leave No Child Behind Act.

In **Chapter Eleven**, the words of Aung San Suu Kyi inspire twenty-six-year-old Charm Tong to journey from a Thai refugee camp—where she and her sister have fled to escape the Burmese army—to England's Parliament, where she decides to testify on behalf of her people and Aung San Suu Kyi, knowing that this testimony may mean that she can never return to her homeland again.

We're inviting you to become a part of this movement for change. The courageous young people in this book are leading the way, showing you how to begin, in five simple steps:

Step 1: Pick Your Issue

First, pick your issue. Find one of the Global Calls to Action that you connect with personally. What are the different pieces of that global call? What things interest you? What things relate to you? Then put your understanding of the issue in your own words. What are you really trying to say?

Step 2: Check Out the Facts

Once you've picked your issue, check out the facts. Take some time to do the research and determine how big the problem really is. Do a little investigating, and focus on the root causes of the problem. There's information to use all around you. You can do a search on the computer, read a newspaper, or use data that any group has already collected about this issue. Have fun with it, and remember to get different perspectives. Don't get all your information from the same place. You want a well-rounded and balanced look at the problem.

Step 3: Dig Deeper

Now it's time to dig deeper. We want you to look, listen, talk to people in your community, and get a feel for how this issue is really impacting things around you. It can be as simple as taking a walk in your own neighborhood. Who is affected by this problem, and how do they feel about it? It's time to get out there and use your eyes, ears, hands, and voice to check out all of the angles.

Step 4: Make a Plan for Action

By now you should know quite a bit about your issue. It's time to create a project. What are some creative solutions to the problem that haven't yet been tried? Remember to take into account the time and resources you have. Then write up your plan—you can use the Global Call to Action project form at the end of this introduction to help you out. Who will the project help? What will it actually accomplish? How will it be done? When will it be finished? And where will it take place? For innovative ideas and inspiration, visit the Global Call to Action Web site (www.globalcalltoaction.org) or the main PeaceJam Web site (www.peacejam.org).

Step 5: Do It!

Now it's time to get out there and do it! Here are a few things to keep in mind:

• Keep notes on what you're doing—that way, you can share your efforts with others. And don't be afraid to ask other people to get involved.

• Work side by side with the people affected by the issue to carry out your project and achieve your goal. You don't want to do projects *to* them, you want to do projects *with* them.

• Finally, remember to do your very best to address the root causes of the problem.

No matter how difficult or complicated the issue is, you *can* find a way to tackle it. No matter how old you are or where you live, there *is* a way to do something.

The world is changing. How is that change going to affect you? Are you going to be part of the problem, or part of the solution? Every great social movement throughout human history has started with the actions of just a few committed souls. Those actions started to add together, drop by drop. Soon enough, those drops formed an ocean, and before long that ocean became a tidal wave, and things changed. The time to begin is now. The Global Call to Action: together, we can change the world. And change starts here.

Ivan Suvanjieff and Dawn Gifford Engle
February 2008

Global Call to Action Project Plan

School/Organization:	PeaceJam Group Name:
Adult Advisor:	Phone: Email:

Global Call to Action You Will Address:

Summary of Research & Investigations:
1. Observe for evidence of the issue.

2. Interview/survey people about the issue.

3. Use data that relate to the issue (e.g., city & national data on water issues).

4. Read the newspapers & watch the news for current information on this issue.

Problem Statement: (Specific issue you will address within the Global Call & at what level)

Root Causes of Problem:

Project Ideas: (Brainstorm some of the projects that can address the root cause of the problem.)

Your Global Call to Action Project : Your Answer to the Call
1. What did your group decide to do?

2. How did your group decide on this project?

3. What are the goals of your project—both service goals (what you hope to accomplish) & learning goals (what you hope to learn)?

4. What is your plan for implementation/how do you plan to accomplish this project?

5. Is this a long-term project? If so, how do you plan to sustain your work?

6. How do you think this project will make a difference?

What About Our Neighbors?

The Dalai Lama & Loden—Equal Access to Water

We are in a new world because of population growth, the crisis of ecology, and the water crisis; all of these things. I think it is a new world.
—The Dalai Lama

Experiencing India

India is an incredible place where almost anything can happen. When you arrive at the Indira Gandhi International Airport, you can't help but be completely awed by the sights, sounds and smells of the teeming mass of humanity. "Overwhelming" only begins to describe the assault on your senses. A raggedy group of children come running up shouting, "Rupees, sir! Rupees!" while desperately grabbing at your sleeves. You feel frightened, confused, excited, and bewildered, all at once . . . then you get distracted by all the motor vehicles honking their horns and the smoke of wood fires permeating your olfactory sense, only to be startled once again by the sight of a stunningly beautiful Indian woman carrying an impossibly huge load of firewood atop her head. Then a cow almost crashes into you while a jet roars overhead and yet another throng of beggars charges at you, yelling . . . and all that was in just the first five seconds after stepping out of the door of the airport. It's as if ten centuries of time is played fast-forward in one breath.

The next ten-centuries-in-one-breath finds you piled into a three-wheeled motorcycle-type contraption zig-zagging through unbelievably crowded streets. We call them "rickshaws of death." Once you adjust, you look to your side and see a family of four all piled onto a tiny motor scooter, a one-year-old in dad's lap as he drives, mom in a brilliant scarlet sari behind him clutching a squirming three-year-old. You begin to shake your head, as

if you are not really seeing this, when a huge truck careens in front of you. You instinctively duck, and the driver of the rickshaw swerves to avoid a withered old man wandering aimlessly through the traffic. That image is immediately replaced by an expensive BMW. The driver is a wealthy man, if you judge by his vehicle, and you start to wonder whether he made his money in the technology boom zooming across this country when your driver screeches to a halt in front of the door to your hotel.

You are greeted by a Sikh dressed in blinding white, his tunic and trousers neatly pressed. When he smiles, you notice he has the whitest, straightest set of teeth you've ever seen, and all you can think is: Where am I?

You're in Delhi, India, in a land of contradictions so abundant and vast it is basically incomprehensible. The chaos of Delhi is encapsulated in the Hindi word *dilliwallah*, which, roughly translated, means "people living in chaos but managing to make it through." And they do! Yes, the poverty is alarming, and the contrasting abundant wealth is mashed up cheek by jowl with it. But there is also a vibrant and burgeoning middle class, and a tremendous sense of hope. There is a palpable, upbeat vibe in Delhi now, as India continues to emerge as a real power in the world. And India's population continues to grow.

Yes, it is the largest English-speaking country in the world, but no, you don't always know exactly what they're saying. The English language here has a different life than the one it has in either the United Kingdom or the United States. When you're finally checked into your hotel room, you flip on the television. The images on the screen are familiar somehow, but the people are speaking Hindi one moment and English the next. Before you know it, you're looking at some manner of elephant with more limbs than you remember an elephant having. The animal is floating through the sky toward a young couple dancing on a cloud of diamonds and gold.

You rub your eyes, look into the screen again, then see the couple in a lover's embrace, kissing behind two flowers as the elephant-creature smiles benignly over them. Meet Ganesha—the Hindu God of Good Fortune and Wisdom, the Remover of Obstacles. Ganesha is seen everywhere in India, painted on walls, sitting as statuettes on the dashboards of taxis. And boy, do the taxi drivers ever rely on good ol' Ganesha!

What you're seeing on the screen is a form of cinema—called "Bollywood"—that is peculiar to India. The basic plot of a Bollywood film may go something like this: lower-caste boy meets upper-caste girl. Despite the differences in their castes, they fall in love. But this is a forbidden love. The girl's parents prohibit her from seeing the boy, so they meet secretly. Soon, however, they are found out. The girl's parents send her to live with her rich uncle and then hire some bad guys to kill the boy. Drama ensues. Finally, Ganesha removes the obstacles in the couple's path, they get married, and they live happily ever after.

After watching part of a Bollywood film, you decide to take your first shower in India. You turn on the water spigot, and a steady stream gushes out from the gleaming showerhead. Don't get a single drop in your mouth! India has different microbes and germs than the ones you are used to, and some people who've merely brushed their teeth with the tap water here became quite ill. But at least they had access to water. Lack of access to clean drinking water is already affecting the lives of tens of millions of Indians. Latest U.N. estimates say that, by the year 2025, 500 million Indians will have no access to drinking water. There is a huge water crisis on the way—India's exploding population and the effects of global warming are about to collide.

Arriving in Dharamsala

Once you get to Dharamsala, which is nestled in the foothills of the Himalayan Mountains, there is indeed a there there. The narrow avenues of Dharamsala teem with brightly hued shops hawking Tibetan items, high-quality pashmina shawls, and T-shirts with the most befuddling slogans. The taxis are bleating like mad sheep, and people are jostling one another as they run their daily errands. Many, many Tibetans are there, too, going about their daily lives.

Dharamsala is divided into two sections—Upper and Lower. Upper Dharamsala is where the 14th Dalai Lama makes his residence, and it is also the seat of the Tibetan Government in Exile. Since the Dalai Lama fled Tibet in 1959, more than 80,000 of his fellow countrymen have followed, and many of them have passed through Dharamsala. The Tibetan refugee community is one of the most successful in the world. Tibetans have been guests in India for almost fifty years—they've dug in, and they're thriving.

Meet Loden and His Friends

We head to Upper Dharamsala, to the Tibetan Children's Village (TCV), one of a series of schools inspired by the Dalai Lama's desire to educate every young Tibetan person he can possibly reach. We are greeted by Tenzin Loden, an eighteen-year-old student at TCV; he's a shy and thoughtful young man who stands nearly six feet tall. He's excited to see us, waving us down and dragging us to the classroom where the rest of his friends are waiting. We meet two other Tibetan boys—Wangyal, a sly jokester, and Desel, who's confident and well spoken—and four Tibetan girls—Dechen, petite and brainy; Palzom, quiet and deep; Tsundu, funny and forceful; and Dolma, innocent and sweet. All of them are going to help with the project.

Loden speaks: "Everywhere the Dalai Lama goes, he is always talking about the water issue. He says that the weather and the climate are changing. It is becoming a real crisis."

Palzom adds, "We met with an environmental leader here in Dharamsala, and she told us that there is a special pain in her heart, and in the Tibetan heart. Tibet has always been called the water tower, and water from the Tibetan plateau gives drinking water to so many countries: India, China, Bangladesh, Vietnam, Cambodia, Bhutan. Now she says that we will no longer be able to freely supply this water. I was shocked."

"We have decided to help some people who have no access to water at all," Tsundu adds.

Desel says, "They really need help. They live in the Churan Ghat slum, nearby."

Wangyal agrees. "The people there really need the water, and they are very supportive."

Loden sums it up. "At this stage we are very much clear about what we are to do."

We say good-bye, and Loden walks us back to the taxi stand. He tells us that he has decided to step forward and act as the leader of this project, because "a leader faces the most challenge, and there is a special joy in facing those challenges; you learn so many new things."

Overwhelmed—once again—we arrange to meet the next morning, so that they can take us to meet the people who live in Churan Ghat. Loden's courage and leadership skills are about to be put to a very real test.

A Water Crisis in Dharamsala

In India, the heartbreakingly beautiful grandeur of the Himalayan Mountains is pitted against some of the most abject poverty in the world. Animals run amuck, unfettered, unattended. A sour smell wafts up from the Churan Ghat slum—the stench of illness caused by the lack of clean water and poor waste disposal, the tragedy of the lives of the impoverished. Loden and his friends have never seen anything quite like it. It is a squatters' camp populated by economic refugees from throughout the country, completely devoid of government services or support. Detritus is strewn everywhere. What prayer do you offer up in this situation? Sister Action jumps up to the rescue, of course. Today these seven Tibetan PeaceJammers are about to go to work.

The young people walk us into the camp and introduce us to one of the elders, Kalu Ram. "There are almost two hundred families here. He says that they do not have even a single water system," Loden translates. "There is a building up there, where they have to go to get water. But the market people have shut off the water. So now the children have to walk very far away to get the water, and often while crossing the roads they get struck by trucks. So he is saying that if there is some way we could help, they would be most grateful."

There's only one water tap in the vicinity of the camp, and it yields the most precious substance on Earth for only two hours each day. Women and children line up for hours beforehand with cans, old pots, and other vessels. Since children have to get water for their families, they obviously aren't going to school. They're not getting an education, not learning anything that may help lift them up from the degradation in which they exist. Waiting for water is a vicious but necessary cycle in lives of these economic refugees. So the first plan of action here, Loden explains, is to run a water line into the camp.

Guidance from the Dalai Lama

By April 2, 2007, Loden and his friends are frantically scrambling to prepare a presentation on their project for the Dalai Lama. They are so nervous they are shaking. Tibetans consider His Holiness the 14th Dalai Lama to be like a god, so to meet him even once is something most Tibetans can only dream about. They dress in their very best clothes, review their presentation one last time, and then start the long walk up the hill to their audience with the Dalai Lama.

Tentatively, the young Tibetans enter the room at the palace, though it's not exactly what you'd expect a palace to be. It's rather ordinary, befitting a humble monk, which is all the Dalai Lama says he is. Yet this incredible example of humanity is much, much more—he's the real deal. He begins his handshake with a long look into your eyes, and there is a certain feeling you

get when he does this. It's like he's looking into the essence of your entire being. He sees who you really are. When he warmly grasps your hand, his eyes locked onto yours, you feel like you are four years old again—a pure human being not yet bent out of shape by life's pliers. He makes you feel that anything is possible.

"We chose an Indian slum called Churan Ghat for our Global Call to Action project," Loden begins. Loden and the rest of the Tibetans raise their heads to glance shyly at the Dalai Lama.

"Oh, I see . . . nearby," the Dalai Lama replies, rocking slightly in his chair.

"They do not have any water," Loden explains. "At first our plan was to provide them with clean drinking water, since there are a lot of waterborne diseases. But we found that this place does not have water fit for any use.

"Our plan has four objectives:

"First, to provide daily access to drinking water equal to what the shopkeepers get—two hours of running water each day.

"Second, to educate them on the prevention of waterborne diseases.

"Third, to give them water containers to store water for later use.

"The fourth one is this—the children will have more time to be educated because they will not have to spend hours carrying water to the camp. We have some volunteers who will come to teach them English, so we are collecting donated children's books for them."

"They are transient? What are these tents?" the Dalai Lama asks. He's looking at the plan the young Tibetans have placed before him on a low table.

"They are very poor, so they live in plastic tents," Loden says. "These people are not locals. About twenty years ago they came from Rajasthan, Punjab, Maharashtra to look for work, thinking that this would be best for them."

The Dalai Lama looks up at the students. "This is very good, don't you think? *Very* good. At its essence, water is a necessity for life," the Dalai Lama says. "And the recipients of your help are these poor people. This is extremely good work and a great service to society. And from a religious standpoint, to help and be compassionate to those who have nothing is one of the most important teachings of the Buddha. To give to them without expecting anything in return is very admirable. That is a very good thing."

The Dalai Lama looks at each of the kids again and says, "The pride and determination to know that you can do it is very important. Otherwise, you will just sit back, thinking, Someone else will do the work. That is a weakness in Tibetan society. It is the same with Indian society. These Indians who are so poor, they just sit back and hope that this suffering will go away. And that is very sad."

Trembling, the students bow and leave the room. Wangyal says he is "on top of the world!" And Loden says, "Now I am more excited than ever before. This gives us more determination and extra energy to carry out our project." Laughing and crying, they float down the hill, prepared in their hearts to meet the challenges that lay ahead. But it's an uphill struggle they face.

The Project Begins

India's bureaucracy is world famous. If you have ever experienced it, you feel like you are in a crazy Monty Python skit, but it's for real—and not funny at all.

Loden is worried. "We got a plumber, but he said that he would not work with us if we didn't get official permission from the government to set up the pipelines. So my big question is, If we don't get the permission by tomorrow, then what do we do?"

As you get to know Dharamsala you realize that there are leaking water pipes everywhere. One environmental expert estimates that about 50 percent of their precious water is lost to leaking water lines each day. Arriving at the water commission's office in Dharamsala, you see two employees playing badminton. Finding them hard at work batting the birdie around on company time does not exactly create a feeling of hopefulness in Loden.

This initial meeting with the Dharamsala water commissioner, Mr. Rajeev Kumar, does not go well. The commissioner impatiently brushes aside any comments or ideas the kids have. Sideways glances are exchanged among the Tibetans, as if to say, This isn't going to work.

They return home in a frustrated heap.

"I thought that we were not given quite the proper attention," Loden explains.

But the Dalai Lama told these young activists that determination is the key to success. So they are going to give it one more try.

Another meeting takes place. "Churan Ghat? They have illegally acquired that land. We are not in a position to provide them with water," says Mr. Kumar.

Loden insists and keeps the discussion going. Finally, there is a breakthrough, and Mr. Kumar agrees to help the young people unofficially. Perhaps Ganesha alighted on Mr. Kumar's shoulder and whispered in his ear.

One roadblock has been removed. But there are still so many things to figure out in the Land of Suchness, as India is sometimes called.

"First, we have to figure out where to buy the pipeline," Loden says.

Loden and his friends head out to locate and secure 250 meters (850 feet) of pipe. Going from shop to shop, they're unable to locate the items necessary to guarantee the project's success. They return home frustrated once more—their heads, hearts, and feet aching.

"At Kangra, they are saying there is a better shop in Dharamsala. In Dharamsala, locals told us to go to Kangra." Wangyal shakes his head. "So we are confused." That's putting it mildly. These young people are bewildered and upset, and it shows.

As the group takes off their shoes, sipping water in the sticky heat of the Dharamsala dusk, they analyze and plan out their next course of action. "At this stage, the project seems quite impossible," Loden admits in a weary voice. Then he takes a deep and hopeful breath and says, "But let's see."

The next day, while the boys search for the pipes, the girls return to Churan Ghat to count the number of households so that they can purchase a water container for each family.

"We need one hundred forty-four containers. Where are we going to find them?" Loden asks. In the Land of Muchness—that's the United States—you simply go to the hardware store or order them online. Procuring the simplest items can be a much tougher challenge in a place like India.

The following day they secure a source for the pipes. But the water containers prove to be a much bigger problem. They speak to many shopkeepers before they identify a supplier in southern India. A collective groan erupts from the Tibetans. The water containers will have to be shipped across the entire length of India, and it will take weeks for them to arrive.

Of course, nothing in this life is free, and the group must figure out a way to raise money to pay for all these items. They are in luck: There's a dialogue between leading Western scientists and the Dalai Lama in Dharamsala this week. They are able to talk to several of the scientists at a local hotel, and in doing so they raise enough funding to pay for the pipes, the plumber, the hardware, and the containers.

They get some more good news—Tibetan Children's Village will donate books for use in teaching English to the children of Churan Ghat.

They then head off to try to find a doctor to teach them about waterborne diseases. But at the local hospital, there are no doctors to be found—it's a Hindu holiday, and they're all on leave.

They finally find a doctor at a Tibetan clinic who gives them hours of his time. He fully understands the nature of tainted water and the effects it can have on the human body. "These people are susceptible to every sort of disease, because of the lack of clean drinking water and proper hygiene. Truly, these people are most deserving of your help," the doctor says. The students listen and learn, and they are eager to share this information.

"We are going to do two presentations to the people about waterborne diseases so that they will know how to keep their water clean," Desel explains, a big smile of satisfaction on his face.

The Big Day Arrives

Finally, after many weeks of worry and delays, the water containers are about to arrive, unassembled. And on the pipeline, all systems are go—everything is in place, and all of the youth are eager to deliver on their promise.

At dusk, the water containers show up via truck driven by an exasperated driver. "Bad traffic," he says. The young Tibetans all load a dozen or so of the vessels on their backs and lug them over to the main meeting tent in Churan Ghat. Many trips are made, and finally the unassembled containers are all in one place.

There's no electricity in the camp, and now it's dark. Flashlights in hand, the Tibetan kids go tent to tent, finally locating someone with a gas lamp they can borrow. The lamp is lit, and you can see the faces of the Tibetans and the children of Churan Ghat glowing with hope.

"We took all of the containers to a tent and started to put the taps onto them," Palzom explains. "The boys were going house to house distributing the buckets, but still some people came to us, saying, 'We still did not get the bucket,' or 'I've told you that I live here,' or 'Me, you did not give a bucket to me.' "

With 144 containers to assemble and distribute, the young people continue working, long into the Indian night.

"They were showing us very aggressive faces, and that was very difficult," Dechen adds. When you have nothing, a simple plastic water container can become a very important thing.

"But at the end, I think that we did quite wonderful," Loden replies, "because at the end, when we were all done, we could hear the words 'thank you.'"

Though they are tired, Loden and his friends return to the camp to start construction of the pipeline. It is a daunting task, as they have to dig through the local paved road in order to lay the pipeline down. And this has to be done at night, when there is less traffic.

Fifteen hours later, the pipeline is almost complete. The residents of the camp start to gather around, waiting in anticipation. The plumber, sweating now, uses his wrench to bang the last pieces of the pipeline into place. He turns the tap, and water comes out. Two small children come to the tap with their father to gather the water in their bucket, and the little ones laugh and splash it about. Loden and his friends sit and watch, almost too exhausted to enjoy this scene, but then they start smiling. They can't help it.

But the project is not yet complete. The water needs to be tested. Dechen and Tsundu have a water-quality kit in hand, and they crouch down to a bucket that's been filled from the new taps. "We tested the water for bacteria, and it was negative. There are no pesticides, and chlorine is also present, so the result is a good one," Dechen says happily.

"All in all, we can say that we have been successful in providing clean drinking water for one hundred forty-four households," Loden says, relieved and smiling. "So it is good."

Final Moments of Grace

Back in the Dalai Lama's palace, Loden sits quietly, reflecting on the experience. "When I told some of my other friends that we were going to build this pipeline, they laughed at me. They said, 'Nice dream.' They said, 'This is India—you can't make something like that happen.' They said it sounded like a Bollywood movie, where there is something impossible and then Ganesha saves the day." He laughs.

The Dalai Lama laughs, too, then asks the kids to describe what they accomplished in Churan Ghat.

"Later on, it would be good to make a report on your project," the Dalai Lama says. "And then make a booklet and distribute it to the other Tibetan settlements to set a good example."

Loden asks quietly, "For the success of our project, please give us a blessing."

"Of course I will pray for it," the Dalai Lama replies. "It is a very good example for Tibetans. It is very good work."

As Loden and his friends receive white kata scarves of blessing from the Dalai Lama, they bow their heads in reverence. It is a dream come true.

India, where anything—absolutely anything—can happen.

This is the Global Call to Action, friends; dig in and get something meaningful accomplished. It is as simple as building a water pipeline for some of your impoverished neighbors.

laureate
The Dalai Lama

In 1935, a little boy named Lhamo Thondup (which means "wish-fulfilling goddess") was born to a peasant family in Takstar, a small village in Tibet, located high in the Himalayan Mountains. Lhamo had one older sister and three older brothers. His family had a small farm where they grew barley and potatoes and kept horses, yaks, sheep, goats, and chicken. The family lived in a typical Tibetan house made primarily of stone and mud.

Lhamo grew up as an ordinary Tibetan boy. He enjoyed ice-skating in the winter and helping his mother around the farm. He would also often make believe that he was going on a trip to Lhasa, the capital city of Tibet, which was

a several-months-long journey from his small town of Takstar. His parents thought this was very strange because they were not sure how Lhamo even knew that Lhasa existed.

One day when Lhamo was three years old, several monks and men from the Tibetan government visited Takstar, looking for the reincarnation of the 13th Dalai Lama. Led by their visions and dreams, the monks searched for a home with turquoise gutters—just like Lhamo's house. After spending time with Lhamo they suspected that he was the reincarnation of the 13th Dalai Lama because of his behavior and some of the things he said. To confirm their hopes, the monks tested Lhama by setting several pairs of objects such as eyeglasses, canes, and prayer beads in front of him. One of each of the objects had belonged to the 13th Dalai Lama, and the others had not. Lhamo chose the objects that had belonged to the previous Dalai Lama, convincing the monks that they had found the next one. Lhamo was going to Lhasa after all.

Lhamo and his family packed their bags and embarked on a three-month trek to Lhasa where Lhamo began his studies with other monks in the Potala Palace. He learned about Tibetan art, culture, logic, and meditation in preparation for becoming the official leader of Tibet on his twenty-first birthday. Lhamo was taught to strive for compassion and sympathy for all living beings, without exception.

In October 1950, when the Dalai Lama was just fifteen years old, 80,000 soldiers from China invaded Tibet. Thousands of Tibetan people were killed because the Tibetan army was no match for the Chinese military. Th people of Tibet needed a strong leader to stand up to the Chinese and to bring peace back to their country. So at the age of fifteen, the Dalai Lama found himself the spiritual and political leader of more than 6 million Tibetans.

The Dalai Lama worked for nine long years to find a peaceful solution to the conflict with China, even daring to travel to Peking under Chinese military escort to meet with Chairman Mao Tse-tung. On March 10, 1959, thousands of Tibetans demonstrated in Lhasa, resisting the Chinese occupation and demanding an independent Tibet. The Chinese soldiers retaliated against the protestors, and thousands of Tibetans were killed. With the situation in Tibet deteriorating, the Dalai Lama knew he had to flee his country. On March 17, 1959, he dressed as a soldier and snuck out of his palace.

The Dalai Lama traveled for many weeks over the Himalayas—the highest mountains in the world—into India. His parents and siblings went with him, as did many of his teachers and other Tibetan government officials. They made their way to Dharamsala, now known as "Little Lhasa," where they set up the Tibetan Government in Exile. The Dalai Lama continued to nonviolently fight for the rights of his people. He appealed to the United Nations on several occasions, and the United Nations General Assembly adopted three resolutions—in 1959, 1961, and 1965—calling on China to respect the human rights of Tibetans and to honor their independence.

The Dalai Lama started more than fifty large settlements for Tibetan refugees in India and created a Tibetan school system to teach refugee children Tibetan language, history, religion, and culture. He founded several cultural institutes to preserve two thousand years of Tibet's arts and sciences and helped reestablish more than two hundred monasteries to keep Buddhist teachings alive.

The Dalai Lama often says, "I am just a simple Buddhist monk—no more, no less." Living in a small cottage in Dharamsala, he rises at four each morning to meditate, attend meetings, host private audiences, and conduct religious teachings and ceremonies. He concludes each day with more prayers. The Dalai Lama has worked hard over the years to bring compassion and loving kindness to the world—even to the Chinese government after all it has done to his people. For him, this is the only way to bring peace to Tibet and to the world.

In 1989, on the thirtieth anniversary of China's invasion of Tibet, the Dalai Lama was awarded the Nobel Peace Prize for his efforts to find a nonviolent solution to the conflict with China. He continues to travel the globe, speaking to world leaders about a nonviolent solution to the Chinese occupation of Tibet. He also speaks with ordinary people around the world, spreading his message of peace and urging all people to live their lives with compassion for others and the earth. The Dalai Lama believes that "in today's world every nation is heavily interdependent, interconnected. Under these circumstances, destroying your enemy—your neighbor—means destroying yourself in the long run. You need your neighbor."

voices of peace

HELPING OUR NEIGHBORS

José Ramos-Horta

"I would say that the fight against poverty anywhere in the world is a moral duty of any of us as human beings. If we see someone, even a stranger, in the street who is hungry, who is shivering because of cold, I think we as human beings should help immediately. The fight against extreme poverty requires leadership at every level. You have to be compassionate."

Rigoberta Menchú Tum

"It is good to know about hunger on Earth, and drought; the sacred liquid is vanishing everywhere. But let's not ignore what we hear from other people. There is a desperate cry from many people, a great human outcry, and we must listen to these people and share their pain. It is said that the more we share the pain of others, the more we are able to be a light to others."

Betty Williams

"If you want to change the world, you have to do it one person at a time. Even in the work that we do; it's amazing what happens because, in the beginning, it's all over the place, and, at the end, it's totally interconnected. I can't say to others what they should be doing unless I'm doing it myself. Peace begins with me, and if everybody knew that, then we could change things within years."

The Dalai Lama

"In order to have a happier humanity and lessen the gap between rich and poor, we must no longer have a narrow-minded, self-centered attitude. We must respect others and think seriously about others' welfare with a sense of brother- and sisterhood. I think society should cultivate a spirit of dialogue, the spirit of reconciliation on the basis of recognizing that others are also a part of yourself."

Ten Things You Can Do to Help

Secure Equal Access to Water and Other Natural Resources

(1) Adopt Your Watershed

Watersheds are streams, bays, wetlands, lakes, and other bodies of water that supply the wildlife habitats, drinking water, and recreation that sustain life. Unfortunately, many are becoming very polluted. Take action by adopting your watershed. Test the water for contamination, report to your local government agencies, clean up trash, and do community campaigns to make sure that it is being protected.

(2) Provide Clean Water for Schools

Many aging schools throughout the world have lead pipes that are poisoning children! Lead poisoning can cause brain damage and lead to developmental disabilities or death. Work with your local schools to test the water in the drinking fountains. Test for lead content and bacteria. If the lead content is high, petition the school board for new pipes. If the bacteria level is high, help the school find better ways to filter the water.

(3) Walk a Mile in Their Shoes

Over 1 billion people do not have access to clean water, and those who do often have to walk several miles per day to bring water back for their families. Help communities to get clean water by fixing or updating existing pipes and educating people about waterborne diseases and how to avoid them.

(4) Seek a Simple Solution

Each year 1.4 million children die from unsafe drinking water. Even if families have access to safe water, it is sometimes stored unsafely in their homes, where it is then contaminated with bacteria. Help communities get plastic or clean metal storage containers with narrow lids and spigots to prevent contamination. Provide clean-water education to community members and disinfectant/purification kits for later use.

(5) Consider Clay Pot Water Filters

A handful of clay, coffee grounds, and some cow manure are all the ingredients you need to bring clean drinking water to many people! Small clay pots—made from combining the clay, coffee grounds, and manure—are fired in an open fire. Water then is filtered through the pores of the pot, which removes about 98 percent of the bacteria. Teach communities how to make these filters to use themselves, and to sell to others in order to bring income to their families.

(6) Investigate Privatization Policy

Private companies are making bids to privatize water and make a profit off it in every country in the world, including the United States. Investigate these companies and check out their track records. Educate the public about choices in water services, and help communities get their voices heard through petitions or letter-writing campaigns.

(7) Fight Water Wars

Dams and man-made canals may provide water and power to some people, but what about those downstream? Work with government officials who are making water-policy plans to ensure that poor communities are not being overlooked, and propose your own alternative plans that work for the benefit of all who will be impacted.

(8) Conserve

Fresh drinking water is a renewable resource that is quickly becoming nonrenewable. Demand for fresh water is starting to exceed the supply, and we need to be mindful of how we use what we've got. Ensure that your home is water efficient by installing low-flow showerheads and toilets, storing water in the refrigerator so that you don't let the water run from the tap to get cold, and making sure that you don't have dripping pipes. Then educate your school and your community about how to do the same.

(9) Keep It Clean

Dumping of toxic chemicals such as paint, soap from washing cars, and motor oil into storm drains dramatically affects the quality of drinking water in many developed and undeveloped countries. Label storm drains in your communities with NO DUMPING signs, and help communities build or maintain water-treatment centers.

(10) Reuse and Recycle

Water is used in the production process of almost everything we consume. Reuse clean water in your home for things like watering plants, but also recycle and reuse other items—such as paper, plastic, metals, and food waste—to save the water that is used in making these products.

How Can I Save My Friends?

Desmond Tutu, Scrooge & Patience—
The Spread of Global Disease

*Six thousand people die every day of AIDS—six hundred to nine hundred
every day in South Africa. Statistics. Who said it was just statistics?
It is somebody's mummy; it is somebody's daddy; it is somebody's son;
it is somebody's child. It could . . . yes, it could be yours.*
—Desmond Tutu

Experiencing South Africa

South Africa is one of the most beautiful places on Earth. The country is host to breathtaking mountains, pristine white-sand beaches, rolling green valleys, and an explosion of flora that can be found only here. For thousands of years, people have managed to thrive and flourish here, and as you wander around South Africa, you are always agog at the beauty and magnificent nature that surrounds you.

So it is always good to be back in South Africa again. Arriving in Cape Town from London, you are jetlagged, smelly, and worse from the fourteen-hour flight. As you descend from the plane to the tarmac, you breathe deeply, taking in the salty fresh air. You are very close now to the fabled Cape of Good Hope, which is surrounded by some of the most treacherous waters on Earth. You're at the bottommost apex of Africa now, as close as you can get to Antarctica.

Seagoing vessels of all nationalities and descriptions port here in Cape Town. International trade is brisk—it is called the "Mother City," and the city's motto is: One City Many Cultures.

This hits you immediately when you view the area's vast and differing races, colors, and cultures commingling all around you.

South Africans are amazing people. They didn't lose hope during the reign of apartheid; they dug deep into their souls to find the courage to stand up against a big and ugly bully. They rose up from the ashes to take back their own identity and country. This is a place where miracles happen, where people have had the strength to forgive, where children are full of hope for a better life to come.

None of the above is lost on one of South Africa's preeminent human rights activists: Archbishop Desmond Tutu. Now well into his seventies, the Arch—as he is called by friends— marshaled the forces for good and for change. The struggle against apartheid was a concerted effort of millions, battling uphill every day. The Arch led nonviolent protests, delivered fiery speeches, and urged his people to employ peaceful actions and then to forgive.

The Arch is diminutive in physical stature but morally twelve feet tall, a giant of a man. His powerful shoulders became that way from carrying so many of his country's burdens. His twinkling brown eyes shine like diamonds when, with his left hand he signs an autograph for you that reads: "You're actually a nice guy! —Desmond Tutu." You discover that the Arch has a wonderful sense of humor.

The Arch has spent years questioning the South African government's policies on HIV/AIDS. He finds the concept of treating HIV with lemon juice and garlic far beyond ludicrous. He has literally screamed at his government about it all, and, for his deep concerns about the health of South Africans, some have called him a traitor. In response, the Arch has said, "I did not fight for the freedom of my country, I did not help to replace one set of tyrants who shut down our voices with another set of tyrants who mean to silence us all."

South Africa now has one of the highest rates of HIV infection on the continent. Desmond Tutu's heart aches at the tragic waste of life, and he is calling out for anyone and everyone to come join him in fighting this essential battle.

Meet Scrooge

A few miles outside of Cape Town lies the poor township of Khayelitsha, where almost a million South Africans make their homes out of corrugated metal or wood. It is a community under siege from the HIV/AIDS pandemic. Forty-eight percent of the people who live here are HIV positive.

We go to Khayelitsha to meet with an intriguing young man who calls himself Scrooge. A nineteen-year-old hip-hop artist, Scrooge has decided to take up Archbishop Tutu's Global Call to Action on the issue of HIV/AIDS. We meet him in the People's Cemetery. Everyone who lives in the township knows someone who is buried here.

Scrooge's weapon in his personal commitment to fight the plague is his gift as a rapper. Walking away from the cemetery, he starts to sway.

"HIV population grows like numbers;
Black people on the streets and the schools are empty;
We need to fill these classes with masses;
They need to understand what we're dealing with, man;
We need to take our time;
We need to rewind the rhyme;
We need to improve ourselves;
We need to understand what we're dealing with."

Scrooge's plan is to communicate through his music, and he asks some of his friends and fellow rappers, the Lampita Clan Crew, to help him out. They walk for miles to reach the local radio station, and wait for hours to meet the manager, Mzamo Ngomana.

Scrooge looks up into the eyes of the station manager, and pleads for a chance to go on the air. "Almost anyone that's around this will be dealing with one thing, and that is HIV and AIDS. So, how could we as musicians and our radio stations come together to help people realize that something is happening out there?"

Impassive, Mzamo Ngomana asks, "What is it that you are wanting to do? What is it that you are trying to say?"

"Just a simple message—use protection, and take the HIV/AIDS test," Scrooge replies.

"Okay." The station manager stands up. "We're having a live show tomorrow at twelve o'clock, an interview show. Come back then."

The next day, Scrooge and his friends head back to the radio station. The DJ, Thabisa, welcomes them with a brilliant smile. "Hey, everybody, we have the youth here in front of us. We have the Lampita Clan Crew and Scrooge. We have a full house of brothers."

Scrooge leans into the microphone. "There are a lot of things that we want to talk about today. The environment we are in today is more infected with the HIV/AIDS virus, and we as the youth feel that we should take part in the community by talking to our people. Because this disease is sitting with us, right here."

The DJ says, "I understand that you talk to the youth. But what do they love more than talking? Don't they love music?"

Smiling, the Lampita Clan Crew jumps up and launches into a slinky rap in Xhosa, the language of many of the people who live in Khayelitsha. And then Scrooge joins in;

"Forty-eight percent of the population where I dwell;

They're affected with a disease called HIV;

This is not even a lie, you can see it on your own TV;

My population each and every day they struggle."

Half an hour later, their time is up, and Thabisa wraps up the show, grinning. "We'd like to thank you guys for coming over. I feel so embraced."

The young rappers race out into the street. They can't stop talking and laughing. Scrooge sums it up, "What we are facing out there is not just musical, it is people's lives. I would love to be close to a lot of people who have HIV to put out a hand and to work with them. That's one of my biggest goals, to be close to these people, to understand them. I want to see a change in the place that I am coming from." He decides to go to a local AIDS clinic tomorrow, in order to learn more.

Harsh Reality Hits Home

Scrooge walks through the crowded streets of Khayelitsha, heading for the local AIDS clinic. He wants to know the facts. But when he meets with Dr. Virginia de Azevedo, he learns enough to break his heart.

"We have a vast health program here in this township," she says. "Last year, we distributed 12 million free condoms, and free antiviral drugs are available for everyone who needs them. But every day there are nine thousand new cases of the disease across South Africa. Too many of them occur right here."

"Men especially are so afraid to be tested. We are seeing cases where the men promise poor young women that they will take care of them if they will carry their child—then when the women comes in for prenatal testing, that is how these men find out if they have AIDS or not."

Scrooge looks up at her and pleads, "So what can be done? This is all so . . . so terrible."

"We are trying to overcome this with a campaign called Know Your Status. We want people, especially young people, to get tested—and if they are *not* infected, to take responsibility for keeping that status, and if they are *indeed* infected, to take the medicine and take responsible actions so that they do not pass this disease along to anyone else."

The phone rings, and she reaches to answer it. Scrooge stands up quietly and walks out slowly, giving a small wave as he goes through the door.

"What I have been doing, it is not enough," he says, shaking his head.

"The moment you talk about HIV to young people, you're talking about something they don't want to hear. If we could find a smarter way of talking, then each and every day we could get at least one person," Scrooge says, a growing light in his eyes. "Maybe we could use a rap concert . . . if the musicians talked about it and even got tested themselves, we could show people the way."

We tell him it is a great idea, it just might work—and does he want to take this new idea to the Arch for some advice?

Scrooge laughs, then stops. "No, I am serious, this is for real."

We tell him that we are serious, too, and the next day, we call and arrange for a meeting between Scrooge and Archbishop Desmond Tutu.

Wisdom from the Arch

Two days later, Scrooge walks up the steps to Archbishop Tutu's small office in Milnerton, only minutes away from Cape Town. Scrooge's eyes are wide, his soul barely believing that he is about to find himself in the company of a living legend.

"Okay, now, who starts?" Tutu asks. "Do you start? Do I start?"

Scrooge and Tutu share a laugh.

"A lot of people know me as Scrooge," the young rapper begins. "I'm a musician, I belong to a band called Resemblance. There's so much that is affecting us as musicians, and there are so many people who are HIV positive in Khayelitsha. We would love to reach those masses in a way we feel that they understand us."

"Yes," the Arch replies, smiling. "It is possible for us to prevent infection—there are things that we can do. And because you are role models for many young people, they are more likely to listen to you, communicating through your music."

Scrooge nods in agreement. "Right now, my mission is to put on a concert in May, the month of rap music. We would focus on HIV, telling the masses that we, as musicians, are as one with them on this. Our plan is to do a live demonstration of HIV testing. The musicians will encourage testing of people in the audience, in the mobile testing vans that the AIDS clinic will bring."

We are the rainbow people. And we make a difference.

The Arch leans back in his chair. "I'm very, very impressed. To say you want to use your gifts as a musician for the benefit of the community, that's very heartwarming. And I'm so glad that one of the things you want to do is to fight against the stigma that so many people attach to anyone who is infected by HIV and AIDS."

"It is my dream that the audience could realize that HIV is something that is living in society—it's not a myth. If we can get people to get tested, then this can be the start," Scrooge says, with hope in his voice.

The Arch is quiet for a moment. "Sometimes, when we were struggling against apartheid and it looked like there was this massive adversary, it didn't seem like we were going to win," he confides. "You had to keep reminding people that the sea is made up of drops of water. One drop coming together with another drop and, hey, presto! You've got an ocean! So your wonderful efforts, when joined with the efforts of others, could become a very significant factor. I want to say, 'Go for it! Good for you!'"

Scrooge exhales, beaming. "Thank you very much!"

Patience to the Rescue

There are only thirty days left until May, so Scrooge calls his best friend, Mzee, and asks him if his sister, Patience, would be willing to help him put together the concert. Scrooge knows that Patience works in an office and has much more organizational experience than he has.

Patience is another South African miracle. Only three and a half feet tall, with legs that do not work at all, Patience has spent her entire life in a well-padded wheelchair. And yet she is a true force of nature—exuberant, sassy, determined, and always ready for action.

When you meet Patience, you are thoroughly charmed by this sparkling twenty-one-year-old, who hasn't let her disabilities get in her way. "Yes, I will help with the concert—there is so much to do!"

At first, the planning seems to be going well. And then, all of sudden, Scrooge stops returning Patience's phone calls. Scrooge has disappeared.

"Scrooge has pitched on me," Patience says, sadly. "I don't know where he is. And I don't know what to do."

The entire burden of coordinating this ambitious endeavor has fallen squarely on her delicate shoulders. Desperate, she calls the only person she can think of, her favorite local musician, D-Low. D-Low is an incredibly warm and compassionate man who is always doing charity work in the Cape Town area. Patience met him once, and she is thrilled to hear that he remembers her and will try to help.

They meet the next day. Patience is beaming. D-Low agrees not only to perform at the concert, but also to act as master of ceremonies. And he gives her the phone numbers for some other local acts, as well. Patience heaves a huge sigh of relief. The concert can still happen.

But the following Monday, things turn sour again. Patience is shocked to learn, when she calls the local AIDS clinic, that someone has stolen one of the mobile AIDS testing vans.

Then she phones the company that has agreed to donate the sound system and lighting, and discovers that no one there logged in the job—it is not even scheduled.

Patience continues to work with urgency, unwilling to give up on her mission. She's acutely aware that, with less than a week before the event, she's not even *close* to being finished with her work.

Late in the afternoon on the Thursday before the concert, Mzee calls to say that he may have found Scrooge. He is back in Khayelitsha, working on the railroad. The sun is beginning to set on the Cape as they clamber into a hired car and head toward Khayelitsha.

Winding around the streets of the township, they locate the house where Scrooge lives. A woman answers the door and tells him that Scrooge is at a friend's house.

They find the address where Scrooge allegedly is visiting, and Mzee jumps out of the car, walks toward the front door, and enters. It seems like hours pass before Mzee reappears.

Then Scrooge slowly walks from around the side of the building, his head hanging down. He's humiliated—he's been ambushed, blindsided. He nervously shifts his weight from foot to foot, eyes cast downward, occasionally peering into the car. His eyes reflect his torment—for a moment it looks like he's about to become angry and lash out at Patience.

But Patience will not take no for an answer. "Just promise me you will be there on Saturday," she insists. The collective blood pressure drops back down to normal when Scrooge agrees to show up for the concert, and to give it his best efforts.

Know Your Status

On the day of the concert, Patience sits near the front door of Khayelitsha's False Bay College, the site of the event. The concert is scheduled to start in a few hours, and the sound system and lighting kits still have not arrived. Patience is a ball of nerves, and she is afraid that no one will show up.

She's tapping numbers into one cell phone, then talking, when she looks up toward the front gate of the college and sees Scrooge walking through. A smile breaks across her face.

Scrooge walks up to Patience and sits down beside her, looking straight into her eyes. "I have to say something. . . . I don't know what happened. I was so overwhelmed that I just ran away from you. I know that I must now earn back your trust, but please, don't give up on me. I want to do this."

Patience looks down at her hands. "You are here. That is something."

"What can I do?" he asks.

"Walk up and down the streets, and get people to come," Patience answers.

Scrooge stands up slowly and says, "I will take Mzee with me." Patience smiles—maybe there will be some people in the audience at this concert after all.

Soon, sound equipment is being assembled on the stage, and lights are being rigged. Then the justifiably famous D-Low walks through the door with a number of the day's scheduled performers trailing along behind him.

It is almost time for the concert to start, and there are only about a dozen people in the audience. Patience dispatches more of her friends out into the township to talk up the show to anyone willing to listen. Soon, groups of people start to enter the venue, and the number of concertgoers really begins to grow.

D-Low takes the stage and grabs the microphone. He welcomes the growing crowd and explains the reason behind the concert, and why it's necessary. "Know your status, people!" he proclaims. The response is quite warm, and the audience applauds loudly. D-Low croons out one of his signature numbers, then welcomes the group Vibe to the stage. They really have their act together, causing the audience to explode in applause and screams.

D-Low then introduces one of the members of the four-man, dynamic vocal group Protégé who has agreed to be tested for HIV/AIDs in front of the entire audience. The female medical technician and the singer sit in chairs facing each other as she administers the test. The audience applauds wildly after the test is completed. They know that it takes great courage to be tested for the disease, especially in front of so many people.

Then D-Low steps up to make the introduction for Scrooge. Scrooge stares deeply into the crowd before beginning his performance:

"I'm a victim of HIV, I'm caught up in a disease

That most black young children are caught up in;
I wonder, would I survive in this society?"
He nails it, and the audience goes wild.

The concert climaxes with a gaggle of different rappers hitting the stage, rhyming together. They're rapping in English, Afrikaans, and Xhosa, spitting out rhymes so fast you can't distinguish one language from another. The concert finally ends with D-Low singing to Patience alone. He smiles as he dances around with the young wheelchair-bound beauty who, through sheer determination and spirit, has pulled off something that was almost impossible.

More than three hundred people flowed through the show today, and more than thirty of those who attended were tested for HIV/AIDs. In South Africa, this is considered a huge success. Maybe Patience and Scrooge really have found a way to get young people to learn their status, and then to do something about it.

A Time to Celebrate

On a cool Cape Town morning a few days later, Patience and Scrooge head out to Archbishop Tutu's office to report in. The South African crusaders are obviously humbled once again to be in his presence. Sensing this, the Arch begins to put them at ease.

"Hi!" the Arch chirps. "It's wonderful to see you again, you're such beautiful people. I remember you were quite taken by the high incidence of HIV/AIDS in your community, and you said you were going to do something about it. So now, you are coming to let me know what you have been up to."

Patience smiles. "We had an AIDS and HIV concert last week Saturday, and we had the mobile clinic getting people tested and some of us also got tested."

Patience places a box on the coffee table in front of them. The three peer down at it."

"I can see a photo of you," the Arch says, "and there are empty chairs at the concert. . . . "

"Yes, this is the beginning of the concert," Patience says.

"Oh," laughs the Arch, "Okay!"

"And this is the college in Khayelitsha, and, as you can see, some other things. . . . "

"Some people being tested," the Arch says, leaning closer to the box, "Um-hmmm."

Patience then explains that they have already devised a follow-up plan. "We have six schools that we're going to work with," she explains. "We will be training student leaders to run workshops and concerts in their communities and to use the mobile AIDS-testing vans, like we did. Each school will have a challenge, and we will continue to follow up with them and help them out. We're empowering the youth to be more involved."

The Arch is now *deeply* impressed.

Scrooge speaks softly. "The concert was so beautiful. It had so many musicians from different backgrounds, and a lot of young people listening to other young people. And the work that Patience does, she's able to do a lot that people who are working on two feet can't manage to do. It's been something very beautiful."

The Arch turns to Patience. "You could use your disability as a very good excuse. People would understand and say, 'Oh well, Patience—I mean, what did you expect, really? She is not as mobile as other people.' But you are not opting out of life. You are saying, there are things you can do. You are a full human being who just happens not to be able to walk."

The Arch is no stranger to debilitating affliction. He was bedridden for years with tuberculosis when he was a child, and he is now suffering from prostate cancer. His empathy with Patience clearly shows.

"I am a full human being, but I do not see properly," he says, smiling. "I am wearing glasses. I am a full human being, but, in fact, I don't hear properly, so I wear hearing aids. And so you are saying, 'Yes, I am a full human being; I am gifted, and I am going to do what I can. I have a disability, but that doesn't make me any less a human being.' You are a great inspiration to us. I salute you."

Now turning to Scrooge, he says, "And I salute you. You use your musical talent and gift. You could be using it only to enrich yourself, to become more famous, but you are refusing to do that. I want to commend you for trying to make the world a better place."

The Arch now addresses both of them. "You're saying you know you can make a difference, and, in this case, you want to slow the spread of HIV and AIDS, and ultimately eradicate it.

"We overcame apartheid when some people thought it would not be possible; we've done that. If we think of this as yet another scourge, we can overcome this, too."

The trio is smiling at one another. This is a land of miracles, this is a land of hope, despite all the vast and seemingly intractable problems. *This* is South Africa.

"Thank you for being who you are and helping to inspire oldies like me!" laughs the Arch.

laureate
Archbishop Desmond Tutu

Desmond Tutu was born in 1931 in Klerksdorp, a small gold-mining town in South Africa. His father was a teacher and his mother was a domestic worker. At the age of twelve his family moved to the large capital city of Johannesburg.

From 1948 to 1993 South Africa had a government policy of apartheid, which upheld a system of unequal laws for people depending on their skin color and background. People were divided into four groups—white, Indian ("Asian"), "colored," and black. Nonwhites had an inferior educational system, inadequate medical care, and substandard public services. The objective of apartheid was for the 4 mil-

lion whites to maintain control over the 23 million nonwhites in South Africa.

White people in South Africa owned most of the land and lived in cleaner, safer neighborhoods. Black and "colored" people were relegated to poor townships, where they lived in shacks with no water or electricity. They sometimes did not have enough food to feed their families and often could not get jobs. They also had to carry a pass with them at all times. If they were caught without the pass, they were arrested and put in jail. White people did not have to carry a pass, and they could go wherever they wanted at any time.

When he was a teenager, Desmond became very sick with tuberculosis, and he almost died. He had to be in the hospital for almost two years. While in the hospital, a white priest named Trevor Huddleston came to visit him often. He would bring Desmond books to read, would play checkers with him, and even tutored him in school subjects so that he didn't fall behind. No white person had ever cared about Desmond or treated him with respect. Trevor Huddleston became a mentor and close friend, and eventually Desmond named his son after him.

After Desmond recovered, he wanted to become a doctor and find a cure for tuberculosis. But his family could not afford to send him to medical school, so he decided to become a teacher just like his father. Because he was black, he could teach only in black schools. He soon discovered that the education that black students received was drastically inferior to the education that white students received. As a result, Desmond Tutu decided that he could not continue being a teacher. "I said to myself, I'm not going to be a collaborator in this scheme. Then I asked myself, What can I do?"

Desmond remembered Trevor Huddleston and how he was able to make a positive impact on people's lives through his work as a priest. So Desmond studied to become a priest. As a priest, Desmond Tutu was able to reach out to the people of South Africa, giving them hope and dignity. Eventually, he became the first black person to hold the post of Archbishop in the Anglican Church in South Africa.

He worked with local churches to speak out against the apartheid government and violence against the black and "colored" people. In 1976, in the town of Soweto, police opened fire on ten thousand high school students who were protesting the unfair treatment. More than five hundred youth were killed during the Soweto Uprising which sparked more violence and retaliation by the South African government. In response, Desmond Tutu led peaceful marches that called for economic sanctions against South Africa. He hoped that, if countries around the world stopped buying goods from South Africa, the government would be forced to end the violence against black and "colored" people and create laws that protected *all* citizens of South Africa—not just whites.

In 1984 Archbishop Desmond Tutu was awarded the Nobel Peace Prize for his non-violent work to end apartheid and bring equality for the people in South Africa. In 1994, after several years of negotiations,

apartheid ended in South Africa. Desmond Tutu and all the other people of color in South Africa could vote together with whites for the first time on April 27, 1994. On that day, Nelson Mandela was elected as the first black president of South Africa.

President Mandela appointed Desmond Tutu as chair of the Truth and Reconciliation Commission. The purpose of the Commission was to reveal the truth of the human rights abuses that had happened under apartheid and to recommend to the government ways in which those who had suffered or their families could be rehabilitated and receive reparations. It was also able to grant amnesty from prosecution to those perpetrators of politically motivated crimes who told the truth about their acts. Many found healing and relief through the commission, and even some perpetrators who admitted to their crimes were forgiven by those whom they had abused.

Archbishop Tutu continues to be a world leader in the struggle for human rights. He believes that all people are God's children, sisters and brothers, members of the same family. He would hope that in that spirit of compassion we would all help each other. He is deeply concerned about the spread of diseases such as malaria, TB, and AIDS.

He longs for a world where there are opportunities for everyone to receive an education, to have access to health care and clean water, to have a house, and to be able to live with dignity. A world where people care for people rather than things, where there is enough for all, and where we can celebrate our diversity of language, culture, and faith.

voices of peace

SPREAD OF GLOBAL DISEASE

José Ramos-Horta

"Globalization will bring about new epidemics that were eliminated in the West but are still prevalent in many developing countries. This is the inevitability of globalization; it is negative, but in some ways it's good because it forces humanity to realize that our destinies are intertwined and that we have to work together for the common good of humanity."

Aung San Suu Kyi

"If somebody falls down and you just look and smile at him, then you're obviously not interested in helping him. If you actually go forward and pick him up and find out whether he's hurt himself, and help him— that shows that you're really concerned. Actions do speak louder than words. It is by action that you show others whether or not they speak your language, that you really feel concern and compassion for them."

Betty Williams

"Those with HIV already are much more susceptible to any kind of infection. So, it's not actually the AIDS that may kill them, but other infections. Tuberculosis is climbing once more, and we've got germs and infections that doctors don't even recognize. These viruses are becoming stronger and stronger, and we're not up to date medically with tackling them, because countries are putting more into arms and ammunition than they are into cures for diseases."

Desmond Tutu

"We particularly in southern Africa are being devastated by the HIV/AIDS pandemic. You almost want to say there is no hope, the world is going down the tubes. But I think, No! There are these fantastic people, the young people, especially, who dream dreams, and I think that is one of our greatest hopes—young people who are idealistic, who really do believe that the world can become a better place."

Ten Things You Can Do to Help
Address the Spread of Global Disease

(1) Provide Mosquito Nets/DEET

Mosquito netting for beds and the mosquito repellent DEET are two simple ways to prevent the spread of malaria. Create a campaign and fund-raiser to purchase netting and DEET for people in malaria-affected areas. Go one step further by providing these materials and a sewing machine so people can make and sell the finished nets, thus earning money to support themselves and their families.

(2) Sponsor Immunizations

The spread of many diseases such as the flu, polio, and measles has been stopped by simply providing immunizations and booster shots. Create a campaign to educate people about immunizations. Work with a company or group of people to sponsor and provide immunizations for children in other countries.

(3) Establish Clean Water and Food Techniques

Waterborne diseases are a large problem for many communities; cholera, typhoid fever, dysentery, and other waterborne diseases account for more than 2 million deaths per year. Foodborne illness similarly affects people throughout the world. Simple filters, treatments, and water-storage techniques can help prevent the spread of waterborne disease. Information on food safety can be distributed to prevent the spread of disease through the improper storage of food and the use of contaminated utensils. Provide materials and education to a community to help them keep their water and food safe.

(4) Educate About Medications/Treatment

Many of the diseases that plague communities can be treated or cured with medications. Educate people on the importance of completing all of their prescribed medications and work with an organization to see if you can help provide funds for people to get the health care and medications they need.

(5) Promote Good Hygiene

One of the most common ways to spread disease is through human contact. Even food can become infected with disease if improperly handled by an infected person. Provide good hygiene supplies such as toothbrushes and soap, along with basic hygiene-education materials, to communities and individuals.

(6) Adopt a Hospital

The spread of airborne disease such as tuberculosis often happens in hospitals and other spaces that do not have good ventilation or air-filtering systems. Because people with HIV/AIDS have an impaired immune system, it is extremely dangerous for them to contract other illnesses. Contact your local hospital, or find a hospital in another country that could use new air filters or an update to its current ventilation system.

(7) Nutrition/Good Health

Healthy habits such as eating nutritious foods, being physically active, and avoiding tobacco use can prevent diseases. Provide basic nutrition and health information to communities, as well as nutritional supplements to mothers and children. Look into food distribution, labeling, and production, and address the bigger issue on a societal scale, too.

(8) Break the Taboos

There are many misconceptions surrounding disease that prevent people from taking proper steps to prevent or treat illnesses. Organize an education campaign to get the facts out about the spread of global disease, the importance of taking and finishing a course of medications, getting proper nutrition, and maintaining good hygiene. Break the taboos around diseases such as HIV/AIDS by hosting a poetry slam, writing a newsletter, or talking openly about the issue.

(9) Encourage Testing

Because having HIV/AIDS affects your partners, your family, and you, it is very important to be tested for the disease. Host events where people can come for free, fast, and confidential HIV testing. Be sure to have people on site who can help counsel an individual who may have had a positive test result. Partner with an agency to provide free or low-cost TB tests as well.

(10) Know Your Status

There is no cure for HIV/AIDS, so the only line of defense is prevention. Implement a Know Your Status campaign in your community to address the issue of HIV/AIDS. Encourage people to get tested. If they are infected with HIV/AIDS, encourage them and empower them to make sure they do not infect anyone else. If they are not infected with HIV/AIDS, empower them to take the steps necessary to keep their status negative.

Reaching Out Despite My Fear

Máiread Corrigan Maguire & Libby — Human Rights for All

*Social justice is a priority for the human family. We have a vision for the human family—
we believe in it with a passion, and we believe that every single nation on the earth is
equal and none are more equal than the others.*
—Máiread Corrigan Maguire

Experiencing Great Britain

The British have long had a passion for the sea. Early on, Great Britain heavily funded its navy. Its other ships, ones used for trade with countries around the world, were some of the largest and fastest sailing vessels ever to sail the oceans blue. They colonized two-thirds of the world in their travels, securing trade routes to India and the Far East along the way.

But the world has changed a great deal over the past hundred years, and most of these colonies have now become independent nations with ambitions and challenges of their own. Nowadays, many people travel globally and enjoy a vast range of cultures. Some people, so charmed by the new country they just visited, pack their bags, leave their home, and emigrate to a nation on the other side of the planet. Life ebbs and flows from one place to another.

Just gazing at the swirling potpourri of cultures when you land at Heathrow International Airport, you know this is true. So many nations are represented here—some came here for opportunity, some came here for safety, but many different kinds of people now call Great Britain home.

We are here in the United Kingdom to visit a spunky group of girls who want to create a project to reach out to some of these people who still feel like strangers in their new, adopted land.

We board the train at Victoria Station in central London and head northeast to a city in the Midlands called Coventry. The gently rolling and picturesque English countryside is beautiful, dotted with farms, horses, sheep, and cattle that graze the deep green pastures and fields.

But Coventry faces all of the same problems many British cities face—a lack of jobs, the growth of gangs, the spread of drugs, and an influx of new people into its mix, including Eastern Europeans, Africans, and Muslims from many different countries. The opening of the European Union's entire borders has changed much in Europe, and evidence is abundant here in Coventry. Being a foreigner anywhere is a challenge, even in a self-declared "city of peace" like Coventry.

Meet Libby

Barrs Hill School in Coventry reflects the city's diverse, growing population. As you enter the school yard, you see young people representing sixty-two different points of ancestral origin studying, talking, and playing—a rainbow nation under one school roof.

It's here at Barrs Hill you meet fourteen-year-old Libby. She has the brightest and loveliest blue eyes you've ever seen, and an angelic face that's framed by beautiful auburn hair. "One of my favorite things to do is hang out with my friends. I guess I'm kind of sociable with people whom I have known for a while, but I hate it when people talk about people behind their backs, and then act all friendly to their faces."

Libby and her pals first attended a PeaceJam Youth Conference at Bradford University in March 2005. The girls—all pretty cynical—hung back from the rest of the participants on the first morning of the two-day event. But then they got the chance to sit down and talk with 1976 Nobel Peace Laureate Máiread Corrigan Maguire, and her warmth and kindness touched them all. Inspired by her genuine interest in each one of them, they came up with the courage to invite Máiread to come visit them at Barrs Hill. They were incredulous when she replied, "Well, I just might do that!" They left the PeaceJam conference on an all-time high.

Six months later, Máiread Corrigan Maguire makes good on her promise.

The girls come bounding down the front steps of the school screaming, "Oh, she really is here" and shouting out "welcome" and "hello" across the courtyard. Máiread looks up at them all, beaming.

Meet Máiread

Máiread Corrigan Maguire lived through "The Troubles" in Northern Ireland. Many of her friends—and family—did not survive. Máiread has learned much from living through those complicated and violent times in Northern Ireland. "We tried to solve these problems through militarism," she says, "and through the government removing many of our basic civil liberties, and all these things didn't solve the problem. Instead, they were adding fuel to the anger and the frustration."

Máiread is terribly aware that the path to peace is a rocky, winding road, and she says, "The whole question of human rights is so important. We're all human, and every human being, I believe, has a sense of what is just and what is not just. If we live with injustice and see no redress to this injustice, no channels by which these things can be put right, then that anger can grow—it can turn into despair, and it can turn into violence. We have seen this in Northern Ireland with terrorist bombs, and we have seen it in suicide bombings in the Middle East."

Máiread is quiet for a moment, and then she says, "In Northern Ireland, we are all still learning, but I think that we also have some things to teach out of our very sad experience of over thirty years of violent ethnic political conflict."

Libby's Project Begins

Libby and several other girls tumble down the school stairs and run toward Máiread, gathering in a tight knot around her. Libby is joined by her friends: Livia, with her punk rock hairstyle; tiny Sophie, who always has an intelligent twinkle in her eye; fiery Laura, who keeps her red hair pulled back in a tight ponytail; thoughtful Emma, with her streaked blond hair; shy Ayan, who is dark and tall; friendly Ellen, who is never afraid to talk to anyone; and brown-eyed Mimi, with her slight Bulgarian accent and her pretty smile. They grab Máiread by one arm and one hand, and almost drag her into their school library, so excited that they seem all to be speaking at once. Máiread is loving every minute of it.

"Delightful to be with you again." Máiread smiles as she sits down at a desk in the library. "I believe that since you've been to the PeaceJam, you yourselves have some ideas for projects working for peace. I'd love to hear your ideas."

Libby sits down beside her. "I looked at the declaration of human rights, and it stated that all people should have freedom of liberty, and freedom of speech, not depending on sex, race, or religion. We want to try setting that up in school because some people here look down on a lot of the other students because they're different. So we wanted to try to create a more peaceful atmosphere in school. Some people have fights with people who are different from them because they feel threatened by them. People should talk to each other, not get into cliques and ignore each other. And we are also trying to reach out to the Muslim community in the school and try and help them and see what they're feeling about all of this."

"In Northern Ireland," Máiread says, "when the Peace People [Máiread's organization, created in response to the violence in Northern Ireland] started, we felt that we had to build friendships and cross barriers, because people were afraid. There were interesting things that started in the North of Ireland to help build up trust and friendship, and one of them was the integrated school, children being educated together."

Libby nods her head. "It's definitely got to start at school. There should be lessons on human rights and accepting differences."

"That's great," Máiread says. "In a world where there's a lot of war and violence, there's also abuse of human rights and civil liberties. I know in Muslim communites in many parts of the world, some Muslims have said they're feeling isolated and marginalized, that their rights are being removed. How do we help the Muslim community to feel part of our human family? How can we come together as people to bring about peace in our communities and peace in our world?"

"Well," Libby says, "I think you have to listen to what they feel they're not getting from the community and what they'd like to see improved. I think you need to listen to what they want and what they need to get fixed and how they're feeling."

"Well, I want to say thank you very much, Libby. You're just a wonderful inspiration. I hope that you all can come to Belfast," Máiread says. "You can meet some people there who are also working for integration and for human rights and justice in Northern Ireland."

The girls are stunned—they don't know what to say. "Really? We could really come to Northern Ireland?" Libby asks.

Máiread just nods her head and smiles, and the girls, giggling and buzzing with excitement, grab her by the hands again and give her a tour of their school for another hour, before they are willing to let her go.

Three-Minute Friendships

The next day we get a phone call from Libby's teacher, Janey Manton. She says that the girls have organized a kind of "focus-group" session, so that they can find out what it feels like to be ostracized because of "differences." We are excited to see what they've come up with, so we head over to their school just before the end-of-the-day bell rings.

It is a warm and breezy spring day, and a group of students is gathered on the steps by the football field. Libby has a clipboard in her hand, and she is starting to ask them questions.

"Do you feel that you get judged by people because of the way you look?" she asks.

"Yes, because they judge everyone and everything," says a girl with straight black hair and goth makeup and jewelry.

"Sometimes I walk down my street and get called racist names," says another girl, who is wearing the black Muslim dress known as an abaya.

The first girl agrees. "You get a lot of abusive comments, and for no reason. You could just be minding your own business and you just get shouted at for being who you are."

A tall, brown-haired girl agrees, saying, "I'm half caste—half white and half Asian—but when people look at me, they just presume that I'm Asian even though I've lived with my mom, who is white, my whole life, and have nothing to do with my dad, who is the Asian one. I feel that I am completely British. I don't even know how to speak Hindi, but people still put me with the category of 'people from India' just because of my skin color."

A girl from Kenya sums it up by saying, "You get judged everywhere you go. You can't avoid it."

Libby stands quietly with her friend Emma, taking notes as the students speak, a look of concern on her face. Then the focus-group session is over, and after offering sincere thanks to all, Libby slowly walks away.

What is she thinking?

We find out the next day when we get another call from her teacher. The girls have a plan.

The girls welcome us into their classroom. They try to explain their new idea to us.

"You know that in every school there are always little social groups. People say that they don't like someone else, basically because they are different. We are going to try to help people to spread out to other people more. You know that speed-dating thing, where people are all at tables, and they move around?" Libby asks.

"You mean three-minute dating?" Ellen answers.

"Yeah, but we could make it three-minute friendships. We could put a little pot in the center of the table with different topics in it. And you pick out a topic and talk about that for a while and just see . . ." Libby looks around for other ideas.

"Or they could each talk about three things that they like to do," Ayan adds.

"That could work . . ." says Mimi, excitedly.

One week later, they put their new idea into effect.

A diverse rainbow of students fills the classroom. The desks have been moved away, and you see a huge circle of chairs facing in, and a similar circle of chairs within that first loop, facing out. Libby starts. "We came up with the three-minute friendships as an idea to try to get the different groups at school to be more aware of one another's feelings and start to interact with one another. Every time I blow the whistle, you have to stop talking to the person in front of you and then move one seat to the right to start a new conversation."

So the whirlwind begins. And the students are loving it. The level of chatter in the room grows and grows, punctuated by huge bursts of laughter and the scraping of chairs as the whistle blows and everyone scoots over, again, to meet their next new friend.

Libby and her friends head home after school, flush with their success. "It went as well as I could have hoped, because everyone seemed to talk the whole time. Mrs. Manton says she wants to have a go with another school in Coventry where there's quite a lot of differences between different ethnic groups and Muslim groups on their own." Libby looks determined as she briskly heads for home.

How Do They Feel, and What Do They Need?

Two weeks go by. Teachers and students at Barrs Hill School report a warming of relations between students, fewer disagreements, more young people saying "hello" as they walk down the halls between classes. Now the girls load into their school minibus and head toward another Coventry school, where the FolesHillfields PeaceJam group is waiting to meet them. The group is made up of mainly South Asian students, around half of whom are Muslim. Will their three-minute friendship idea work here? Libby and her friends say that they have decided to start an Amnesty International club at Barrs Hill, too, and that they are going to add that to the mix this time. After the FolesHillfields group leads some conflict resolution games, they will do a joint project—letter writing on the human rights issue each student cares about most.

There is apprehension in the air as they head up the steps to a second-floor classroom, where they meet a group of young students, some wearing black headscarves (hijabs). They range in age from twelve to seventeen, and they are there with their youth leader, Fatima Mangera, who wears a hijab as well. The girls hang back, suddenly uncomfortable and shy.

"Right," says Fatima, seeing that she needs to get things started. The students all work together to pull the desks out of the way, and the atmosphere in the room starts to warm up a bit. The chairs are placed into a circle, and one of the young Muslims leads the first game. Soon there are smiles and laughter from almost everyone. After the three-minute friendship excercise, the students pull the desks back into rows.

Now comes the time for letter writing. Each young person is given paper and a pen, and is asked to write about the human-rights issue about which he or she cares most. The room instantly falls silent.

When the allotted time has passed, the teacher asks if students will read from their letters. The letters from the Barrs Hill girls cover a broad range of topics: from "blood diamonds" to global warming to domestic violence. But it is the letters from the Muslim, Sikh, and Hindu students that cry out in the most poignant way:

"My name is Hasina and I am fifteen years old. I am concerned about racism in our country."

"My name is Mitesh, and I am writing to say that people should stop judging other people."

Another reads, "I am twelve years old, and I have concerns about war."

And another, "I feel there are many people who are deprived of the rights they should have—people are being locked away for no reason at all! They are locked away for things they have never done. These people are let out later, but by then their reputation has been ruined."

The evening ends on a silent and thoughtful note, and the Barrs Hill girls are quiet again as they walk down the stairs and file into the school minibus. Several days later, we receive a call saying that the girls are going full steam ahead with their Amnesty International projects—but that they do not want to work on the issues raised by the South Asian students. We wonder at this, and we also wonder what will happen when they travel to Northern Ireland.

Belfast

"Welcome to Belfast," Máiread trills as she throws open the doors to the Peace House, a rambling and historic old home that is the headquarters of the Peace People.

Máiread and her Peace People colleagues have organized an evening of food and festivity to welcome their young friends from Coventry, England. They have prepared a simple and elegant meal, and dozens of people crowd the warm living room of the Peace House.

Students have come to meet with the girls and teach them some good old-fashioned Irish dance. After supper, traditional Irish music pours from a boom box, and someone explains the art of Irish dancing. Shyly, the contingent from Coventry joins in, with the exception of Libby—who sits alone fiddling with her cell phone—and before long the Peace House is rocking out.

The Coventry girls also have a chance to meet with Máiread to discuss their human-rights projects. The eager young group has taken on many issues—like the plight of Burma's freely elected leader Aung San Suu Kyi. The girls have written letters condemning the brutal oppression of the people of Burma and requesting freedom for Aung San Suu Kyi.

They have agreed to toil for Tools for Self Reliance, an organization that sends tools to Africa to empower African craftsmen to set up their own businesses. They have organized a campaign to collect these items from friends at their school and in their community. They'll also expend further energy on a letter-writing campaign against the insanity of the production and trade of the aptly named "blood diamonds" in that continent.

The Barrs Hill girls think globally, but they also want to act locally, they tell Máiread—they want to organize a local campaign to tackle the ever-worsening domestic violence they've seen and experienced in their own lives. Máiread is most impressed with these young girls from Coventry, at their energy and their commitment to act.

But she has a question for them, too. "I'm deeply concerned about a letter I've read here  from one of your fellow Muslim students, from the first letter-writing session you held together. When I read this letter, I can't help but feel that she suffers so much, is in need of so much understanding and help. What are you thinking to do to help her, and the other Muslims in your community?"

You could hear the drop of a pin in the silence that meets Máiread's question. Eyes cast down and away from the concerned Nobel Peace Laureate, they sit in a collective silence that speaks loudly of the fears in the Western psyche. It's a very uncomfortable moment in the room, and the girls hope some other question will soon be asked, something that will get them all through the awkward chill.

Máiread sits very still, waiting for an answer that never comes. "Okay," she then says. "I would very much like to show you around Belfast tomorrow. Does that sound good to you?"

The girls brighten up immediately, nodding their heads and saying, "Yes, yes!" They make plans to meet up the next morning to begin their Nobel-guided tour of the city.

Learning the Lessons of Northern Ireland

Think about what it takes to change things for the better: and one of those things is determination. You don't win the Nobel Peace Prize without a great, unwavering dose of that, right? And in Máiread Corrigan Maguire it is pure unadulterated determination you see this morning. To solve a problem one must first admit that there is a problem—a leap of faith the young girls from Coventry haven't yet made. She knows she needs to convince them that there is not only a problem in ignoring the Muslims' issues, but a viable solution. But how is she going to convince them that they want to be the agents of change?

"Just to explain a little bit of a very complicated situation," Máiread says, as the girls get out of the minibus near the walls that divide Máiread's old Catholic neighborhood from the

Protestant one a stone's throw away, "in the 1960s a lot of Catholics and some liberal Protestants, they began realizing that the Catholic community didn't have basic civil liberties. So when the civil-rights movement started, they began to ask for these basic civil liberties, because the root cause of their suffering was this injustice.

"We had a minority Catholic community in a region where the majority Protestant community held all of the power. So it was really a struggle for human rights, for equality, for justice. Tragically, that nonviolent civil-rights movement developed into a situation where violence broke out because people were frightened. There was a deep fear between the two different communities. Why do you think people were so frightened of each other?"

The girls look around at one another, and Livia finally chirps, "Because they were different from each other?"

"They were different from each other"—Máiread nods—"and they didn't know each other, and they lived apart. I feel so sad because I feel very close to people on the other side of this wall. We've shared so much, and we've more in common than we have that divides us. I want to see the people of Northern Ireland living together without walls between them. Do you think you have something to learn from this wall?"

"To try to get along with people?" Ellen says hopefully.

"To try to get them to be friends?" Mimi adds.

"Indeed." Máiread smiles.

"This area is still 100 percent Catholic now, and that area over there is 100 percent Protestant," Máiread continues. "Because tragically in The Troubles, people were so frightened that they moved into communities that they felt safe in."

Máiread pauses here, carefully choosing her words. "People have to be *included*," she says, driving home the essential point, "not *excluded*. If you exclude any community, you're feeding fear and separation and isolation and marginalization, and people feel that their voice is not being heard."

"It's just not right being like that. I don't like it," says Livia as the girls clamber back into the bus. Sophie agrees, adding, "They should just be able to, like, speak to each other instead of there being a wall between them."

The girls take a good, hard look, and you can see it in their faces: *Who would want to live like this?*

"And you know, there's more than physical walls," Máiread says. "We need to take down the walls in our minds."

Libby nods at the rest of the girls. They nod back. It's all sinking in and making sense now—a very sad sense—but sense nonetheless.

Final Reflection

The bus snakes its way up a long and winding road, around cows, goats, and sheep that are the natural denizens of the cliffs that look out over Belfast. The minibus pulls up a dirt road toward a house that perches at the top of the cliff, and the girls tumble out to a panoramic view of the city that reveals everything in one breath, dividing walls and all.

This is the site of the Quaker House, which looks like so many of the quaint, bucolic cottagelike structures that abound across the countryside of Northern Ireland. The Quaker House is used as a counseling center for the families of Belfast.

Libby sits in a quiet corner, and has an opportunity to reflect on everything she has learned since she started her project on the issue of human rights.

"Belfast is really different from Coventry because it's got all the divides—actual divides you can see. I knew there was a problem between the two groups, but I didn't think it would go so far as putting up walls to stop people from talking and finding out about each other," she says thoughtfully.

"It's kind of a different world here than it is in my country." Libby goes on, "I really think we should try to listen to other people—not just the Muslim community, though they are a part of it. I think we should just try to talk to people about how they are feeling and how they think things are being handled before it has time to become a real problem," Libby quietly concludes.

And then she runs off to join the rest of her friends, with a new understanding of the importance of social justice and human rights, and a new resolve to do all that she can to reach out to those who are different from her, despite the fears that so many of us face.

Three months later, we hear some great news—Libby and her crew will be traveling with their new Muslim, Sikh, and Hindu friends from the FolesHillfields project to attend the upcoming PeaceJam Youth Conference together. All we can do is smile.

laureate
Máiread Corrigan Maguire

Máiread Corrigan Maguire was born on January 27, 1944, to a Catholic family in Belfast, Northern Ireland. She grew up with her parents, five sisters, and two brothers in a very poor Catholic ghetto. Her father supported their family with the very small income of a window washer. From her youth, Máiread was deeply involved in social work among children and teenagers in various Catholic neighborhoods of Belfast.

The history of Ireland is full of conflict from the time of the twelfth century, when the English began invading Ireland. Religion became a part of the conflict in the 1600s when British Protestants began moving into Catholic Ireland. Conflict and violence continued between these communities until Ireland was split in two in 1921: the Republic of Ireland as its own country in the South, and Northern Ireland as part of the United Kingdom in the North.

The conflict in Northern Ireland continued after that point, and the period from 1969 to 1998 has been known as "The Troubles." The Troubles in Northern Ireland were not about the differences between the Catholic and Protestant religions. They came from different ideas about how Northern Ireland should be run. The Nationalists—people who wanted Northern Ireland to be part of the Republic of Ireland—were mostly Catholic. The Unionists—people who wanted Northern Ireland to stay a part of the United Kingdom—were mostly Protestant.

Northern Ireland was a deeply divided land. Many communities were divided between Protestant and Catholic, and there was a great deal of fear and mistrust between the people. Catholic people and Protestant people shopped at separate stores and went to separate schools. This was true all over Northern Ireland, and Belfast was a very strong example of this tension and division.

Máiread became a part of the peace movement because of a tragic event. On August 10, 1976, four children—Máiread's nephews and nieces—were struck on a street corner in Belfast by the getaway car of Danny Lennon, a gunman from the (Nationalist Catholic) Irish Republican Army. Their mother, Máiread's sister Anne, was badly hurt in the crash. Only one child survived. The car was out of control because the driver of the car had been shot dead by British soldiers (who were Protestant). It did not make sense to the community to blame either the Nationalists or the Unionists in the deaths of these children; instead, they were shocked and outraged about how needless the deaths of these children were.

Because the community was so upset, they came out in crowds to mourn the deaths of the children. People throughout Northern Ireland and around the world focused their attention on the senseless deaths and the senselessness of all of the violence of The Troubles. Máiread connected with Betty Williams, another woman from the community who actually witnessed the accident, and a journalist friend, Ciaran McKeown, and together, they organized very large weekly peace marches and demonstrations.

More than half a million people from Northern Ireland, Ireland, and England attended these rallies to demand an end to the violence. These were some of the largest peace demonstrations ever held in the history of Northern Ireland, and they happened in 1976, the time with the highest number of killings during The Troubles. They also took place in Belfast, London, and many other cities, and much international attention was focused on these marches. Máiread, along with Betty and Ciaran, also founded the "Community of the Peace People" to continue the peacemaking programs that grew out of these rallies. One of the main ideas behind the Community of the Peace People was that true reconciliation and the prevention of community institutions, such as schools and recreation centers, as well as residential areas.

As an adult, Máiread dedicated her life to promoting a peaceful resolution of the conflict in Northern Ireland. For more than thirty years, Máiread has communicated a simple message: nonviolence is the only way to achieve a peaceful and just society. Working tirelessly with community groups throughout Northern Ireland, as well as with political and church leaders, she has sought to promote dialogue between the two deeply divided communities of Catholics and Protestants. She has continued to work for peace, long after the media stopped paying attention to their movement, and in the face of being mocked and ignored for her work.

Máiread has also understood for a long time that peace is not important only to Northern Ireland. She has dedicated her life to working toward a future of global nonviolence.

In 1976, Máiread Corrigan Maguire and Betty Williams were awarded the Nobel Peace Prize for their work against violence in Northern Ireland. Their Nobel Prize acceptance speech stated, "We are for life and creation, and we are against war and destruction, and in our rage, we screamed that the violence had to stop. But we also began to do something about it besides shouting."

Through her speaking engagements, her writings, and her participation in grassroots peace initiatives, Máiread has helped to keep the flame of hope alive around the world.

voices of peace

REACHING OUT DESPITE MY FEAR

Máiread Corrigan Maguire

"We have a vision for the human family—we believe in it with a passion, and we believe that every single nation on Earth is equal and none is more equal than the others. We've got to create a culture where we recognize that every human life is sacred and precious . . . that sanctity of life must be the link between the spiritual and the political life, that it must be the ultimate value in society."

Shirin Ebadi

"Globalization can be positive only if it decreases the injustice in the world and brings an end to the violation of human rights. I dream about a world that does not have poverty, prejudice, ignorance or oppression in it. In this dream, I see the globalization in the hearts of people—a globalization where everyone can feel compassion for the pain of others."

Jody Williams

"We can't just feel emotion about the injustice of the world. It is wasted emotion unless you do something to make it different. It is our special responsibility to do something about the foreign policies of a government that is destroying the environment, that is destroying a belief in human rights and international law, which thinks that it has the right to do whatever it wants in the world."

Desmond Tutu

"Sometimes we forget—human beings are fundamentally good! This is a world that is part of a moral universe. It is that justice, goodness, love—all of those things one day will triumph over their ghastly counterparts. There's no way in which injustice, oppression, evil will have the last word."

Ten Things You Can Do to Help

Ensure Human Rights and Social Justice

(1) Get Informed

Making sure that you are informed on an issue is extremely important to being able to think about it, talk about it, and address it. Go online or to the library—or even conduct community interviews—to get information on social injustice. Go online to check out the latest Amnesty International Report regarding the human-rights meltdown. Most of all, just make sure you're in the know!

(2) Put Your Pen to Work

Letter-writing campaigns have been effective in stopping some of the most horrific human-rights abuses throughout the world. Start a letter-writing campaign, a fax campaign, a petition, or a calling campaign of your own or join one that has already been established.

(3) Use Simulations and Visualizations

So often, people turn a blind eye to the human rights and social-justice abuses that are happening throughout the world. Creating a simulation—installing an art exhibit, showing a film, hosting a photo exhibit, doing dramatic readings, or putting on a play—is a great way to humanize the issues and inspire people to take action.

(4) Take It to the Streets

Peaceful protest can be a very powerful tool, and many of the rights and freedoms we enjoy today were gained because people were prepared to go out on the streets and protest. Get connected with people in your community to organize a peaceful protest, solidarity march, candlelight vigil, or other public gathering for or against an issue you are interested in taking on.

(5) Support Human Rights Legislation

Laws and rules reflect a society's beliefs as well as dictate acceptable and unacceptable behavior and actions. Passing legislation that protects human rights and stands for social justice is one way that we can ensure that everyone understands collective values and expectations. Find out what legislation is being discussed in your area, or work with local agencies and legislators to get the issues you care about on the ballot.

(6) Stand with Those Who Stand Alone

We all feel a little better taking a stand when we are not taking a stand alone. Building a solidarity campaign can be a way of showing support to people whose voices are not being heard. Solidarity campaigns exist for issues including political prisoners, civil rights, and a multitude of other social justice or human rights movements. Campaigns of Solidarity send a clear message to those who are being treated unjustly that you are on their side, that you will fight for their cause, and that they are not alone.

(7) Put Your Money Where Your Mouth Is

Companies and corporations can be some of the biggest abusers of human rights in the world. Various Web sites and companies monitor the human-rights practices of companies and create reports for consumers. Your dollars speak loudly to companies, and your refusal to purchase from companies that violate human rights can go a long way to making a difference. Don't forget to support those companies that make a point of upholding human rights, as well!

(8) Promote the Universal Declaration of Human Rights

The Universal Declaration of Human Rights was created by the United Nations in 1948. It outlines the basic human rights of every human being and calls for us all to uphold those rights and bring them to the forefront at all times. Take a look at the U.N. Declaration of Human Rights at http://www.un.org/Overview/rights.html, and then check to see if your country has signed on and ratified the document. If so, send letters of appreciation to your local government leaders and ask them to continue with their good work. If not, create a project to let people know and start putting pressure on your government to sign and ratify the declaration.

(9) Understand the Connections

Working for human rights and social justice means many things to many people. Understanding the fact that these terms serve as an umbrella for issues having to do with a variety of topics such as racism, labor, distribution of resources, gender, ethnicity, etc., is important in moving forward on a project or an idea. Also, it is very important to understand the connections between each of the issues so that movements can work together and build from one another. Check out Internet sites and books to gain a perspective on the vast movement for human rights and social justice.

(10) Shed the Light in Cyberspace

People can't do anything about a human-rights violation if they don't know it's happening. Create an online resource where readers can go to find information on human-rights abuses, human-rights issues, social justice, and events in your community or throughout the world. Use social-networking platforms to spread the word and connect with other people who are working for a common cause.

We Need Jobs and Training

José Ramos-Horta & Vidal—The Challenge of Extreme Poverty

*If those in power, wherever we are, whichever country but also at whatever level in society
that we are leaders, began working together, we would eliminate abject poverty and
ensure that poverty becomes history in twenty years from now.
It's a moral duty of any of us as human beings.*
—José Ramos-Horta

Experiencing East Timor

Imagine the most remote and faraway place in the world. What would it look like? A tiny island, surrounded by rough shark-infested seas? A steamy jungle, with exotic vegetation cascading down? An impossibly mountainous terrain, with only a few treacherous roads to link the remote villages that are dotted along the way?

Welcome to East Timor, which is all of these things . . . and more. East Timor is the farthest place we've ever traveled to, and the journey itself is quite an adventure. Even by air, it takes several days to get there, and at least four different planes. East Timor is located along a string of islands just north of Darwin, Australia, and to the west of Papua New Guinea. It is so far away that it is seventeen time zones ahead of us—when it is 4:00 P.M. at our house in Colorado, it is already 9:00 A.M. the next day in East Timor.

When you get off the plane at the Dili Airport, you walk down the steps to the tarmac with weak rubber legs. The dense, humid air hits you as you stagger toward the tiny building that serves as Dili's airport terminal. Inside, the air-conditioning is functioning, but not as well as you had hoped. A man stamps your passport—a simple oval stamp with the letters RDTL inside (for República Domocrátia de Timor-Leste), truly representing the humble democracy that is East Timor.

We have come to this impoverished and far-flung country in order to work with an energetic young college student who wants to take on the problem of extreme poverty in his beloved homeland.

The Impossible Dream of East Timor

There are very few countries in the world that have faced more difficult obstacles than the land of East Timor.

The Portuguese began trading with the people of East Timor in the early sixteenth century. Before long, a group of Portuguese decided to take over and colonize the place. Dutch sailors were not far behind, and soon the Dutch and the Portuguese were fighting over the island. In 1859, the western half of the island was ceded to the Dutch. Then from 1942 to 1945, during World War II, Japan occupied East Timor. After the war, Portugal once again took control. And that was the state of affairs until November 28, 1975, when the people of this small island nation banded together and declared their independence, which they enjoyed for nine days—until the Indonesian army launched a brutal invasion and took over the country by force.

East Timor is a tiny place, with a population of just over 1 million people. But the people wanted to be free. The Indonesian military did everything in its power to quell the uprisings of the people, killing almost 250,000 East Timorese in the process.

One young East Timor man, who hoped to become a journalist someday, was dispatched to New York City in 1975, in order to tell the world what was happening in his homeland. That young dreamer was José Ramos-Horta, and he was destined to spend the next twenty-seven years of his life as the "representative" for a country that did not exist, pleading his people's case to anyone who would listen. Everyone at the United Nations told him that his cause was lost. But he refused to give up, slowly developing a network of support for his impoverished and destitute people. He traveled to one hundred different countries to plead the case for East Timor.

In 1991, there was a tragic massacre in Dili when a gathering of young people, marching silently in support of freedom, was confronted by the Indonesian military. The army opened fire, and the crowd rushed toward what should have been a safe haven, the sacred cemetery of Santa Cruz. But instead, they were slaughtered, more than three hundred of them dying on the spot. Hundreds of others were hunted down in the hills surrounding Dili, and many others were taken from the hospitals they had crawled to for help and never seen again. The press was able to capture the incident on film, and José Ramos-Horta and his network worked tirelessly to use this to galvanize world opinion on the situation in his country.

By 1999, world opinion had turned strongly against Jakarta's generals, and the United Nations forced Indonesia to hold a referendum in East Timor to determine whether the people wanted to be an independent country or to continue to live under Indonesian rule. In August, buoyed by the presence of the U.N. peacekeeping troops, the people voted overwhelmingly for freedom.

But when the Indonesian army was finally forced to leave, they didn't leave quietly or peacefully. Nearly the entire country was burned to the ground. The electrical grid was destroyed. Cattle and other livestock were killed and thrown into the fresh-water supply in order to poison it. The few existing cash crops (like coffee) were almost completely burned out. Nearly every building on the island was left a pile of useless rubble. The East Timorese were faced with literally building their fledgling democracy from the ground up.

The poverty in East Timor simply staggers the imagination. The vast majority of the people here subsist on an income of less than $1 per day, and the majority of the people have never received any decent education or training. The unemployment rate is in the stratosphere, and most of the people here are younger than eighteen years old.

Refugee camps tell the sad, lingering story of a country on the mend. The United Nations has provided tents, fresh water, rice, and other staples to the seventy thousand refugees, but it isn't quite enough. Only 60 percent of the land is arable, and yet more than 90 percent of the people survive on the subsistence farming that they are able to eke out of this mountainous land. Most of the dwellings are either tiny concrete-block constructions with tin roofs or wooden structures. Wood is a highly prized commodity and resource on this island.

And yet one of the biggest challenges that the people face is a psychological one. José Ramos-Horta, who returned to East Timor in 2002 to help rebuild his ravaged country, sees it this way. "For many generations, the people were subject to constant humiliation,

robbed of their dignity and pride. They often had to cheat and lie in order to survive; often they had to spy on others in order to survive. They saw friends and parents killed with their own eyes—hardly any family here escaped the violence during the Indonesian occupation.

"One of the legacies of the Indonesian occupation is what we are harvesting today," José continues. "A lot of people are traumatized. We have rampant domestic violence. It's not just an issue of poverty. It's an issue of marginalization. You have a collective trauma in the country that needs to be healed."

Meet Vidal

Sitting in the lobby of Hotel Timor, you hear a strong and confident voice shout out, "PeaceJam—Change Starts Here!" You turn around to see a charismatic young man, beaming across the room. Meet Vidal! He was one of ten young people selected to attend the Tenth Anniversary PeaceJam Youth Conference in Denver, Colorado, as part of a youth delegation from East Timor in 2006, and he has been on fire ever since.

Vidal is quick to smile and is eagerly optimistic by nature. Through sheer pluck and determination, he has managed to create his own opportunities despite the toughest of odds. "I am the last one born in my family—we are only two. I have one sister, and my mother died when I was one year old." His father left soon after, so from an early age, Vidal and his sister depended on the kindness of their aunt for survival.

When he was sixteen years old, his entire world began to crumble. As the Indonesian military started to pull out of East Timor, they destroyed every village along the way, including the remote outpost where Vidal's family lived. "I have no home," Vidal explains. "In 1999, it got burned down by the military. I ran into the mountains to save myself." Vidal and several other boys from his village survived on roots and fruit for several months before they found the courage to come out of hiding. When they returned to their village, there were no homes left, no families. Then Vidal reached deep down and made a momentous decision; he would find a way to travel to Dili, the biggest town in East Timor. He knew that he had a relative there—maybe someone would take him in.

It was a very long walk, with many terrors along the way. But somehow, he made it to Dili and a cousin did help him out. By the time the United Nations fully recognized his country as a new, independent nation, in May of 2002, Vidal was attending school, and he had made plans for the future. "I am preparing myself to be a teacher," Vidal says confidently. "I really like to work with young people, so that, in the future, they can know how to do things for themselves." He has just enrolled in Dili's only university, and he is full of hope, despite all the horrors he has seen.

Another Crisis on the Horizon

Vidal wants to do a Global Call to Action project that will address the extreme poverty in his country, especially among young people. There is a growing problem of gang violence in East Timor, and he feels a desperate need to reach out. Already, he has found a job as a facilitator and project coordinator at Ba Futuru, a local organization whose name means "for the future." But he feels the need to do much more.

Looking at his devastated country, he sees a cycle of extreme poverty that has continued, generation after generation. How can this cycle of pain be transformed into a wheel of progress? How can his homeland move from extreme poverty to some semblance of prosperity? That is the question, and Vidal is determined to find some answers.

Vidal goes to meet with José Sousa-Santos, who is working as youth liaison to the prime minister of East Timor (who just happens to be Nobel Peace Laureate José Ramos-Horta). He's called Big Ze by everyone, and he towers over Vidal, his dark eyes smiling down.

Vidal knows a thing or two about gangs—he lives in the poorest and toughest part of Dili, a neighborhood dominated by gangs, and he wants to know what can be done to change the future for these disaffected young people.

"You're dealing with traumatized youth here," Big Ze says, looking around. "A lot of these groups were used by the resistance during the Indonesian occupation.

"Once Timor had independence," Big Ze continues, "you had this huge semiparamilitary youth gang, but they were forgotten about by the leaders. There was nothing for them to do; there was no work for them, no hope for education. Even the ones who do get education have no hope for work at the moment because there's no industry, no jobs.

"We probably have one of the largest youth demographics in the world in regards to population, and a booming population as well." Big Ze says that this spike in population is about to create another crisis for the country.

"Everyone here uses wood to cook their food, to build their huts, right? Entire forests have been cut down for firewood. With a booming population, that clear-cutting will only increase. If we lose our trees, we lose the topsoil; it will just wash out into the ocean. We will really have problems surviving then."

Vidal looks up at him, a shocked expression on his face.

"These kids still believe that they can have a good future," Big Ze concludes. "They believe that Timor can be like any other modern part of the world. They've got the energy to do it, and because they are the largest demographic here in Timor, they should be able to do it. They should be able to change things. They just need support."

"But what can I do to help?" Vidal asks plaintively.

"Well, José Ramos-Horta is always talking about reforestation, about starting a youth corps to plant some trees. Would you be interested in hearing more about that?"

Vidal nods his head twice and says, "I would really like to work on this project, especially for our people and the new generation."

"Well, all right then." Big Ze smiles down at him again, and then picks up the phone to set up a meeting for Vidal with José Ramos-Horta.

Some Guidance from José

Vidal joins up with several other PeaceJammers from East Timor, and together they make the long trek to the elegant but humble abode of Prime Minister José Ramos-Horta. It is located half a mile from one of the beautiful beaches that surround East Timor, and it's constructed of wood, with a huge thatched roof hanging over it in traditional East Timorese style.

"Welcome, my friends," José says, a crooked smile on his face and a warm twinkle in his eye. "Come in, come in."

Vidal and his friends all gather around, eyes wide, hands fidgeting, to discuss what can be done to thwart the extreme poverty that has the country in a stranglehold.

José Ramos-Horta is keenly aware of the problems his country is facing. "The fight against poverty is a moral duty of any of us as human beings," he begins, looking around at the eager faces in his midst. "The fight requires leadership at every level—not only governments, but civil societies, church, academia, youth—all of us who are more fortunate than those who struggle every day just to have a basic meal, or who do not even have access to proper clean water, let alone electricity.

"What this country needs," José says, "is a reforestation program. The tree planting as I visualize it has multipurposes—one immediate impact is to create jobs and put money in people's pockets. At the same time, it creates incentive for them to plant trees. Long-term trees like teak and sandalwood will take generations to grow. Yet in forty years, they will represent a good measure of income for the country because you can sell the teak and sandalwood and export it.

"So through this program, you achieve many things," José explains. "You immediately distribute cash to people who don't have money. You keep them busy because they will work and at the same time learn to preserve nature and water. I believe that with a program like this, in twenty to thirty years we can turn East Timor completely green again."

The excitement is building at this proposition. Vidal says, "Yes, we will plant the trees, the young generation, in order to make East Timor, our beloved country, green and covered by trees—with shade everywhere!"

Plans are made, appointments are scheduled, and, being a good teacher, Vidal knows that the key to accomplishment is to be a good student. He knows he has something to learn.

Vidal's Project Begins

Vidal has promised José that he will gather a group of young people and work with them to plant a thousand trees on the island. The first question, of course, is where to find one thousand saplings. Vidal is completely clueless, and the frustration shows on his face.

He checks around with everyone he knows, yet after a few days, he still hasn't solved the problem.

Traveling into Dili a few days later, Vidal spots a house where it's obvious that the owner

knows something about landscaping. Vidal spies all the hallmark signs of a master gardener: pots, shovels, a lush garden, many trees. Vidal strides up to the gate and knocks loudly. A good-looking man in his early thirties comes out and walks slowly toward Vidal. He asks Vidal what he wants, and then smiles at Vidal's questions, inviting the young student into his yard.

It turns out that this young man, Fabio, is indeed a professional landscaper. Born in East Timor, Fabio emigrated to the United States as a child but has returned home as an adult, with a burning desire to help his homeland. Both young men see the opportunity each presents to the other, and it is here Vidal voices his initial concern.

"I don't know how to plant a tree," Vidal freely admits, adding, "*honestly.*"

It turns out that Fabio, being passionate about landscaping and ecological issues, is a good and thorough teacher, too.

"Before you start any kind of planting," Vidal's new mentor says, "you've got to inform yourself about climates, weather, and temperature; and you have to do a lot of work with soil conditions."

"Second of all, you have to protect each tree not only from pests but from the animals.

"We're working with a mountainous terrain, which is very difficult," Fabio adds. "It's not dangerous; it's just a lot of work. We have a lot of uphill battles. This is East Timor, and there is no nursery where we can just go buy trees and start planting, so we have to find what is doing well and take from that and make more."

Vidal seems overwhelmed at all the challenges that lay ahead. He didn't know it would be so complex. Vidal shakes his head, saying, "I don't know where we will find the trees."

Fabio not only knows where to find trees, but also how to make cuttings, pot them, nurture them, and get them ready for planting. "We need to start working really quick. Given that it is rainy season, it'll be a bit helpful because we won't have to do as much watering," he says as he drives Vidal home. "But it'll take us some time."

Fabio glances around. "You live in a dangerous area," he says. "I think it's pretty brave of you to get out of there and actually do something for East Timor."

Vidal just lowers his head and offers his hand to Fabio, grateful that he has found someone willing to help him make a start.

The next day, the education of teacher Vidal continues. Fabio is going to show him exactly how to choose a spot to plant a tree, how to dig the soil, how to cover the roots, how and when to water it, and how to take care of the sapling in general.

Fabio surveys the grounds and says, "Hey, Vidal, that looks like a pretty good spot." The rusty blade of the ancient shovel first strikes the earth. Vidal stands to the side, leaning down, watching him work.

"The soil here, as you can see, is pretty rocky," says Fabio.

Vidal looks at the mounds of rocky, sandy soil near the small hole Fabio has dug, and then asks, "Do you think the tree will grow?"

"Oh, it'll grow." Fabio grins. By now, Vidal is down on the ground helping to dig, and he's digging it.

"It *has* to grow!" enthuses Fabio. "We'll make it grow."

Fabio is now spreading fertilizer around the base of the thin trunk of the would-be tree. Vidal joins him in this task. Once the fertilizer has been spread, the two begin watering the tree.

"Thank you!" Vidal says. He's very happy to get the project rolling, to learn by experience.

On the ride back to his home Vidal says, "In the couple of months coming, if we plant a thousand trees, it will involve twenty youth. Maybe I will be the one to show youth the way, and how to plant a tree."

Training a "Green Corps" for East Timor

So many things must be facilitated—land, seedlings, water, and of course, the young people who will become the first "Green Corps." Vidal also wants to educate the participants in conflict resolution and leadership training. So Vidal calls upon José Ramos-Horta's personal organization, the Peace and Democracy Foundation, for help.

Vidal speaks with the foundation's director, Estanislau, at their new headquarters in Dili. Vidal explains the tree-planting project—what he hopes to do, what is necessary to implement it—and Estanislau receives this information openly. This is a man who cares.

The Peace and Democracy Foundation agrees to help Vidal identify young people with strong leadership skills to begin planting the trees. "Our role will be to facilitate this process," he tells Vidal. "We will select people who are between twelve and twenty-five years old. And we will pick people who seem to have a strong commitment to make changes in their own communities."

Vidal is visibly relieved.

But several weeks later, he is in despair. The trainings cannot start because of a new outbreak of violence in Dili. Poverty, lack of education, the gangs, the violence are all interconnected. These outbreaks of violence cause a halt in the job training for the reforestation program, and Vidal's project is many weeks behind schedule as a result.

Finally, the first training is held at the Peace and Democracy Foundation office. "We need to make a lot of effort in explaining to people how this process will take place so that they can develop a sense of ownership of the trees," Estanislau tells Vidal. "Even in these small groups, some members still don't understand the process."

Vidal stands in front of the room full of new Green Corps members, energetically explaining that they need to look up instead of down, keep moving and keep learning—that they need to educate themselves so that in turn they can educate others. The students respond with hope.

It is here that you grasp a greater sense of the entire country's potential. It lies right here, in the hands of the young.

Soon Vidal and Fabio lead their new students up the mountainous countryside to find the best location to plant the trees. The arduous trek finds them all a bit worn out. But there's much hard work ahead, and they cling to their mission and its importance. Finally, after much deliberation, inspection, and discussion they decide that here on this mountain they will make their stand—with a stand of one thousand baby trees.

Fabio gives instructions about terrace planting on the hillsides, explaining the complexities, the reasons for terrace planting, and the nuances of it all.

Fabio says, "Dig around a little bit more and place rocks, bigger rocks around here. One rain in Timor will just wash this away, so by creating this terrace effect with big rocks, it'll help to keep some of the dirt and allow the roots to go farther and deeper into the mountain."

Vidal notes, "The water source is around 150 meters [492 feet] from here," so it will take quite a bit of effort to keep watering these seedlings on a regular basis.

Eight weeks go by. It is the dry season now, and some of the trees have started to die. Animals are starting to eat the leaves off the little trees. Members of the Green Corps struggle to save the trees—but they also ask local people in the area to help, knowing that much nurturing is still necessary, and that they cannot do it all on their own.

Lessons Learned

Vidal, Fabio, and the crew return to the site at the end of their three-month-long Green Corps project, and Fabio inspects the vegetation in the area.

He walks from tree to tree, inspects each one, then says, "On just this one hillside, we have eight different varieties of trees. We have a bit of fruit, we have some fuel trees, and we have some shade trees. This is very good."

Vidal turns to the young crew and praises them. "I think you did a good job. You did a very, very good job."

Estanislau says, "With the effort that we made, people now seem to understand that these trees are very important for us."

Despite the lack of saplings, the heat, the outbreaks of violence, and the roaming hungry animals that Vidal, Fabio, and their crew had to contend with, 836 of the trees survived. They are all amazed and happy—they have succeeded mightily, and word gets back to President Ramos-Horta, who wants to see for himself what some of the youth of his country have been up to.

As his small motorcade pulls into the village, the entire population is out in full force. They have pulled out all the stops, and the gala celebration of the project brings José Ramos-Horta (who has just been elected president of East Timor) to the microphone to address the crowd.

"For a long time, I have been a lonely wolf crying in the night, crying out to look after the land, the environment," José says. "I hope that you will continue to care for the trees and to care for the poor."

He turns to Vidal and says, "I personally will do whatever is in my power to support the continuation of this very good project."

Vidal beams.

"Yes, I want to continue this work," he tells you. "We need to train many many thousands more of our young generation to plant the trees, to care for the trees."

And in your heart, you know that he will.

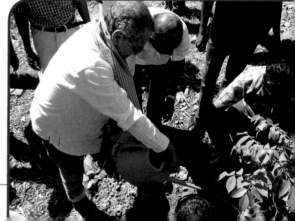

laureate
José Ramos-Horta

O ne of eleven children, José Ramos-Horta was born to a Timorese mother and Portuguese father on December 26, 1949, in Dili, East Timor. His father was a member of the Portuguese navy and was exiled to East Timor after protesting Portugal's military dictatorship. His mother survived the devastating invasion of the Japanese military during World War II, during which she lost all but one member of her family.

José was educated in a Catholic mission school in the remote hills of East Timor. He grew up without television and was therefore not heavily influenced by media or stars of the day. He also was not influenced by musicians,

although he did listen to the Beatles and the Rolling Stones, and was impressed not so much by their music, but by the widespread acclaim they received.

When he was eighteen years old, José met the same fate as his father, being exiled to Mozambique for comments that were deemed "subversive." These statements, made among friends, questioned Portugal's control over East Timor because of the poverty and underdevelopment of the country. After a brief time back in his home country, he was exiled again from 1970 to 1971 for his activism, which again spoke out against the Portuguese military rule.

In 1974, when José was twenty-five years old, Portugal gave up its colony and East Timor declared independence. Though many people in East Timor were excited about the newly gained independence, they were also worried that Indonesia had other plans for their tiny country. Their fears were not unwarranted, and, despite all of their best efforts, Indonesia invaded and began its brutal occupation of the tiny country. José spent the next twenty-four years in exile, trying to bring the story of East Timor to the world.

As one of the youngest people ever to address the United Nations, he was successful in convincing U.N. representatives to pass a resolution supporting the independence of East Timor. Despite this victory, Indonesia continued its occupation. José continued to push the United Nations and other world leaders to convince Indonesia to allow East Timor to regain and maintain its sovereignty.

In 1992, José formally presented a three-stage peace plan to the European Parliament.

The plan called for the withdrawal of Indonesian troops, the release of political prisoners, the respect for human rights, and the stationing of U.N. peacekeepers in East Timor. The final phase of the plan called for a period of time during which East Timor would be independent, followed by a United Nations-supervised vote, allowing the East Timorese to choose among being independent, becoming a part of Indonesia, or being associated with Portugal.

In December 1996, José Ramos-Horta was awarded the Nobel Peace Prize for his sustained efforts to stop the oppression of his people. In the year 2000, the people of East Timor won their struggle for independence and became the world's newest democracy. When the East Timorese people held their vote to decide the fate of their country, independence won overwhelmingly. In response, the Indonesian army burned and destroyed all that they could on their way out of the country, leaving the people with nothing.

José was able to go home for the first time in twenty-four years to see firsthand the devastation of his beautiful homeland, but also to the hope of his people. Despite the fact that four of his eleven brothers and sisters had been killed by the Indonesian military, José believes that peace can come to East Timor only through reconciliation and forgiveness. He says, "Just remember that violence leads you nowhere. We have to learn not to be violent if we want to have power. Compassion, generosity, humility, and tolerance are real power."

Xanana Gusmão, East Timor's first president, appointed José Ramos-Horta to serve as the country's first foreign minister. José was then elected President of East Timor in 2007.

On February 11, 2008, after returning from his morning walk, José Ramos-Horta was critically injured in an assassination attempt outside his home in Dili. Only two months after nearly losing his life, José Ramos-Horta returned to Dili to resume his presidential duties. Despite the assassination attempt, José continues to connect and engage with the people of East Timor on a very personal level. He stated that the primary effect of the attempt was a reaffirmation of his own personal conviction to lift people out of extreme poverty. As a president who has been known to ride public transportation—buying everyone aboard the minibus a meal at a street café—his deepest sadness as a result of the incidents is that his increased security protection will hamper his ability to be as close to the people of East Timor as he once was.

As he was preparing to leave the hospital to return home, José Ramos-Horta stated "I am returning home in the next few days, to do all I can to realize my dreams for East Timor—to continue lifting the Timorese people out of poverty, and to create a Zone of Peace where all forms of violence are abandoned."

voices of peace

WE NEED JOBS AND TRAINING

Máiread Corrigan Maguire

"We have a world where the rich are getting richer and the poor are getting poorer, and you can't have peace when you have injustice and inequality. So we have to put that right. My greatest hope is that people, throughout the world—the human family—will be able to find a way of working together to solve the great problems that we are now facing."

Desmond Tutu

"We see eliminating poverty, ensuring that people are healthy, providing education and things of that kind to others as not being altruistic; it's the best form of self-interest. It means that we're safe. Actually, I say that we can be human only together. We can be prosperous only together. We can be free only together. We can be secure, ultimately, only together."

Adolfo Pérez Esquivel

"What we are trying to do in the villages emerged as a need to raise awareness, value, and self-esteem. The first step in any process of liberation is that every man and woman acknowledge each other as persons. Rather than wasting billions and billions of dollars on the arms race and war, we have to make sure those resources are used to fight hunger—hunger that today affects almost half of humanity."

Rigoberta Menchú Tum

"I think that the cause of all the disorder that there is in our world is the lack of equality between he who has a lot of money and accumulated wealth—and does not care about others—and all the millions of poor people who surround him. In every country there is a zone of rich people and one of poor people. One place for those who exploit, and one for those who are exploited."

Ten Things You Can Do to Help

Address Extreme Poverty

1 **Encourage Microlending**

Microlending is a leading strategy in ending extreme poverty. Individuals, small groups, organizations, and banks have created small loans to give to families or individuals in countries where extreme poverty exists. These loans empower people to start a small business, enabling them to lift themselves out of poverty. You can join a microlending group in your community, or start one of your own.

2 **Provide Basic Job-Skills Training**

In places torn apart by war and poverty, there is a dire need for job skills training. Work within your local neighborhood, businesses, or universities to organize a group that can provide training and apprenticeships for youth, women, and others who can then help to build the infrastructure of their communities and provide income for their families.

3 **Promote Education**

Education is a very important factor in working to eliminate poverty. Many people who are affected by extreme poverty are not able to receive any level of schooling. Directly supporting schools—sending books and supplies, sponsoring students, or contributing financially to the building of a school or library—can create opportunities and access to jobs that can help end extreme poverty.

4 **Support Fair Trade**

Fair trade is a model of international trade that promotes fair pay to workers, generally in the realms of textiles, coffee, cocoa, handcrafts, fresh produce, and production of items such as electronics. Often, the people working in these jobs earn very minimal wages and work in horrible conditions. Creating a fair trade network, purchasing fair trade goods, and writing letters to companies insisting that they abide by fair trade guidelines can go a long way toward ensuring that the people are treated equally, work in safe conditions, and receive fair pay.

5 **Put Pressure on Governments**

Governments around the world need to make the commitment to getting rid of poverty. If the governments with more resources committed even 1 percent of their GDP, extreme poverty could be eliminated in our lifetime. Individuals need to put pressure on their own and other governments to commit to the elimination of poverty. Create a campaign to raise awareness and write letters to your own government and other governments to do the most they can do to fight poverty.

(6) Promote Debt Relief

Many countries whose people live on less than $1 a day are heavily in debt to other nations. The idea of debt relief is for developed countries to partially or completely forgive the debt of those countries who owe them money. This leaves more funds for the governments in developing countries to invest in the needs of their people. Write letters to your elected officials regarding debt relief, and join organizations that promote this strategy.

(7) Encourage Targeted and Effective Aid

Direct aid, such as sending money, materials, or volunteers to an area in need, is a good way to address many issues. Partner with an individual village, family, or organization to find out exactly what is needed and how to get it to the people who need it most. For more impact, try to build long-term partnerships.

(8) Promote Gender Equality

A key to ending poverty is to promote and guarantee gender equality, giving women access to education and jobs. Create a program to support schooling for girls, job training for young women, or aid in creating their own businesses to sustain themselves and their families. You can also campaign for equal pay for women and fair and safe treatment in work environments.

(9) Support Infrastructure Building

Poverty is not just lack of money; it is the lack of basic resources needed for people to survive. Whether it's providing clean drinking water, building a school or library, educating on health and sanitation issues, or developing businesses, projects that bring basic infrastructure to communities and homes help eradicate poverty.

(10) Eliminate Corruption

All too often, money and goods that are donated do not get into the hands of the people who need them most. Corruption is a massive problem that is keeping people in poverty throughout the world. When creating a project with or through another organization or government to eliminate poverty, ensure that the group you are working with is free of corruption. Put pressure on your local government officials to eliminate corruption and join the numerous groups that monitor corruption.

CHAPTER 5

We Want to Feel Safe

Oscar Arias Sánchez, Maria & Karla— The International Arms Trade

A world where $1.15 trillion are spent on arms and soldiers is a completely irrational world. The truth is that there is no justification. If our greatest enemies are illiteracy, inequality, poverty, and the degradation to the environment, we must modify spending in the world economies, the same in richer countries as in poorer ones.
—Oscar Arias Sánchez

Discovering Costa Rica

The Costa Rican national motto is *"Pura Vida,"* which translates to "Pure Life." On the plane ride in to San José, we are hoping to find that this phrase will still ring true.

Costa Rica, a tiny nation sandwiched between Panama and Nicaragua in Central America, reflects an amazing mixture of the natural and some of the most innovative political ideas mankind has to offer.

Its tropical rain forests teem with an astounding array of life forms. Stunningly primal flora and fauna that exist nowhere else in the world flourish here. Its pristine beaches run in sandy bands down both sides of the country, along the Pacific and Caribbean coasts. The spine of the country is dotted with volcanoes. In the jungle, luscious, ripe, verdant vegetation grows freely, just as it did thousands of years ago. Gazing up into the rain forest canopy, you see a mother monkey with a baby clinging to her as she forages among the trees. A brightly colored toucan flaps by, alighting on the branch of a tree only feet from you.

But these incredible rain forests are being threatened by pollution, global warming, and the encroachment of man. Dozens of species of animals and vegetation are disappearing from the region, and at a much more alarming rate than was first predicted. Scientists are in a race to save the natural wonder of the Costa Rican rain forest, and the Costa Rican government aggressively supports this effort. In fact, for its work to save the rain forests and for investing in clean technology designed to lower carbon emissions dramatically countrywide, Costa Rica has just been ranked fifth best nation in the world for excellence in environmental performance (2008 Environmental Performance Index), right behind Norway, Sweden, Switzerland, and Finland. Quite an achievement for a modest little country like Costa Rica.

This is the same kind of innovative thinking that inspired the people of Costa Rica to abolish their army in 1948. Ever since, they have had no standing military at all—instead, government funds have been invested in education, housing, health care, and environmental preservation, and as a result, the people of Costa Rica have been able to live in relative peace and harmony for more than sixty years.

"Tico" is the affectionate nickname for a citizen of Costa Rica. And this peace and harmony is the special something that Ticos are talking about when they describe their national ethos as *Pura Vida.*

Yet many Costa Ricans are now afraid that their very way of life may soon be endangered, much like their beloved rain forests. Guns and gang violence are spreading throughout Central America today. And slowly but surely, these weapons are starting to permeate Costa Rica's borders, to creep into its cities and towns.

Meet Maria and Karla

We are here in Costa Rica to meet with two seventeen-year-old students, Maria and Karla. They fear that their country is changing—that it will be a tranquil and peaceful place no more. December 2007 was the most violent month in many years, with a record number of gun-related deaths reported. Police have confiscated more than six thousand weapons, but this has not stopped gun violence in the streets. Maria and Karla are shocked as they watch the nightly news on TV and witness the rise in gun violence. As PeaceJammers, they have decided that they are going to do something about it.

Maria runs her fingers through her shiny brown hair. Her almond-shaped eyes are full of concern as she describes her fears in rapid-fire staccato Spanish. Everyone knows that you can purchase a machine gun in neighboring Panama for next to nothing. How long will it be before these devices of death get dragged illegally over the border?

Karla's quiet intensity catches you off guard. She speaks softly, measuring her words and thoughts. There is much at stake here—she knows the deep, nonviolent past of her country could easily be shattered, destroyed by illegal arms. She pulls her long hair back into a ponytail and glances up, and Karla's quick smile immediately charms you into wanting to know more.

"Guns are a danger to society," Karla says. "We want young people to understand that all of this is bad, so as they grow up, they will try to prevent everything related to the use of guns."

Maria jumps in. "Just having a gun close by is a dangerous thing. In a mere moment, life can disappear with the use of a gun. It is incredible when you think about what can happen, not just to you—mentally, physically—but to your family, your friends."

Maria and Karla have been working on a project to educate their generation to say "*Armas no gracias*"—"No thank you"—to guns. It is a vital project, because some people in Costa Rica are reacting to the rising level of violence in their country by going out and purchasing guns of their own. Maria and Karla know that some of their peers are starting to see guns and violence as cool, as more and more violent images are being force-fed to them via music, video games, and movies. They tell us that they want to create a new ethic of nonviolence for their generation, like the one that inspired their great-grandparents to abolish the Costa Rican military sixty years ago.

"We are meeting at the Arias Peace Museum tomorrow to finish the planning for our project. Why don't you come, too?" Maria asks. Moved by their passion and concern, we enthusiastically agree.

How Can We Convince Our Friends?

Karla and Maria attended the PeaceJam Tenth Anniversary Youth Conference in September 2006 and listened carefully as their president, Oscar Arias Sánchez, delivered a speech on controlling the proliferation of weapons, globally *and* locally. They are gathered at the museum today along with several other students who were with them at that event, and they have two goals in mind: to develop their "*Armas No Gracias*" campaign for Costa Rica, and to lay out a timeline for implementation.

Karla begins. "This project started after we returned from the PeaceJam. In February we met to talk about the idea of creating a gun prevention campaign to raise society's awareness of the real causes involved, and the consequences."

A tall, ruggedly handsome student named Marco speaks up. "After returning from Denver, well, we met people there from all over the world: Tibet, Guatemala, Argentina. So we thought, We're not alone—there are really a lot of us working on this. Basically I'm scared, because we know that besides the guns there are many gangs coming down through Central America, through Guatemala and El Salvador. We really have to do something."

"Yes, that's right," says an athletic young man named Rafael. "This project's most important goal is to raise young people's awareness about guns, to change their thinking to see that guns always bring negative consequences, because there can be many conflicts, many problems behind a gun."

"I think that is the most important thing," Maria agrees, "the perception we have of guns, and that we can really change this perception. That is the most vital part, changing the current way of thinking for young people."

Rafael nods his head. "People have to realize that guns are bad from the moment they are built, even when they haven't been used. When guns are built they're also sold, and that money could be put to other uses, like helping poor children or for education."

Karla smiles. "So what can we do to create a network that will increase the number of us who are opposed to guns? My idea is that, after we work with young people, they should be able to teach other kids everything we've shown them in these workshops. What we want is for the chain to grow, so we can eventually educate all young people—and the country as well—to be opposed to guns, and to be more of an example to others in Latin America."

Maria asks, "What activities do you think we could use?"

Karla says, "We could play some games to raise their awareness—like one about guilt. You could have a gun-related accident, and then the question is, *who is responsible?*"

"Yes," Maria agrees, "responsibility would fall on each person, the one who bought the gun, the one who supplied it, the one who used it—and they all dodge the issue. Then we can ask each student's view on the question. That would be perfect."

Karla asks, "What else?"

Rafael speaks out. "Some advertising clips, like the ones they have on TV in other countries."

Karla nods her head. "We could ask the Arias Foundation if they have any that they could share with us. What else?"

Marco raises his hand. "Ask if anyone has had any experience with guns. They can tell us about it, about their own personal stories."

"Great!" Karla smiles. "This is already an hour; in order not to tire them out too much, each workshop that we present should take about an hour, so they pay attention, because remember that—"

Maria completes the thought. "They are students."

"That's right," Karla laughs. "Now we need to decide where."

Rafael says, "How about in Guanacaste, Heredia, San José, and Cartago, too?"

"And one more idea," Marco says. "Once we've implemented the program in many different schools, we could do a final closing campaign—an *Armas No Gracias* training camp."

"It would be the beginning of a broader campaign against guns?" Maria asks.

"Yes," Marco replies. "It would be the closing of the initial campaign, and also the beginning of a countrywide chain to educate more people who can then educate others."

"Perfect. That is so powerful!" Maria says with a smile.

"Yes," Rafael says, "it is a revolution, but a different kind of revolution—one without guns."

Everyone laughs, and they work late into the night, writing down the plans that could make their exciting vision come true.

A Meeting with the President

The country of Costa Rica is helmed by a most extraordinary man—Oscar Arias Sánchez. He was the president of his country once before, from 1986 to 1990, a violent and tumultuous time of many wars throughout Central America. He negotiated the regional peace treaty that brought an end to this devastation, and for his tremendous contribution, he was awarded the Nobel Peace Prize in 1987. After many years leading an international campaign to halt the spread of weapons, he was coaxed out of political retirement and was asked to run for president once again, this time in 2006.

He won the election and is once again helming his country. Oscar Arias Sánchez understands that he has his work cut out for him, but he's a great leader and a man who is ready, willing, and able to roll up his shirtsleeves and get down to the task at hand.

Today, Maria and Karla and their friends are going to get the incredible opportunity to meet with President Arias, and to tell him about their *Armas No Gracias* campaign.

Karla and Maria hop into one of the many taxicabs that zip through the city, through the clogged and colorful streets. The driver asks where they are going, and they reply in unison, "To the president's house." The driver zigs and zags around buses, transport trucks, and other traffic as the young women talk excitedly about their project. Arriving at President Arias's home, the driver then asks, "Now where?"

The two grin as they say, "Just drop us off here; we have a meeting with President Arias." The arched curve of the driver's eyebrow causes the girls to laugh even more. Yes it's true—they're meeting with the president. And sixteen more of their PeaceJam friends are going to join them.

The students are in awe as they walk slowly into the handsomely appointed home. President Arias enters the room smiling, and he shakes hands with the young activists. He sits down in a beautiful brown leather chair and invites them to sit on a matching couch. The conversation begins.

"First, I would like to congratulate you for these programs you have in mind. They will help this society to be more peaceful and less violent," Oscar says. "But of course, as Einstein put it, everything is relative, right? Violence here is certainly very low when compared to other sister countries like Guatemala and El Salvador. We have the fortune of not having had wars during the 1980s like our brothers. That is why these places became filled with weapons, and this is in part why they have armies . . . armies that are too big, in fact."

"We have had the good fortune of not having an army since 1948," he continues. "We were a visionary country, and we showed a lot of courage in abolishing the military. Think about how much we should be thanking God for the foresight of our ancestors in getting rid of our army."

"Yes, yes." Maria says. "We want to take our project to the whole country, and then to take it beyond our borders. Our brothers and sisters in Guatemala and Honduras, for example, have a lot of problems with weapons in the hands of young people."

"You always want the best for your neighbors," Oscar Arias Sánchez replies. "A desperate neighbor often takes desperate actions, many of which can be violent.

"I want Costa Rica to be a moral force," the president continues. "For many years, my Arias Foundation has been working on the weapons proliferation problem. We have also created another project through the Arias Foundation, one that the United Nations has now adopted. The National Assembly at the United Nations has recently voted for a group of experts to be assembled to create a treatise on the arms industry. This treatise would work to control the spread of weapons. There is nothing that arouses passion in me more than pacifying, diminishing, and attenuating the military conflict and violence that is sweeping the whole world."

Karla and Maria listen quietly and then look up, shyly. "Our program is based on prevention overall," Maria summarizes. "To educate about all the negative consequences related to weapons: deaths and damage to friends and family. One stray bullet can change our lives entirely. It can ruin our dreams and wreck everything. So disarmament is our main objective, and it is overall a campaign focused on prevention."

The president stands up and offers a warm handshake to each one of them. "I think that being able to introduce a program that is focused on getting weapons out of the hands of individuals is a great thing. I want to congratulate you. I think what you are doing is marvelous."

Camp Armas No Gracias

Six months later, we find the dedicated duo of Maria and Karla preparing for the final event of their campaign, their *Armas No Gracias* training camp. They are sitting amid a messy pile of posters, sign-in sheets, balls of string, workshop signs, rolls of masking tape, T-shirts, and brightly colored balloons—all part of their preparation for the big weekend. They have already presented their workshop in dozens of high schools throughout Costa Rica, and we ask them how things have gone.

"Well," Karla starts, "what we have done in these schools is a program with a series of activities designed to stimulate them, to spark their interest in knowing the consequences, in knowing that this could happen to anyone. We have helped them see that they shouldn't use a gun thinking that it will make them safe, because at any time that gun could be used against them."

Maria says, "The most interesting thing was seeing how little information young people had on this issue. They would come up to us and say that they had never heard this information before."

"Many of them were really shocked," Karla adds. "We showed them videos, and they had never seen a gun wound close up, and they were like, 'What's that? Ughhh!' But that is what happens; weapons kill."

"For example," Maria explains, "we heard about an eleven-year-old boy who killed his mother accidentally. In a video there was a boy who was lying in a bed; he's a paraplegic—he couldn't move his hands, just his legs. He said, 'I could have solved the conflict in a different way, but I had a gun in my hand, and that was that.' We asked the kids if they'd had any confrontations, any contact with guns. And many said yes."

Karla shakes her head slowly. "I think the hardest part was learning about other people's experiences with guns, that their lives as children came to an end, that because of a stray bullet they lost their family, they lost everything. It was so hard to hear them tell their stories, and the totally negative and tragic consequences that they now face."

"It was also very difficult to get started," Maria adds. "At first the schools were like, 'You want to come and talk to us about guns?' They were surprised, and they resisted a bit because we are only students ourselves. But once we got in the door, and as the workshops progressed, the students really started to open up more and more. For me, doing this project was quite an experience. It was very valuable, because in the end one learns to see many different points of view, and one learns from that."

Karla nods. "The most important thing was the issue that we wanted to present. We didn't know if the young people would grasp the meaning or if they would want to participate in our workshops. What we found was that many of them already had their own ideas. The workshops really raised the question of looking for an alternative to violence, finding nonviolent solutions—like talking or negotiating, or asking their parents not to have a gun in the house. Little by little, the young people themselves are making a moral commitment to this."

"It was so great to see how the kids really liked the activities, and how in the end they thanked you," Maria says, her eyes glistening. "In Heredia, a boy came up at the end of the workshop and he thanked us, saying that he learned a lot . . . so it kind of fills you up, and gives you an incredible sort of energy to go on with the project."

Both girls are quiet for a moment, and then they glance at the messy room around them.

"So now," Karla says, laughing nervously, "we are finishing the signs, getting all of the materials ready for the games, so that everything will be perfect for our camp."

"What we are really hoping to do this weekend," Maria says, "is to bring together all of the schools where we did the workshops to have a general conclusion and have them mingle, to be together and to know that they are not the only ones who have these ideals."

"And the idea is really to reach out to other kids who may not have heard the *Armas No Gracias* message yet, and to take it to every town in Costa Rica," Karla adds, and then she starts laughing. "There is so much to do . . . we are all going to be up very late tonight!"

The next morning dawns cold and bright, and students from all over Costa Rica head to Campo Escuela Nacional Iztarú. Located outside San José in the mountains surrounding the city, Iztarú is one of the oldest and best known Boy Scout camps in Costa Rica. The view from the camp over the rolling, verdant valleys is breathtaking.

The hero of the day is Marco; he's been a Boy Scout all of his life and knows this venue well. He has a cell phone jangling in his pocket and a heavy black walkie-talkie stuck to his ear. He walks up and down the hills between the small wooden buildings, helping students to register, herding young people from one activity to the next. Karla, a Girl Scout herself, is right at his side, a highly competent deputy in running this unique and inspiring issue camp for kids.

The camp culminates with a live theater performance, created by some of the students themselves. It starts with two central characters—two young boys—who are watching a violent television cartoon. The boys laugh as cartoon characters get sprayed by bullets, have limbs hacked off with machetes, or die in fiery car wrecks. At first, the young people in the audience laugh along with the television-watching boys, because they are giving completely over-the-top performances.

Suddenly, behind these two performers you see another set of actors, and they are not aware of the two boys watching television. They are engaged in an entirely different play—based

in real life—to illustrate the actual consequences of violence. Three stories are woven together in a moving montage behind the television. In the first, a woman is continually abused by a man who acts as if he loves her, yet he keeps beating her until, one day, he finally kills her. In the second, some young men exchange words as they pass each other on the street of a small town; the situation escalates quickly into confrontation and results in one boy bleeding to death on the road. In the third, two young children, a brother and sister, find a gun in their parents' bedroom and start to act out all of the funny things they have seen on television—and the little girl is accidentally shot, just as their mother enters the room to find out what the fuss is all about. The boys watching television at the front of the stage continue to laugh at the violence on the television set they're glued to, oblivious of the reality being enacted out behind them.

Slowly, sadness spreads through the audience, and several young people wipe away tears as a sheet is placed over the youngest gunshot victim. The actors receive a long-standing ovation for their emotional performances, and the lesson on the effects of "fictional" violence is very well-received.

Then the camp is over, but before the young people leave for home, they all sign a giant white sheet with their names and their own personal pledge to carry the *Armas No Gracias* message home in their hearts. Then there are smiles all around, and they goof for the camera as dozens of photos are taken of the determined young people who came together in such an extraordinary way today.

Karla and Marco are sitting together as the buses and minivans pull out of the parking lot; they are both sweaty and exhausted and happy.

Marco says "That play, it really let us see how everything we watch on TV leads us to look at guns as something normal. But it's not so—it's not normal to have guns."

Karla nods her head, and then she speaks out in her thoughtful way. "What we want to do is to continue, to have these young people act as receivers for the message we want to transmit, and for the chain to continue to expand, because this is not a problem that is just going to disappear. We have to go on, we have to create a new culture of nonviolence in order to eradicate the problem. And we are the ones who can make this happen."

As the sun sets over the green hills of Iztarú, her quiet voice rings out, powerful and true.

Creating a Shift in Consciousness for a New Generation

Two days later, Maria swoops by our hotel and whisks us off for a final meeting with the president of Costa Rica. She is full of life as she enthusiastically explains the plans that she and Karla have made for the future, and how they want to get many, many more young people involved in this cause.

Maria jumps out of the cab and runs to catch up with Karla and Marco. Then the three of them walk confidently into the Costa Rican "White House" to give a final report on their project.

Oscar Arias Sánchez greets them warmly. "Hi. Glad to see you again. How are you?" Then he asks them how things are going, and if they have graduated from high school yet.

"I just finished, thank goodness." Maria laughs.

"I have a year left," Karla replies.

And then they bubble on about their plans to continue their project (more workshops for every grade level, an advertising campaign for TV, an interactive youth conference via satellite countrywide), as the president of Costa Rica sits with them and smiles.

"That was thrilling!" Maria almost shouts as they leave the meeting room. "He spoke such encouraging words, and he said that he would do all he could to support us. We like that, because we are going to continue with this project."

"I feel great," Karla agrees, "because I have never spoken like this before with the president, so close, and he told us that our work was so worthwhile. He said that he would give us support as we go forward."

"I feel happy," Marco adds, "because I feel like we really accomplished something. You know, sometimes my friends ask me, 'Why are you doing this? You are not getting paid anything. You are wasting your time.' But this is important. If everyone could just do something like this to help their family, their town, their country, this would be a very, very different world."

Maria and Karla look at each other and beam, and then the three of them link arms and head out the door. Nothing can stop them now.

laureate
Oscar Arias Sánchez

Oscar Arias Sánchez was born on September 13, 1940, in Heredia, Costa Rica. Heredia is known for its beautiful tropical forests, waterfalls, roaring rivers, and coffee plantations. Arias Sánchez was born to one of Costa Rica's richest coffee-growing families. When he was just seven years old, Costa Rica made the historic decision to be the first country in the world to abolish its standing army. Thus, Oscar grew up in Central America's only country that had no army and did not rely on military might to ensure its security.

After studying at the Colegio Saint Francis in San José, Oscar went to the United States to study medicine at Boston University. He returned to Costa Rica in 1969 and started teaching political science at the University of Costa Rica. Three years later, he entered politics. In 1986, he was elected president of Costa Rica for the first time and served until 1990.

The day he took office was not a day of celebration. Oscar wasted no time in making sure the leaders of the other countries in Central America understood his mission to create peace throughout the region. On his election day, the presidents of nine Latin American countries came together to hear Oscar's plea for democracy and liberty. He revealed his plan to remove Central America from the middle of the cold war that was being waged between the world's two superpowers—the United States and the USSR. By supporting various governments and armies, these superpowers had fueled the civil wars that killed more than one hundred thousand people in Guatemala and aggravated unrest in El Salvador and Nicaragua, as well as increased border tensions between Nicaragua and its neighboring states, Honduras and Costa Rica.

What soon became known as the "Arias Plan" called on leaders to limit the size of their armies, assure freedom of the press, and hold free and open elections. As the leader of a politically neutral country, nestled in a region turned upside down by political conflict, Oscar came to be known for defending personal freedoms and limiting the buildup of military power.

In his Nobel Prize acceptance speech, Oscar stated, "we seek in Central America not peace alone, not peace to be followed some day by political progress, but peace and democracy together, indivisible, an end to the shedding of human blood, which is inseparable from an end to the suppression of human rights. . . . We believe that justice and peace can only thrive together, never apart. A nation that mistreats its own citizens is more likely to mistreat its neighbors."

His work as an international diplomat culminated in 1987 when all the Central American presidents signed the Procedure to Establish a Firm and Lasting Peace in Central America. Oscar also achieved great things for Costa Rica and was a very accessible president, often mingling in the streets without bodyguards. Unlike most world leaders, President Arias often dined in public restaurants and drove his own car. Oscar felt safe in Costa Rica, a country whose stability was measured not by military power but by success in the areas of education, health care, and elections.

Oscar's tenacity and loyalty to his people elevated him to the status of a national hero. The world recognized him for his courageous efforts in the Central American peace process in 1987, when he was awarded the Nobel Peace Prize.

Being showered with fame and praise did not slow down his efforts to promote peace. If anything, it encouraged him to expand his attention from the recovering region of Central America to the entire world. He is actively involved with peace-promoting organizations around the world. With the monetary award that comes with the Nobel Peace Prize, President Arias established the Arias Foundation for Peace and Human Progress. Aiming to promote peace, justice, and equality in Central America—and serve as a model in these areas for the rest of the world—the Arias Foundation has been one of the leading organizations in Central America when it comes to post-war reconstruction in the region.

The foundation has focused largely on disarmament and the end of the international arms trade, but has also taken on many of the toughest social problems that plague the conflict-prone region. Concerned with the well-being of those most often victimized by the trafficking of drugs, arms, and people—namely women and youth—the foundation has launched numerous programs in the areas of human security, peace, education, disarmament, and government.

Currently, the Arias Foundation is in the midst of revisiting the disarmament plan that resulted in Oscar Arias Sánchez winning the Nobel Peace Prize. In addition to collecting data on what has been accomplished, the foundation plans to examine what needs to be improved as well as fill in any gaps that may have been overlooked in the original agreement. From this extensive research, the foundation plans to come forward with an agenda that will bring much-needed attention to the fragile region and continue the work for peace and stability in Central America.

Oscar Arias Sánchez strives to get the people of the world to understand security as something that is not based on having a huge army but on education, jobs, and health.

A few years ago, the Costa Rican people "reinterpreted" their constitution in order to allow Oscar Arias Sánchez another run for president. He won the election in January 2006 and is currently serving as the president of Costa Rica once again.

voices of peace

WE WANT TO FEEL SAFE

The Dalai Lama

"I think war is outdated and is not relevant. The whole world should be acting like this one body, so they should treat all parts of the world as they'd treat parts of themselves. Some conflict is always there, yet the method to solve this conflict—using force—is out of date. The new practical, realistic method is through talk, dialogue—and the spirit of reconciliation and compromise."

José Ramos-Horta

"Land mines, torture equipment, cluster bombs, and chemical weapons are designed to inflict pain and death to human beings. Most victims are civilians —women and children. How can arms manufacturers, weapons designers, plant managers, politicians, all of whom have families of their own that they love, be so insensitive when it comes to the suffering of other human beings?"

Adolfo Pérez Esquivel

"Rather than wasting billions of dollars on the arms race and war, we have to make sure those resources are used to fight hunger—hunger that affects almost half of humanity. When one talks about safety, we talk about the army, the police, repression, we talk about making more rules, building more weapons, and locking ourselves in our homes. I believe that this generates more insecurity than security."

Jody Williams

"Arms control and disarmament are not esoteric issues that only a few military powers of the world are capable of handling. Any discussion related to weapons must include the humanitarian perspective as well. The impact of any weapon or weapons system on individuals, communities, and whole countries must be an integral part of any arms control and disarmament discussions."

Ten Things You Can Do to Help

Address the Issue of the International Arms Trade

(1) Educate Yourself

Small arms, light weapons, large arms, munitions, cluster bombs, landmines, surplus stockpiles . . . the list goes on. The international arms trade is massive and complex. Do research to make sure you are in the know about arms trade issues and create your own opinions as to what to do to address the complications, conflicts, and problems that occur as a result of this global-weapons industry.

(2) Educate Others

Do people in your community know what is happening as the result of the international arms trade? Do the people in your community know about the impacts of arms on *their own* community? Organize a group of friends to pass out information about the effects of arms locally and globally. Create a petition regarding small arms to take to your local leaders, and ask people to sign, letting those with influence and power know that you want things to change.

(3) Make an Impression

Every year thousands of people are killed worldwide by handguns alone. Over 12 billion bullets are produced each year. Visual representations of large numbers often help put these statistics into perspective and get people to act. Create a visual representation of the number of deaths or injuries due to handguns each year. The representation can be an artistic piece such as a painting, a dramatic interpretation such as a play, or simply a chain of paper clips with each clip representing one person who died as a result of firearms that year.

(4) Choose Your Weapons

The issue of the international arms trade is so expansive that it's easy to get overwhelmed! It may be helpful to create or jump onto a campaign in a specific arms area. For example, you could decide to work specifically on cluster bombs, nuclear weapons, handguns, or automatic weapons; or you could work on creating laws that crack down on arms trading in general. Once you've got one issue down, move on to the next!

(5) Demand Safe Storage or Destruction

Civilians pay the price with their lives when weapons fall into the hands of criminals or other armed groups. Around the world, tens of millions of small arms and ammunitions are kept in poorly secured conditions. Demand that your country and others safely secure weapons stockpiles.

If safe storage cannot be provided, demand that the weapons stockpile be destroyed to prevent the weapons from falling into the wrong hands.

⑥ Support the Arms Trade Treaty

Oxfam, Amnesty International, and the International Action Network on Small Arms have worked together to create an Arms Trade Treaty that calls for "an international, legally binding treaty to ease the suffering caused by irresponsible weapons transfers." Join their campaign and their "Million Faces" visual petition. Visit their Web site at www.controlarms.com to find out more.

⑦ Say Thanks, but No Thanks

Over $1 trillion are spent annually on military expenditures and arms worldwide—including both legal and illegal weapons sales or trading. Illegal trade of small arms is very prevalent in many regions affected by terrible instability, as are legal sales of arms from industrialized nations. Demand that leaders not sell weapons to politically or economically unstable governments, and also put pressure on leaders to turn down offers of arms, especially in turbulent times.

⑧ Encourage Responsible Use

Though the complete abolition of personal firearms may not be in our near future, something must be done to address the fact that nearly thirty thousand people are killed by handguns each year in the United States alone. Promoting responsible gun use, requiring training, and enforcing tough laws on the types of firearms that are legal for an individual citizen to own are all ways to reduce the number of injuries and deaths caused by these weapons.

⑨ Keep the Peace

One of the biggest issues with arms control is the fact that gangs are heavily armed in most places. Many community leaders and organizers have worked together to negotiate cease-fires between gangs in residential neighborhoods, parks, or entire communities. Pull together a group of people to discuss how a cease-fire could be established and how community members together can raise their voices against violence.

⑩ Make Pledges and Encourage Amnesty

Create your own pledge never to use guns and circulate the pledge throughout the community. Work with your local law enforcement or government officials to develop an amnesty period—a period of time during which people can come to a secure and confidential place and turn in weapons without fear of punitive repercussions.

Racism Is Against the Law!

Rigoberta Menchú Tum & Fernando—The Problem of Racism

Greed, envy, individualism, and an excessive materialism are altering the human experience and causing a lack of equilibrium in the world. I believe the inequality has also generated racism, the sickness of discrimination. This world has lost values and it must begin again. Beginning again means much humility.
—Rigoberta Menchú Tum

Guatemala

Nestled between Mexico and Belize, Guatemala is a country with a lengthy history. Evidence of the first people in Guatemala dates back ten thousand years, and descendants of those indigenous people—the Mayans—make up a majority of the population in this Central American country.

In March 2007, we flew to Guatemala to meet up with Fernando, a high school senior who is working to create a fundamental shift in consciousness in his country on the issue of racism—which is primarily directed at the Mayan Indians. According to the Mayan spiritual tradition, much of the world will begin to change in the year 2012. Mayans say that 2007 is the "Gateway Year" to the auspicious year of change that is 2012. We are fascinated, and anxious to learn more.

As we drive out of Guatemala City, we begin to see the true beauty of this place. The countryside opens up into some of the most fertile agricultural land in the world. Speeding

down the highway, we see miles of rich green sugarcane fields. Guatemala is the third-largest sugarcane producer in the world, but Guatemala's yield per acre is number one. A national joke: Guatemalan soil is so rich that you can plant a rock and a tree will grow from it. Just fourteen degrees above the equator and enjoying extensive rainfall, it is a country that agriculturally should be able to provide not only for itself but for many other countries as well.

But the struggle of Guatemala's indigenous people to earn even a decent living from their work in these fields is a tale of great struggle, strife, violence, and woe. For years the Mayans have endured subsistence wages and terrible living conditions. Yet a change is coming, they believe—a change that has the potential to alter the entire future of humankind. And one of the strongest voices speaking out for this change is Rigoberta Menchú Tum, recipient of the 1992 Nobel Peace Prize.

Mystical Mayan Time

Diminutive in stature but overpowering in presence—that's the first thing you notice about Rigoberta Menchú Tum. She won the Nobel Peace Prize for leading her people in a nonviolent movement against the military government that had embroiled Guatemala in decades of devastating war. Ever since, she has summoned her will and her poetic magic to speak directly to hearts and minds all over the globe. Her messages are plain common sense combined with ancient Mayan teachings, and she is wise enough to know the delicate balance needed to bring her points home gale force.

"For us, the Mayas, during the years from 1992 until 2012," Rigoberta says, digging deeply into her cultural background, "space is devoid of time. Time is totally dispersed, and people have different objectives, different jobs, different missions. But overall, they are all waiting for a common ground.

"These years, right now, are the darkest time for humanity—we call it 'No Time.' There is no perspective," Rigoberta says carefully, pausing momentarily. "People lack confidence in themselves, in their endeavors. We all think we are doing our best, but we are not reaching the solutions for the problems facing mankind. We have lost the concept of solidarity, of amity, of collaboration, of sharing.

"Greed, envy, individualism, and an excessive materialism are altering the human experience and causing a lack of equilibrium in the world. We see no equilibrium anywhere. We see women divided or with no rights at all. We see poverty and hunger, and on the other hand a great deal of opulence. All of these negative aspects are affecting human culture in general. We are hoping for a new day."

And you think: Who isn't hoping for a new day? Day-to-day life is more than daunting, and when you add politics and problems such as racism, intolerance, lack of human rights, and economic disparity into the mix, you want to go to bed and pull the covers over your head.

But Rigoberta's faith is greater than her fear, and you are inspired as she rolls out more Mayan prophecy.

"According to our Mayan ancestors, a new time is drawing near," Rigoberta confirms. "It is like the coming of a new dawn. So it is important to maintain the light shining in these days. We need to reflect upon what can be done."

Having spent time with this courageous woman—who has just launched a bid for the presidency of her country—you hope that this brilliant new era arrives soon.

"The era is to be approximately 5,125 years long," she goes on, "and it will begin around 2012. In this new era, for the very first time, male and female energies will be united. The duality of life will be united. We are all dual creatures, but we have forgotten this duality."

You're reeling now. What you're hearing is some deeply serious thought about the long-term future, something you can barely comprehend. Then the notion of "duality" makes you realize how incredible the Mayan vision of the future really is. What will this new era look like?

First, you think of the luminous spiritual nature of the Mayan people. But then you question the wisdom of a Mayan woman—no matter how strong and brave she is—running for her country's highest office, which puts not only herself in mortal danger but everyone around her as well.

In many parts of the world, we've seen great progress in terms of equality of races, sexes, and sometimes, religions. But these are totally new and strange concepts to a place like Guatemala, where men and *only* men—and certainly not an indigenous woman—would share power. *Any* power. Guatemala has been a patriarchal society for centuries. Can things here really change?

Meet Fernando

Hurricane is a word whose etymological roots are Mayan in origin. The Mayas have given the world much, and now many of them are trying to deliver something new: an indigenous female president. The storm is brewing and the winds of change are swirling, and you wonder just how hard the rain is going to fall.

Fernando is part of this storm. He's seventeen years old and just about to finish high school. He hopes to be a communications major when he enters university, and from there, pursue a career in journalism. Fernando has dancing brown eyes and effortless charm, and you can easily imagine him as a television reporter or anchor. He's *that* charismatic.

Fernando's father runs a small auto-parts business and his mother runs a beauty salon.

Their income is a bit above the national average, but they are not wealthy. They work hard and are a tight-knit family who share the day to day in the tradition of so very many.

Fernando's parents are more than aware that simply being middle class, with enough money to own their own home, does not guarantee the success of their children. This is readily apparent as you get to know Fernando. His parents have worked hard to instill in him a highly developed sense of right and wrong, of good morals and of civic duty.

Fernando also has a gift for communication. He leads all handshakes by looking the person directly in the eye. He smiles easily, bringing people rapidly into his confidence. Whether Fernando is talking to a presidential candidate or a regular person on the street, he takes great delight in engaging people, winning them over with his easy smile and his candid and lively questions. He makes you feel as if you've been best friends for years.

That Fernando has chosen to take up a Global Call to Action project that fights racism and helps Rigoberta in her run at the presidency—with his parents cheering him on to do so—says a mouthful about the Gateway Year that is 2007. Few Ladinos have come to the aid of Guatemala's indigenous people at this juncture in history. But Fernando takes up the cause with vigor and verve. He's just like a farmer who is planting the seeds in Guatemala's fertile soil, and he's going to nurture the goodness that springs up with every campaign leaflet he distributes to Mayas and Ladinos alike.

Fernando hails from Coatepeque, a picturesque rural community in Guatemala. He attended PeaceJam's tenth anniversary in Denver in 2006, and he pledged to work to eradicate racism in his country. Fernando knows there is much for Guatemala to overcome.

"Well, before going to PeaceJam, I didn't realize that my country needed things from us, *things from me* in order to change," he says. "Thanks to PeaceJam, and the words from all the Nobel Peace Prize winners, I realized that, my country, much like myself, needs a change overall.

"My own views have changed: I've opened myself up, and I've been to a lot more reunions and conferences because I know I have to do something for my country. I know that it's a very important change in me."

This inner change is leading to outward action on a national scale.

A Historic Campaign

Fernando plans to start from the simplest idea and then attack with something strong. He wants to catch them young—presenting this topic to elementary-school students so that they can dissolve attitudes of racism bit by bit and hopefully grow into adults who care about ending racism.

In addition, he wants to launch a ten-year national advertising project targeted toward young people between the ages of fourteen and thirty. This project would include five campaigns—each campaign lasting two years. The first two years will focus on fostering a sense of patriotism and encouraging people to speak out in favor of what everyone wants—a united Guatemala. The next campaigns will focus on culture, equality, and pluriculturalism.

The morning sun beats down on Coatepeque's quiet streets as the town's denizens drink their morning coffee. A humid breeze carries the sound of motorcycles and automobiles buzzing through the streets as Fernando explains his plan of action to his parents over breakfast.

"I believe that the younger the person is, the better the chance of this work having a deep, long-term set of consequences," Fernando says, sipping his coffee.

His mother is at the stove, spatula in hand, flipping the eggs that are in the massive cast-iron frying pan. As he talks, she continues to prepare the meal, nodding and smiling as Fernando rolls out his plan.

"With the younger children," he says, "I'll create puppet shows and have the characters act out situations where someone is being racist to one of the puppets. The other puppets know that one of their own is being extremely offensive. Through dialogue and acting the characters will teach the offender the error of his ways, and they will explain racism and roots of racism."

"But that can't possibly be enough!" Fernando's mother says.

"Of course it isn't," Fernando agrees. "I'm also going to design games about racism. We'll create an art project with the students about what a world without racism would look like. I'll have them work in journals where they can describe acts of racism that they see daily, and have them write down solutions to these daily acts of stupidity. Mom, there is so much to work with here!"

Fernando Goes to School

A typical Guatemalan torrential rainfall greets Fernando a few mornings later as he heads from home to the very first public school he will work in. His mother pats the shiny, tightly curled hair on his head, and hands him an umbrella. Fernando kisses her cheek and then bounds out the door. He has to be punctual. There is no time to waste.

Over the last few weeks Fernando has enlisted a couple of his friends to help out. Standing in front of the elementary school, Fernando sees the fear on his friends' faces, and says, "Look—we have a lot of work ahead of us. That's all. If we put our best efforts forward, we can't fail."

Energized, Fernando and his team duck into the first classroom. The children sitting before them are at least ten years younger than the teens, and they are of course giggling, talking, and goofing around. Fernando gets their attention, and announces that he and his friends will perform a puppet play.

The teens begin manipulating the puppets. In this play, two puppets—obviously meant to represent Ladinos, as indicated by their coloring and clothing— abuse a third puppet that is adorned in native Mayan clothes. At first, the young students laugh as the Ladino puppets run their nonsense on the Mayan doll. But as the taunting grows in fever and pitch, the students begin to squint and frown as if to say *I'm sure glad it isn't happening to me*! As the two main characters in this small play keep antagonizing the third, the class's laughter dies off. It's not funny, after all, they decide.

"Why did you stop laughing?" Fernando asks the class after the play is finished.

All the classmates are fidgeting, shuffling their feet and wiggling their knees. Then a boy raises his hand. "Because it's wrong," he says.

"That's right!" Fernando says. "Why is it wrong?"

The small boy at the back of the room is now staring at all the faces that have turned around in their seats to stare at him. He chokes out, "It's wrong because they are picking on him." Murmurs rumble through the room.

"Has anyone ever treated you like that?" Fernando asks the class.

This launches a boisterous discussion among the students. Some say that they get bullied simply because they happen to be standing there. One little girl says that people get picked on simply because they are Mayan. This notion ushers in another round of spirited discussion. Slowly but surely, the students are beginning to see the light.

Fernando Hits the Street

Today, Fernando decides to do some research in Guatemala City, so he heads out into the center of the city with a small film crew to document his efforts. He wonders if the good idea of an indigenous woman running for president is just that—a good idea. As he receives positive responses to Rigoberta's campaign, he is delighted. Few say that her run is foolish; most are openly supportive. Fernando concludes later that maybe, just maybe, the tables are turning for the indigenous in Guatemala. But the election is still months away, and there are thousands that Fernando must speak with before they vote. This is a tall order for such a young man.

One week later, at campaign headquarters—which is Rigoberta's home—Fernando finally has a chance to put aside the campaign for a moment to sit down with the revered Nobel Peace Laureate to explain his efforts in his Global Call to Action.

"I'm developing a youth project on racism," he tells the presidential candidate. "I saw in the newspapers that you also want to work with racism, so I thought, Great! I want to work

with schools, mainly first- and second-graders, to instill in them personal values and values with regard to others."

Rigoberta nods as she listens to Fernando. She likes his idea, and then she tells him, "I think this is where there is much that you could do!"

"Yes!" Fernando agrees.

"Racism is also a psychological illness, it's a mental illness, it's a spiritual sickness," she continues. "Much of the racism that exists is spiritual, it's that people are not balanced and that is why they apply racism."

"You know, this really makes me happy," Fernando says, revving up his motor. "I think women are being given the chance to grow, not just spiritually, but to work, especially for Guatemala, don't you think?" Fernando says.

Rigoberta nods and says, "Yes!"

"As a young person, I have many goals," Fernando explains, "and it really makes me sad to read in the daily paper about eight deaths, two rapes. So I start thinking, and I put myself in the shoes of the person who is suffering, and I say that there must at least be something that a young person like me, who represents the present and who will be the future of Guatemala, can do to make a change."

Rigoberta says, "Yes, yes, that is very true. The biggest obstacle would be people not having ideals and goals, in spite of everything. The obstacle would be adults keeping the same convictions they've had for many years, without changing their way of thinking, and continuing to discriminate in spite of everything we've done; for young people not to think things through and to discriminate simply because they imitate their parents."

Then the two start laughing as Rigoberta's four puppies run across the room, and they spend the next few minutes playing with the puppies together on Rigoberta's front lawn.

On the Campaign Trail

It's now June 2007. Fernando has become a volunteer on Rigoberta's campaign, and he is riding in a truck with Rigoberta Menchú Tum who's on her way to videotape a thirty-second commercial on the bridge that crosses the gorge in a section of Guatemala City called El Naranjo. But before we cross that bridge, let's get some background in place so as to better understand the situation in this country.

El Naranjo is a very impoverished section of the Ciudad de Guatemala. It is a place where fear, drugs, and violence have ruled for far too long, a place too far from all the great hopes of humanity, from humanitarians like Rigoberta Menchú Tum.

Densely populated, beset by all the problems you'll find in any ghetto, the citizens of El Naranjo suffer greatly from drug abuse, violence, and gangs. It is estimated that Guatemala holds over four hundred thousand gang members in a country whose population is around 13 million. Many of them are affiliated with the Mara Salvatrucha 13 (MS-13, on the street), the most desperately violent and feared gang in Latin America.

This is only one reason that Rigoberta's bodyguards are heavily armed as they escort her into El Naranjo for the video shoot. The other is the potential for political assassination. The first round of the presidential vote—basically, a primary election—is still months away, and already two candidates have been assassinated.

Arriving on the windswept El Naranjo bridge, you're not thinking much about politics and racism, you're trying hard not to stare at the submachine guns Rigoberta's bodyguards carry. Taping on the bridge is deemed impossible because of the wind and the cars, trucks, and motorcycles screaming by, so everyone hikes down the goat path at one end of the structure. It's a steep downward descent until some concrete and stone steps are found that are level enough to set up tripods and assemble equipment. Someone attaches the lapel microphone to the presidential candidate, and the taping begins.

A small crowd of locals has gathered to watch it all, and Rigoberta speaks with them on the way up out of the gorge. These people tell Rigoberta that not only is she brave to be in the infamous gang-infested gorge below the bridge, but also that they truly appreciate her presence in El Naranjo.

"No other candidate would ever dream of coming here," says one young man. "They're too afraid."

"And if they aren't afraid," says another, "they just don't care about us here. The other candidates have no compassion, no plan to help us get out of poverty."

These residents of El Naranjo are in awe of the Nobel Peace Laureate who has arrived unannounced to their barrio. They thank her profusely, and we all leave, happy and unharmed.

The Challenge Ahead

The year 2007 ushered in a new notion of national leadership for Guatemala—the notion that an indigenous female could run the country. Resounding joy can be found in the simple fact that people like Rigoberta Menchú Tum are strong enough to stand up, run for office, and be counted. That Guatemala is even considering voting for a female indigenous person for the presidency clearly indicates that things could indeed change one day.

"I have many things in my mind," Fernando offers in his final conversation with Rigoberta about his project and his personal commitment to ensuring that change will happen in his homeland. "They are long term, but I think that if I set myself to it, if I fight for my goals, I will achieve them. But I don't want to work alone, I want people to help me, to support me; I want people to be proud of their country. I want for young people to proudly say 'I'm from Guatemala, I'm Guatemalan in my heart,' you know?"

Rigoberta's beautiful spirit is reflected in her heartfelt response. "I have no doubt that there are young persons like yourself in many corners of the world. There are young people like you right here in Guatemala. These young people have a long road ahead of them, and if we can forge a bit of that path for them, well, I think that is what we are doing," Rigoberta tells Fernando. "I wish you a lot of success and that you will be a model for youth."

Fernando blushes, and then he says, "Our hopes for this campaign are that everyone— children and adults alike—change the idea shaped over the course of many years, change the pattern, break it, speak for themselves and overcome the fears that exist within each of them, and destroy the stereotypes."

Remember, it took four decades from the time an African-American woman (Shirley Chisholm) first ran as a major party candidate in the U. S. to the time when an African-American and a woman had an honest chance of actually becoming president. It took almost forty years, but someone needed to have the courage in 1972 to open that door so that others could walk through it.

Now, Rigoberta Menchú Tum has done the same thing for her country and her people. It may take a century more, but eventually, Guatemala can achieve racial equality, too—with young people like Fernando leading the way.

And if anyone can spark this change, Fernando can.

laureate
Rigoberta Menchú Tum

Rigoberta Menchú Tum was born to a poor peasant family in January 1959, in Chimel in northwestern Guatemala. She was raised in the traditions of the Quiche Indians, who are a specific group of Mayan Indians. Her father, Vicente Menchú, was a community leader, and her mother, Juana Tum, was a midwife and a traditional healer.

Rigoberta was the sixth of nine children. Her childhood memories are of a small homestead in the beautiful mountains of Guatemala where her family lived. The mountains were an untouched paradise that could be reached only by horseback. The Mayan Indians were very poor and could not grow enough food in the mountains to survive. So most years, Rigoberta's family had to leave their community for six months to work on cotton and coffee plantations that lined the southern coast of Guatemala.

In addition to her economic struggles, Rigoberta had to face a larger violent conflict in her country. During the cold war, the United States was fearful of communism, so the CIA helped plan the overthrow of the socialist government in Guatemala. This sparked over thirty years of war and violence. Over this time two hundred thousand Guatemalans were murdered. The military focused especially viciously on the Mayas, destroying hundreds of Indian villages and creating a million refugees.

The military began harassing Rigoberta's village by setting houses on fire, destroying property, and killing animals. They tried to scare them out of their homes and off their land. Rigoberta's father began organizing the community, and he put together a small resistance that was able to capture a soldier during an attack. They told the soldier their story and asked him to explain their plight to his commanders and companions, and then they let him go unharmed. This story exemplifies the Maya Indians' ingenuity and commitment to nonviolence.

Because of her father's resistance, the family was accused of being part of the guerrilla movement. Her father was accused of murdering a local plantation owner and was kidnapped, tortured, and jailed for fourteen months. When he was released he joined a new organization called the Committee of the Peasant Union (CUC), which worked to secure for the Mayan people basic rights like fair wages and protection of their land. He took Rigoberta to the city to introduce her to people working on this movement and to teach her nonviolent strategies for organizing people. He knew that the government was planning to kill him for the work he was doing, and he felt confident that Rigoberta, even as a young girl, had the strength, smarts, and courage to continue his work.

During a protest against human-rights abuses by the military, her father and other members of the CUC were killed. Soon afterward her younger brother was kidnapped, tortured, and killed by a military death squad. Just a few months later, her mother was kidnapped, tortured, raped, mutilated, and killed. In total, Rigoberta lost both parents, two brothers, a sister-in-law, and three nieces and nephews to violence in Guatemala. In the name of her brother, father, mother, and all the Mayan people, Rigoberta vowed to continue working hard and nonviolently for the rights of her people.

Her efforts caught the military's eye and she was targeted for arrest. Soon, it became impossible for her to remain in Guatemala, and she fled to Mexico.

In exile she became the world spokesperson for her people—the Guatemalan poor—and a powerful voice against the terrible oppression they suffered. She participated in founding The United Representation of the Guatemalan Opposition (RUOG) in 1982, and then in 1983 she told her life story to Elisabeth Burgos-Debray in recorded interviews. These were developed into a book that, when translated into English as *I, Rigoberta Menchú*, drew large international attention to the horrors occurring in Guatemala. Following the release of the book, Rigoberta joined the National Coordinating Committee of the CUC in 1986, and then she narrated a gripping documentary film named *When the Mountains Tremble*, which was about the pain and suffering of the Mayan people. Rigoberta tried to return to Guatemala several times, but she always arrived to death threats.

In 1992, Rigoberta Menchú Tum was awarded the Nobel Peace Prize in recognition of her work for the rights of indigenous people. She was the first indigenous person ever to receive the award and one of only a handful of women to ever win it. Her nonviolent work contributed to the 1996 Peace Accords in Guatemala, which ended Guatemala's thirty-six-year civil war and gave many rights back to the Mayan people.

After the civil war ended, Rigoberta fought to have the Guatemalan political and military establishment tried in a court of law. After many years, the Spanish courts finally agreed to try the case, and in December 2006 they called for the extradition of seven former members of the Guatemalan government on charges of torture and genocide against the Mayan people of Guatemala.

Rigoberta also became actively involved in the health care reform movement, trying to provide inexpensive drugs to all in need. She is the president of Salud para Todos (Health for All) and the company Farmacias Similares. In 2004, she accepted President Óscar Berger's offer to help implement the country's Peace Accords and took on the role of goodwill ambassador. In 2007, Rigoberta Menchú Tum ran for president of Guatemala, campaigning around the country for the rights of all Guatemalans.

voices of peace

ENDING RACISM AND HATE

Aung San Suu Kyi

"People who are spiritually developed do not think of others in terms of their differences, but in terms of what they have in common. That is why a spiritually developed person is full of compassion: because he can think of every other human being as the same sort of person that he is, basically, with hopes and fears. He can feel a lot of compassion for others."

Shirin Ebadi

"Those whose interest is in setting fire to the world and creating wars declare that there exists a clash of civilization of the east and civilization of the west, and that this is a clash that cannot be cured, whereas Muslims have lived among Jews, Christians, Buddhists, and other religions for years and years. There are many commonalities among the religions. The Muslims and Jews lived peacefully for centuries in the Middle East together."

The Dalai Lama

"We need unbiased compassion—regardless of what attitudes are toward others, still recognizing them as human brothers and sisters and understanding that they have every right to overcome suffering, to overcome problems. On the basis of that kind of recognition, then you can develop a constant sense of caring. I really appreciate and admire all different religions."

Betty Williams

"I now know that the only way to change anything in the world is to make every single human being important. Everyone has a reason to be here. Our Creator sent us for a reason. We're not just born and thrown into the world. There's a reason for every child born."

Ten Things You Can Do to Help
Address Racism and Hate

1 **Begin a Campaign**

Racism and hate often come from biases and prejudices developed early on in life. It is the responsibility of individuals to question and challenge these biases and prejudices to prevent racism and hate. Begin a Pledge to End Hate campaign in your school or community. Encourage those who participate to hold one another responsible for their pledge.

2 **Host a Film Festival**

Film can be a powerful tool to help build empathy and understanding. Host a film festival centered on ending racism and hate, and invite fellow students and community members to attend. Hold discussions after each film that you show to address the issues it brought up and to more closely connect the people who choose to take a step toward ending hate.

3 **Encourage Community Dialogues**

It is harder for people to hate one another when they have had a chance to get to know one another and work on a common project together. Bringing together groups of people for a community dialogue can be a great way to build these relationships. Host a monthly community dialogue addressing issues of racism and hate.

4 **Make It Against the Law**

There are many groups of people throughout the world who are not given equal opportunity in various aspects of life. Specifically, racism and hate can affect people's ability to get quality education, good jobs, access to social services, home ownership, and equal treatment at stores and restaurants. Help local political leaders to create and pass Equal Opportunity and Non-Discrimination legislation to make unequal treatment against the law.

5 **Deconstruct Racism**

The ideas that fuel racism and hate are often horribly misguided and based in fear and power. Hold a series of teach-ins, workshops, and symposia that will address the history of racism as well as the issue of hate in general. Invite people from your community and others to explore their own biases and prejudices, and to discuss what can happen if these beliefs go unchecked.

(6) Remember Where You Came From

One lasting and devastating impact of racism and hate is that the culture, history, and traditions of those who are the target of racism and hate get lost or destroyed. Cultural preservation addresses the need to protect, restore, and honor all forms of diversity. Hold events that incorporate and honor language, stories, songs, dances, skills, sacred or important sites, artifacts, arts and crafts, and forms of subsistence.

(7) Take a Stand

Make a personal pledge to speak out whenever you see someone being treated unfairly, whenever you hear a racist joke, or whenever someone uses language that promotes racism or hate. Create a school- or community-wide pledge and provide stickers, T-shirts, or buttons for people who have signed the pledge to take a stand against hate.

(8) Look at Language

Popular language and slang often incorporate derogatory terms and put them to everyday use. Walking down the halls in your school or down the street in your neighborhood, you often hear some form of slang for which the original use was an expression of racism or hate. Challenge yourself and others to examine the language used on an everyday basis and make it consistent with the elimination of racism and hate.

(9) Own Up

We all have a responsibility to check our thoughts, feelings, beliefs, and behaviors—examining and challenging ourselves constantly—to ensure that we are not unknowingly slipping down the slope of hate. Also, it is important for us to examine and own up to our history, our privileges, and the power that we have in any given situation.

(10) Start Young

Ending hate begins at an early age. If young children can be taught to celebrate diversity, they may be less likely to hold racist or hateful beliefs when they become adults. Create an educational program about valuing diversity for local elementary schools. Incorporate cooperative games, stories, and activities that you can teach once a month, or even once a week, that can start getting young people on the path to creating a future that celebrates what makes us different.

CHAPTER 7

What Kind of World Will We Inherit?

Betty Williams & Sonny Ray— The Crisis of the Environment

You have to work one person at a time. That may sound ridiculous, but if you're going to do anything new, you have to start right at the root core of the problem, and if you don't take action from the bottom up, then the problem won't be solved.
—Betty Williams

Welcome to Colorado

Have you ever heard the song "America the Beautiful" which contains the line "Purple mountains majesty/above the fruited plain"? Wellesley University professor of English Katharine Lee Bates came out to Colorado in the summer of 1893 to teach at Colorado College in Colorado Springs. She and a group of visiting professors endeavored to scale Pikes Peak, and Bates, from her vantage point overlooking both the mountains and the plains, was so inspired by what she saw that she wrote those famous words.

Colorado is a truly beautiful state. It is the eighth-largest state in the country, and roughly half of it is mountainous terrain. The capital, Denver, which sits at the base of the Rocky Mountains, is a sprawling metropolis. Colorado's second-oldest city is Arvada, where gold was first discovered in the state, a find that quickly drew many thousands of people from the eastern region of this country to the west in the mid-1800s—it wasn't called the "Gold Rush" for nothing.

Denver eventually became a railroad hub. Countless trains passed through, bringing workers, building materials, and other necessities to the people of the new outpost. Initially, there were all the problems that you could imagine in the developing "wild west" frontier town: lawlessness, gunfights, prostitution, and extreme public drunkenness. There was also the tragic story of the treatment of Colorado's first citizens, the indigenous people who were pushed off their lands and even massacred. Slowly Denver grew from these dangerous and bad seeds into a beautiful flower of a city over the next hundred and fifty years.

Flash forward to the year 2008. Denver's mayor, John Hickenlooper, has been called "One of the Top 5 American Mayors" by *Time* magazine. Colorado's governor is a man named Bill Ritter. He and his wife served in the Peace Corps in Africa after college.

For many years oil and gas money drove Colorado politics and this has dictated public policy in this mountainous, resource-rich state. But a new sense of ethics and innovation has stepped to the forefront. Colorado is voting progressively, and the governor and the mayor are part of this new rise of spirit and hope in the new American west.

Meet Sonny Ray

Everywhere we travel we find young people who are more than concerned about what's going on in their countries—they're downright scared. Whether it's the flow of guns into tranquil Costa Rica, the loss of human rights in the United Kingdom, or unequal access to water in India, young people are frightened by what they are seeing, and, even worse, by what they might be forced to deal with in the coming years. This deep concern is found not only in foreign countries—it exsists right here in the United States, too.

At Foster Elementary School in Arvada, Colorado, we meet up with a young student named Sonny Ray. Sonny got his start as a PeaceJammer in fourth grade, when his teacher, Dawn Axelson, taught his class the PeaceJam Juniors curriculum.

Sonny lives with his mother and two brothers in a tiny two-bedroom apartment in Arvada. After having broken free from an abusive spouse, his mother works hard to support them on her own. Sonny is all too aware of their difficult situation, and when we take him to lunch to discuss his Global Call to Action project, he asks if he can take some food home. But he is concerned about more than just his family.

His primary concern? Global warming.

And why does he care?

On Sunday, September 15, 2007, ten Nobel Peace Laureates sat on a stage in Denver, Colorado. Three thousand youth and five thousand members of the general public attended this public talk. To recognize their work as PeaceJammers, Sonny and his classmates were asked to kick off the event by presenting each of the laureates with a single flower. The sometimes shy and sometimes boisterous Sonny Ray presented an exquisite red rose to the Nobel Peace Laureate from Northern Ireland, Betty Williams.

Betty is an incredible bundle of Irish-grandmother-activist energy. She's a storyteller in the grand Irish tradition, a great chef, a homemaker, a rabble-rouser, and more.

When Betty spoke, she described in horrific detail the plight of those she has encountered who will suffer the most from the effects of global climate change.

"What I've seen in refugee camps is death and destruction on a huge scale. I couldn't number the babies that I have held while they were dying. Every time I've held a child like that who's dying . . . it seems to be that they're asking you why. Maybe that's only my take on it, but I always ask them to forgive us for what we've done, because the gross cruelty of that is beyond belief. And with global warming, so many more innocent little babies are going to die from the effects of drought, from hunger and disease.

"I don't see governments taking steps to stop global warming. Not enough of us are up there yelling, 'Stop this!' Maybe people don't realize the depth of what's wrong in our world, and it's only maybe when it hits them that they'll have a voice to change it."

Betty's passionate speech about the implications of environmental degradation and global warming shocked Sonny Ray. How could all this be happening? What could be done to thwart it, to fight against it?

Becoming an Agent of Change

When Sonny returned to school the following Monday, he began asking questions. He was looking for serious answers to some very vexing questions—he fretted over his future, over what would happen to his friends and family, and over the fate of the entire world.

He began to research global warming, which left him only with more questions. He watched the award-winning documentary *An Inconvenient Truth* with a dropped jaw. It became frighteningly clear to him that the future of everyone on the planet was in danger. He was tired of sitting and asking questions, now he wanted to do something about it.

But, as has been shown throughout history, making an impact can also make one the subject of scrutiny and even ridicule. For Sonny, the ridicule for his newfound sense of activism comes from family—his older brothers. These two pull no stops harping on the baby of the family. They both play a bit with the gangsta lifestyle. They have dropped out of school, and they have decided to start giving Sonny a hard time.

Sonny's mom does her best to give emotional support to her youngest, but working all day and night to provide for her boys' basic needs doesn't leave much time. One afternoon, Sonny decides he can't take it anymore. He runs away from home, away from school, away from his Global Call to Action project. His mom, lost and worried, calls PeaceJam to see if he's contacted anyone in our office. A few hours later, he does turn up at PeaceJam. Upset and downtrodden, Sonny needs a pep talk to get back on track. And after a few inspirational words from PeaceJam staff member Rudy Balles, Sonny heads home with renewed energy and enthusiasm.

A Steep Learning Curve

Back in the saddle, Sonny Ray, and his fellow classmates, decide to talk to some experts to assess the situation in the metro Denver area, their state, their country, and the rest of the world.

They embark on an arduous information-gathering expedition that will take them from their modest school all the way to Boulder, Colorado, and eventually to the state capital itself.

Their first stop is NCAR, the National Center for Atmospheric Research. NCAR houses experts in the topic of atmospheric chemistry, climate, cloud physics, and interactions between the sun and Earth—as well as research about the role of humans in creating climate change.

Visiting NCAR is like stepping into a time machine and launching yourself into the future. The building is full of super-computers that calculate enormous amounts of data in a fraction of a second. This incredible technology allows for real-time, 3D images of the globe to be produced and shown on plasma screens throughout the facility.

There is one particular screen that Sonny can't take his eyes off. It shows what the effects of climate change will be if nothing is done to slow the process of global warming. It has several different images that flash: one of the greenhouse emissions produced by each country, one of the temperature changes over the last two hunded years, and, most frightening of all, one of the rate at which the polar ice caps are melting. It's chilling to see these images in succession.

Their second stop is at Environment Colorado, an environmental advocacy organization in Denver, where they pay a visit to the executive director, Matt Baker.

Sonny Ray wastes no time whatsoever diving right in. "When looking at global climate change," Sonny begins, "what concerns you most?"

"I'm most worried that the United States won't do anything about climate change unless we make an enormous effort right now," Matt flatly states, driving right to the heart of the situation. "The effects of climate change can be devastating. Between the United States and Western Europe, we're responsible for about two-thirds of the carbon pollution that's been put into the atmosphere.

"A lot of people are saying that it'll be difficult for places like Africa to grow wheat after 2050, and that the impacts of flooding and drought are going to make life very, very difficult in places. I think that it's a moral issue, that the United States has a moral obligation to help prevent this impending catastrophe.

"One of the scientists who released the International Panel on Climate Change report was quoted as saying, 'If you drove your car into somebody's living room, you'd have a responsibility to clean up that person's living room. The developed world, led by the United States, is driving our car into the living room of the rest of the world, and we have an obligation to do whatever we can to prevent that and to clean it up however we can.'"

Our responsibility to clean it up, you say? Sonny takes this to heart and after a few more probing questions wraps up with a zinger. "What are the politics surrounding global warming?"

"I think there are two impediments," Matt says. "One is that we've all grown up living a certain way and getting our energy a certain way and using it a certain way.

"More important than that is the opposition of the fossil fuel industry, which has an enormous stake in preventing action on climate change. In places like Colorado, the coal industry is very powerful, and some of the utilities don't want to have anything to do with climate change. The oil and gas industries have been dragging their feet—and through the pressure they've been able to create (both in Colorado and the rest of the country), we're in a position where our politics have basically been frozen in time."

Sonny gives Matt a synopsis of his own vision, his quiet voice hinting at a greater power than you'd expect from a person his age. He asks, "Since this is a youth project, what do you think the young folks can do?"

"The most important thing that anyone can do is vote," Matt asserts. "But unfortunately, the system is weighted against the people who are going to have to deal with this. So I think young people should be out in the streets *screaming*, 'This is our future; wake up people!'

"What I'd like to see right now is a young person rise up and say, 'Hey, this is our world, and you guys better get moving because we need to take action and do something about this.'"

Matt continues. "You have to go out and make change on your own. I think it is important for folks who can't vote to do what they can to reduce their carbon footprint. They also need

to get involved in the larger politics, more so than any generation in history. The folks coming of voting age today are the ones who will be living with this the longest—*and* are the least responsible for it. So their voices need to be heard more than anybody's."

Hearing this grim scenario firsthand makes everything seem more real, and much more pressing. Something needs to be done, and Sonny Ray knows that he is the one who needs to do it.

Focusing on Foster

Sonny Ray decides to go back to his old friends in his PeaceJam group at Foster for help. He meets with the group and presents a bright new idea.

"What if we made Foster the first green school in Colorado?" he proposes to the eager group of third- and fourth-graders. One student, Irving, is particularly excited about this prospect.

The group quickly goes to work looking at the environmental impact of their school. They find that they waste massive amounts of water every day as a result of students' turning water on full blast to wash their hands. They find that they spend approximately $12,000 per month on electricity and gas. That's a big impact for a single school. If Foster can reduce their use of resources, perhaps other schools will follow suit? Imagine what the impact might be then.

The group devises a plan to help the school save water. They create a visual aid of forty empty gallon containers tied on string to show how much water is wasted per day when students wash their hands. They then split up and go class to class explaining ways to conserve water in their school. Water usage drops significantly the following month.

Then the students begin a Lights Out campaign. They create placards to be placed next to every light switch in the building reminding the last one out of the room to turn out the lights. This again is followed by demonstrations and presentations, which result in reductions of electricity use as well.

Finally, they decide it would be good to transfer their knowledge from their school to the homes in their communities. They create brochures on energy-saving techniques for the home and contact the local hardware store for a donation of energy-saving compact fluorescent light-bulbs—enough for one per family at Foster Elementary School. These bulbs are sent home with the energy-saving tips so that families can save money and the environment. Not bad at all for a ragtag band of school kids!

Changing Colorado

While the PeaceJam group continues to work on reducing the environmental impact at Foster, Sonny Ray keeps digging deeper.

Itching for more answers, Sonny Ray decides to take his questions to the top—the Colorado state government. His friend Irving offers to lend a hand, and together the two boys head down to Colorado state senator Gail Schwartz's office to interview her. Senator Schwartz enters the office, walking at a brisk pace. She smiles at the boys and says, "Hello, I'm Gail Schwartz."

Irving takes the lead, saying, "What is your biggest concern when it comes to global climate change?" Apparently the boys are going to address the Big Picture first.

"Certainly we have a lot of concerns for Colorado because so much of our economy depends on our climate—our hunting, fishing, and winter sports," the senator says. "More important, our agriculture relies on the climate and the water that we have here in Colorado—it depends on our using the water wisely and also having enough snow to produce water for the crops in the fields all summer long. That's a main concern for me, certainly, for Colorado, and that's one of the reasons I'm working so hard in the Senate.

"Globally, what concerns me the most is the rising sea levels and how many countries will be impacted. Oftentimes, our poorest nations live along coastlines and have very few alternatives. When it comes to climate change, we have a lot of work to do—*but* we also have to be concerned about a lot of people who have a lesser ability to control their future."

The young environmental Jedis stay on target, and they think globally but remain local when next they ask, "What is Colorado doing to address these issues?"

"The biggest bill that we have passed," she tells them, "was called House Bill 1281. It asks utilities for a commitment to provide energy from renewable sources."

"Do you think Colorado could do more?" they ask, knowing that the House Bill 1281 was just a small step. "And if so, what more could the state do?"

"I think Colorado could do a lot more," Senator Schwartz acknowledges. "I think that making a commitment to finding ways that everyone can move to using renewable energy in their everyday life—I think that's a commitment to make. How can Coloradoans do it? We can drive less, ride our bikes more, be more efficient when we're building new buildings or fix-

ing our old buildings. We can buy hybrid cars.

"Everyone can make a difference," she says. "We just have to choose to do that. Young people can say, 'Hey, this is our world to inherit! You'd better start taking better care of it to provide for our future.' We can also do it through state laws. We want to encourage people to create a new sense of urgency that this needs to be changed."

After a very candid and positive interview with the Senator, the boys decide to wind up their courage and go for the big time. Colorado governor Bill Ritter has agreed to a meeting with this dynamic duo. Though the governor is busy, he is eager to meet with these young men and to hear what they have to say.

Sonny starts off with the confidence that he had been mustering all morning. "We are scared for the future," he says. "Scientists have shown that the climate is changing at an alarming rate and that humans are responsible. We are taking action on this problem and want to know what you are doing to address these very big issues."

"Actually," the governor says, "we are creating an office on climate change. Part of what we set up in the office is a climate change coordinator coming in to look at this issue and ask the question, 'What part of climate change is caused by humans?' and then 'What are the things we should do in Colorado to address the human causes?'"

The boys give each other a surprised look of approval; this is really great news!

Having done his research, Irving jumps in with a burning question. "Can Colorado sign on to the Kyoto Protocols or make them a state priority?"

"The Kyoto Protocols were an international agreement that the United States helped craft—and when George Bush became president, he made a decision not to sign," the governor explains. "So, the question is, What can states do? States can look at the Kyoto Protocols and put the same kinds of standards in place. You can't sign the treaty, but you can agree that those Kyoto Protocols are something that you as a state can live up to. Part of what we're doing in our state climate change program is to ask that question: Are there things in the Kyoto Protocols that we can live with as the standards in Colorado? And the answer is probably yes."

Without missing a beat, Sonny asks, "What steps do we need to take in order to make this happen?"

"I need to get my people in this office working. We have to be careful not to shut down industries because of the standards. The state gets a lot of money from the production of natural gas and oil and coal, and what we've said is that we're going to keep producing oil, gas, and coal, but we want to make sure that we take care of the environment. Having the right people in place to determine how we obtain those resources and at the same time protect the environment is what we're doing right now—it's part of our plan."

"So what can we do to help?" the boys say almost in unison.

"You can educate your class members. For you and your classmates to know that there's a connection between the electricity in your home that you're burning and the consequences to the environment of having to produce that electricity by burning coal—that will help."

The boys leave the interview with a renewed confidence. They may not be doing everything possible yet, but they're getting the ball rolling, and that is reassuring for these two diligent investigators.

Shortly after their meeting, Governor Ritter announces a plan to "green" Colorado. With a combination of executive order and legislation, he promises to reduce the state's waste by 75 percent by 2020, reforming farming practices to reduce greenhouse gas emissions, and calling on every Colorado citizen to conserve, reduce waste, invest in renewable energy, and recycle.

Sonny Ray and Irving are thrilled, and they rush to share the news and to write letters of thanks to their new partner in the effort, Governor Ritter.

A Grandmother's Advice

In an unexpected twist of fate, the instigator of Sonny's Global Call to Action project is once again visiting Denver for a PeaceJam Youth Conference. She has heard about what Sonny Ray's been up to and wants to talk to him directly.

"So, Sonny, tell me about your project." Though Sonny Ray is nervous, the grandmotherly glow of Betty Williams sets him at ease.

"This project is about climate change," Sonny says, in a matter-of-fact manner. But then, as if a faucet has been turned on, it all pours out of him.

When Sonny pauses to take a breath, Betty jumps in. "What did you find? Can I read it?" She reaches out to Sonny's shaking hand to look over his Global Call to Action report.

"Go ahead!" he exclaims, excited to show off his hard work.

Betty reads aloud: "'Global climate change is an issue that affects us all,' you say. And you're right!" She continues reading, "'It has the potential to negatively impact the life of this planet to a very large degree.' So what have you decided to do about it?"

"Well, our big dream is to make my old school a green school, run by renewable energy.

We are still trying to do that," he says softly.

"And what about that water conservation project? You started that and I'm so proud of you for doing so."

"Well, it wasn't all just me," Sonny said modestly. "Some kids found out how much water they were wasting, and then found out it tied in to global warming, like what we're talking about."

"So you can wash your hands in a trickle of water and you won't waste how many gallons of water?"

"I think it was one."

"So you save a gallon of water—so with forty people washing their hands, that's forty gallons of water wasted! Now, what else do you want to do? Besides the water issue, I mean?"

"Mostly, I want to stop people from polluting and making greenhouse gases in the air. And to provide a solar power system for our school. Also, educate the community about global climate change issues by developing easy projects and guides on how to conserve energy."

"I heard the governor here is really into the ecology. What did you find when you spoke to him? Were you impressed by what he was doing?" Betty inquired.

"Yes! And talking to him was really exciting! He listened to us! He said there were more things Colorado could do to work on global warming, and we want to keep working with him to make Colorado a green state."

"Do you know the one thing I know that's going to happen from your project? The children will educate their parents. They'll go home from school and tell their parents, 'Don't waste all that water running your faucet—you can do the same with just a trickle!' I think it's fabulous what you're doing—I'm telling you this from my heart. I'm extremely proud of you. Thank you, Sonny, for what you do."

Now Sonny Ray has a question for Betty. "For kids of the future, how can we work for peace?"

"Since I was awarded the prize thirty-two years ago, I've been traveling and educating young people like you that violence leads only to more violence, and violence leads only to death and destruction. My message to the young people is this: I want young people to be for life and creation and not death and destruction. I also want to say to them: If you really love your country, you won't want to go out and die for it, you want to go out and live for it and make it a better place to live. You're on that path now. If we hurt Mother Earth, it is a severe act of violence and we all pay for that."

"Yeah. That's crazy. That's all I had to say and that's my Global Call to Action project."

But that's *not* all—because of the example set by Sonny Ray and Foster Elementary School, other local schools are now looking into their impact as well. The plan to set an example is working. And even though Sonny's dream to create a fully green school hasn't happened yet, they're still pushing to make Foster the first school in Colorado to be run on solar energy. And we've got a hunch that they *will* make it happen.

Betty and Sonny Ray part with a giant hug, a connecting glance, and two ear-to-ear smiles. Sonny walks away with a bounce in his step, his plan to change his little bit of the planet tightly clutched in his own two hands.

laureate
Betty Williams

Betty Williams was born in Belfast, Northern Ireland, on May 22, 1942. She was baptized a Roman Catholic, despite the fact that three of her four grandparents were not Catholic (two were Protestant and one was Jewish). When Betty was only thirteen years old, her mother suffered a massive stroke. Betty dropped out of school to take on the role of caring for her mother and raising her younger sister.

Like many families in Northern Ireland, Betty's family was touched by violence. Her Protestant grandfather, a riveter in a Belfast shipyard, was thrown down the hold of a ship that was under construction simply because his son was marrying a Catholic woman. Her cousin Daniel was killed at the age of eighteen, when Protestant extremists shot him as he stood at the front door of his house. Another cousin was killed when a booby-trapped car, abandoned by members of the IRA, exploded as he was driving past it. In Betty's words, "The Protestants killed one of my cousins, and the Catholics killed the other."

Betty joined the Irish Republican Army in 1972, but "didn't remain a member long." After witnessing a British soldier be shot in front of her in 1973, she knelt and prayed beside him. She was criticized by Catholic neighbors for showing sympathy for "the enemy."

On August 10, 1976, a runaway car driven by IRA member Danny Lennon, who had been fatally shot while fleeing from British soldiers, crashed into a family of four who were out for a walk. All three children were killed. Their mother, Anne Maguire, was critically injured and later committed suicide in 1980. Betty Williams, who heard the crash, was one of the first to arrive on the scene.

Betty immediately began to circulate petitions against the violence and, in less than forty-eight hours, had over six thousand signatures. When Máiread Corrigan, the children's aunt, heard what Betty Williams had done, she invited her to the children's funeral. On August 13, 1976, the day of the funeral, Betty Williams and Máiread Corrigan met with journalist Ciaran McKeown, who joined the two women in cofounding the Peace People, an organization dedicated to nonviolence in Northern Ireland and throughout the world.

Betty and Máiread organized a peace march that was attended by ten thousand Protestant and Catholic women. The peaceful march was disrupted by members of the Irish Republican Army, who accused them of being influenced by the British. The following week, thirty-five thousand people marched with Williams and Corrigan to show their support for ending the violence in their country.

In recognition of their extraordinary action to end the sectarian violence in Northern Ireland, and for their dedication to building a foundation for a peaceful future, Betty Williams and Máiread Corrigan were jointly awarded the Nobel Peace Prize in 1976.

In her acceptance speech, Betty said, "That first week will always be remembered for something besides the birth of the Peace People. For those most closely involved, the most powerful memory of that week was the death of a young republican and the deaths of three children struck by the dead man's car. A deep sense of frustration at the mindless stupidity of the continuing violence was already evident before the tragic events of that sunny afternoon. But the deaths of those four young people in one terrible moment of violence caused that frustration to explode and created the possibility of a real peace movement. . . . As far as we are concerned, every single death in the last eight years, and every death in every war that was ever fought, represents life needlessly wasted, a mother's labor spurned." She also said, "The Nobel Peace Prize is not awarded for what one has done, but hopefully for what one will do."

True to those words, since receiving the Nobel Prize, Betty Williams has traveled the world, working tirelessly with fellow Nobel Laureates where peace, and especially the safety and well-being of children, is at risk. "I had no concept of the depth of the children's suffering until witnessing their pain. Yet in a world that we know can feed itself, more than 40,000 children die each day from conditions of malnutrition. Surely we must question why we are allowing this to continue," Betty Williams stated. Betty currently serves as the president of World Centers of Compassion for Children (WCCC), whose mission is to provide a strong political voice for children in areas afflicted by war, hunger, and social, economic, or political upheaval, and to respond to their material and emotional needs by creating safe and nurturing environments. Their work includes "the determination to feed, clothe, and nurture children while creating an environment in which we can help reconnect the child to the family, the family to the community, the community to the nation, and nations to one another—resulting in environments that are capable of sustaining themselves according to high human ideals." The WCCC has recently announced that they will be building their first "City of Compassion" in southern Italy. This city will be a rehabilitative and safe community for children who are most susceptible to the horrors of hunger, war, disease, and abuse—providing homes, nutrition, education, rehabilitation, love and compassion. This city is meant to serve as a prototype that, once perfected, can provide healthy and healing homes for suffering children throughout the world.

voices of peace

WHAT KIND OF WORLD WILL WE INHERIT?

Adolfo Pérez Esquivel

"My hope is to return to thinking about humankind's relationship with Mother Nature because we are losing Her; this little planet called Earth is being destroyed."

The Dalai Lama

"We need knowledge to care for ourselves, every part of Earth and the life upon it, and all of the future generations as well. This means that education about the environment is of great importance to everyone. Scientific learning and technological progress are essential for improving the quality of life in the modern world. Still more important is the simple practice of getting to know and better appreciate ourselves and our natural surroundings, whether we are children or adults. If we have a true appreciation for others and resist acting out ignorance, we will take care of the Earth."

Oscar Arias Sánchez

"We speak of saving the planet and we poison the air, poison the water of the rivers, the water of the seas, and we fell the trees of the forests. We speak of peace and we make war. This double-speak is evidence of the hypocrisy and cynicism of this political class, the lack of transparency and sincerity between discourse and action, between what is preached and what is done."

Rigoberta Menchú Tum

"The hope of the future is in the signals given to us by Mother Nature. There are earthquakes, hurricanes, suffering. But through all this we can reflect, we can think it over. My hope for the future is our capacity to humble ourselves before life, before the ages and times. That is my hope. That people return to thinking about life and the future, and once again consider their surroundings."

Ten Things You Can Do to Help

Address Global Climate Change

(1) Know Your Footprint

An ecological footprint measures the land area required to support your lifestyle; including the food you eat, the housing you live in, the energy you use, and the consumer goods and services you require. The bigger your footprint, the more resources your lifestyle is using up. Find an ecological quiz online to help you calculate your footprint; then, work to make it smaller. Let others know about the various ways their lives affect the world we all share, and teach them ways they can reduce their impact.

(2) Evaluate Your Eating Habits

Energy and resources are used not only in food production, but also in transporting it to your local markets. Look for locally grown and produced food to cut down on transportation costs, and consider seasonal fruits and vegetables to cut down on the energy required to grow them. Also, harsh pesticides and chemical fertilizers pollute our ground and water. Organic food is grown without such harmful substances.

(3) Multiply Your Efforts

Multiply the effects of your personal efforts by joining with others. Creating a recycling program, organizing a carpool, and working in community gardens are some of the ways you can connect with others and increase the positive impact you have on the world around you.

(4) Save Water

Water is an extremely valuable and finite resource. The amount of water that is available to us is the same as it has always been, but our population continues to grow very rapidly. With more and more people needing access to this precious resource, it is important to conserve. Fix leaky faucets, shorten your showers, and collect excess water to water plants; adopting these measures can save hundreds of gallons of water a month.

(5) Investigate Renewable Energy

Much of the energy people consume comes from nonrenewable sources, such as fossil fuels. Renewable energy sources—which include hydro power, wind power, solar power, biomass energy, and geothermal energy—are becoming more widely used. If possible, work to convert your home to use more renewable energy sources. Find out if there is an energy provider in your area that offers green energy. If not, contact your local energy provider and insist they provide sustainable energy options.

(6) Practice Energy Conservation

There are many ways you can use less energy. Turning off lights and appliances when they are not in use is one of the simplest ways. You can also make sure that you keep your house equipped for the weather in your area (insulation, weather stripping, etc.). Another very simple way to conserve energy is by changing to compact fluorescent lightbulbs. Teach the people you know about the benefits, both financial and environmental, of these energy-saving techniques.

(7) Clean It Up!

Pollution and litter damage our Earth. Cleaning up the pollution around you is an important step to helping the environment. Find out when a community cleanup is taking place, or organize your own! Create a group that cleans up different places regularly, so that the buildup of litter and pollution does not accumulate and cause more damage.

(8) Have Some Fun!

Invite family and friends over for an ecofriendly house party. Prepare environmentally friendly foods, use environmentally safe dishes and utensils, and clean up with natural cleaning products. Give your guests information about how they can have their own environmentally friendly get-togethers and about how they can make changes in their lifestyles that both help the environment and save them money.

(9) Spend for Green

Encourage companies to be more environmentally friendly in their practices and products by spending money on them and by encouraging people you know to support them as well. Let companies know that you are supporting them because of their ecofriendly practices and products. Also, write those companies that are not particularly green, and let them know you will not support them unless they change their practices.

(10) Enlist Government Cooperation

One person can make an impact on the environment by taking steps to live a greener life and encouraging others to do the same. Work on encouraging the government to commit to adopting greener policies and practices. Work with local and national governments to adopt legislation that will require more environmentally friendly policies. Also, work with them on ways they can reduce their own negative impact on the environment as they are conducting the business of government.

CHAPTER 8

Why Isn't My Voice Equal to Yours?

Shirin Ebadi & Mymoena—Equal Rights for Women

Not only is a woman a citizen, but she is also a mother who nurtures future generations. In my opinion, the conditions toward women around the world are prejudicial, but in certain places, they are worse than in others. Success for women is when prejudice is removed everywhere in the world.
—Shirin Ebadi

Imagining Iran

Of all the countries highlighted in this book, the only one that we have not visited yet is Iran—a place we really, really want to travel to and experience. We suspect that you might be a bit shocked as you read this, thinking, Don't you know there are heavy international economic sanctions on that country? Don't you know they might be trying to develop a nuclear bomb? Don't you know how they treat women?!

Yes, we're keenly aware, and we agree that all of this is bad news. But the two of us are from Detroit, Michigan, a city awash in problems. Once a bustling, highly productive industrial city, once the gleaming Motor City, it has now become the infamous "Murder Capital" of the United States.

Our hometown has a bad reputation, but we still love it dearly. Detroit's a great city with a great big heart. The people are incredibly resilient, the city has a deep cultural history, and Detroit's contribution to modern music cannot be underestimated.

There are so many perceptions and misconceptions about Iran and its capital city of Tehran—just like Detroit—that it's staggering. Both cities boast rich histories, rich traditions, great food, and tremendous artistic accomplishments. This chapter is about Iran, and this will be the focus, but for us, it all relates pretty directly back to Detroit (which, by the way, boasts the largest middle eastern population of any city in the United States).

So you're a human being, right? You have hopes and fears, doubts, aspirations? Iranians are the same as you. More than half of Iran's population is under twenty-five years old. These young people are interested in the same things you're interested in. They desire to be hip, to be cool, and to listen to great music. They want decent educations so they can find a good job, make money, have a family, and create a happy life—just like you. And we believe this is possible—both for the people of Detroit and for the people of Iran.

A Human Rights Powerhouse

Once you meet Nobel Peace Laureate Shirin Ebadi, you start to understand why we have so much hope for Iran. Barely five feet tall, she's a lawyer by trade and a relentless human rights activist. And this is in Iran, a country that yields very few rights to women.

As she tells you her stories of life inside her country, her warm brown eyes smile with an intelligence and a sense of deep responsibility. Shirin is a powerhouse who has stared down the powers that be. In the 1970s, she graduated from law school and was later appointed as the first woman judge in the courts of Tehran. Iran was more moderate at that juncture in history, and women held lofty positions, positions that they certainly earned based on their education, training, and skill.

But things took a dramatic turn in 1979 when a surge of unrest swept throughout the country. Seemingly overnight, Iran's monarchy was overthrown and replaced by a new form of governance—an Islamic republic that melded theocracy with politics. This new form of government was overseen by the Ayatollah Khomeini, the "supreme leader." This is the highest office in Iran, and the supreme leader handles everything, including choosing the heads of media sources, military, and judiciary systems and selecting the six-member Guardian Council, which has been given powerful veto rights. If the Guardian Council so desires, it can stop politicians from running for office, and all governmental legislation must be approved by the council. There are no women, of course, on the Guardian Council.

This is the Iran that Shirin dwells in now, and she hopes to help reform it. She herself was a victim of her country's changing views on women: once a respected judge, she was removed from the bench simply because she was female—demoted to a secretarial position along with all other women holding the post of magistrate. And she did not take that sitting down, of course. She made so much noise in public about it that, eventually, she was sent to prison. And she said, "Fine! Throw me in prison. I'm unafraid to go there! You can jail me but you will not change my mind."

Being barred from the bench did not sway Shirin from working for justice. She petitioned repeatedly to be able to practice law, and she began her own law firm in 1993. Boldly defending some of the most controversial human-rights, children's-rights, and censorship cases in the country, she became an even more prominent figure in the international lens. Despite the continuous threats to her well-being, Shirin Ebadi has continued to work for human rights, a cause for which she was awarded the Nobel Peace Prize in 2003.

Of course, she didn't stop there—helping and empowering people throughout Iran is a big task, and there are still many struggles ahead. Shirin is one Nobel Peace Laureate who is most definitely up to the challenge.

Meet Mymoena

To help secure equal rights for women, Shirin Ebadi travels around the world. Today, she will arrive in Cape Town, South Africa, in order to work with three hundred young PeaceJam leaders, many of whom are Muslim. These young people are on fire and committed to working for change. A young Muslim girl named Mymoena has stepped forward and volunteered to create a Global Call to Action project in support of the efforts of Shirin Ebadi.

Mymoena is a thoroughly modern Muslim girl. She's forthright, direct, funny, detail-oriented, and very opinionated, though this last quality is always rendered delicately and diplomatically. Mymoena has learned that to be effective, diplomacy is of ultimate value. When she speaks, her voice is soft and unassuming, but she always manages to get her point across.

Knowing that her heroine, Shirin Ebadi, will be the featured Nobel at the PeaceJam Youth Conference, Mymoena is sitting front row center, on the edge of her chair, filled with anticipation as the event begins. After a rock-star greeting, Shirin begins to speak.

"First, I want to tell you about the current political and social situation for Iranian girls and women. More than 65 percent of our college students are girls, meaning that Iran is a society where its women have become more educated than the men. Iranian women were first given political rights a very long time ago. They have had the right to participate in elections, enter the parliament, and play many other leading roles in Iranian society.

"The most painful day of my life was after the revolution in Iran, when I read the new laws of Iran. When I read them the first time, I thought I was reading them wrong. I read them once again. I couldn't believe it.

"Today in Iran a husband has the right to restrain his wife from traveling—from going anywhere—simply by going to a government office and signing a piece of paper. The same rules apply for a girl or for a single woman, except it is her father who has that power.

"Women have to sit in a segregated section at the back of the bus as if they are second-class citizens.

"While women can divorce their husbands, custody of their children is given automatically to the father in almost every case.

"If a woman dies or is injured in an accident, insurance companies pay only half of what they would pay to a man for compensation—a woman's life is valued to be worth only half of a man's.

"I have been involved in the field of law for more than thirty-five years. I was a judge and a lawyer. I'm a Nobel Peace Prize winner. I have defended many different political prisoners. But if I want to give my testimony in a court, because I am a woman the court will not hear me alone. However, the court would accept my client's testimony—because he is a man. These laws are simply not fair.

"I grew up in a family where there was really no difference between a man and a woman. My father always gave me the same freedoms and rights as he did to my brother. But when I read Iran's new sentencing laws for the third time, I understood that the laws were as bad as I have just explained for you. And that was when I understood that I would have to change my life. I couldn't live in a country where it is written in the law that a woman is only equal to half of a man."

Shocked by what she has just heard, Mymoena leans forward, eager to hear more.

"There is a new movement in Iran today, a feminist movement which has recently launched a new objective to collect "One Million Signatures" from Iranian men and women who oppose the discriminating laws in Iran. These average Iranian citizens are demanding equal rights for women and reform of our current laws. Through this petition we want to tell the world that these discriminating laws are not accepted or agreed to by hundreds of thousands of people throughout our country."

Shirin finishes powerfully with a simple idea that lodges firmly in Mymoena's mind. "Ensuring women's rights is the best way to begin to create a true and lasting system of democracy in a country," Shirin says. "Ensuring women's rights is the best way to begin to build a better future for the people of Iran."

Mymoena Steps Up

Mymoena, after hearing about the state of affairs in Iran, is compelled to do something, anything, to help this articulate and passionate woman. Overcoming her nervousness, she approaches Shirin as she makes her way off the stage.

"Dr. Ebadi. Hello! Your speech impacted me quite a lot, and I want to do something to help women in Iran."

Shirin stops and turns to face Mymoena, smiling. "Hello to you, too. And what is your name?"

"My name is Mymoena," the young woman says, now almost frozen with fear as she stands face-to-face with her role model.

"And where are you from, Mymoena?" Shirin asks, taking Mymoena's hand.

Mymoena takes a deep breath, and then she says, "I'm from right here, Cape Town, South Africa, and I am Muslim, too. But we do not have laws like this in our country."

Shirin walks over to sit in the front row, leading Mymoena with her. "As you know, there are different interpretations of religious laws, of things like Sharia law, in different countries and different cultures."

"Sharia law?" Mymoena asks.

"Throughout history," Shirin explains, "there are many nations that have incorporated some degree of Sharia or Islamic law, which is based on the teachings of the Koran. It would be interesting to know what role Sharia law plays for Muslims here in South Africa," Shirin continues.

"Well, yes, I guess it would," Mymoena replies. "And what is happening with the "One Million Signatures" campaign? Is it really helping?"

Shirin answers thoughtfully. "It should. It is our best hope right now. It is very difficult because the government is set in its thinking, but we must force the issue. When we raise the issue enough, eventually, they will change."

"Then they will change?" Mymoena asks.

Shirin smiles. "They will be forced to change."

"Yes." Mymoena says enthusiastically. "I want to help this change to come."

"A human being is most happy when helping the happiness of others," Shirin says warmly. "If you want to help, we would be glad for your help."

Mymoena shakes her hand again and skips across the room, heading for the computers at the registration table. She gets permission to use one to do a bit of research, the gears already turning in her mind. She needs a plan.

To Mymoena, the first step seems pretty clear—prominent people need to jump on the bandwagon and lend their names to the cause. If you're looking for prominent people, Nobel Prize winners are a great place to start. Mymoena decides that her "goal number one" will be to get as many living Nobel Prize winners as possible to agree to sign the One Million Signatures petition.

She is also intrigued by Shirin's questions about the law of the land in South Africa. It will take a lot of research, but she decides to learn more about the rights of Muslim women here in her own country, and just how those rights developed during the hundreds of years when the vast majority of people here had very little protection under the law at all. Mymoena sets as her "goal number two"—finding out how Muslim women in South Africa won their rights. It is a history and an example that could really help the brave young women who are working on the "One Million Signatures" campaign in Iran. If South Africa can do it, Mymoena thinks to herself, Iran can, too.

Before the weekend is over, Mymoena stands in a long line of enthusiastic students, waiting for her chance to speak to Shirin Ebadi once more.

She finally makes it to the front of the line, and she quickly explains her basic action plan to Shirin.

"Wonderful! These are very good ideas, Mymoena!" Shirin says.

Mymoena beams and pledges to start on her project right away.

"You might want to join us in Dublin—we will all be gathered for a women's conference there this May," Shirin offers.

Mymoena is so excited she can barely speak. "No! Really?"

"Really." Shirin smiles back.

Mymoena pinches herself to see if she is dreaming as she files out of the auditorium with the rest of the crowd and clambers aboard the buses heading home.

Going into Action

Two months later, Mymoena is stuck in a rut, and she can't get out. She needs to pick up the phone to call leading Nobel Prize winners, and she is frozen stiff with fear. Only two Nobels have replied to the dozens of e-mails and letters that she has sent, and time is running out. She is set to leave for Dublin to meet with Shirin and the leaders of the "One Million Signatures" campaign in ten days.

Mymoena stares at the phone, and it seems to grow in size. She picks up the receiver. She puts it back down. Then, with millions of butterflies in her stomach, Mymoena picks up the phone again and begins calling holders of the Nobel Prize to ask them to add their names to the "One Million Signatures" campaign.

"Hello, my name is Mymoena, and I am a student in South Africa," she says softly. "Did you receive my e-mail? I am really trying to help the cause of women's rights in Iran."

The first twenty-two phone calls are a complete failure. "I couldn't even get past the secretary to talk to them!" she cries.

But phone call number twenty-three is a success. Nadine Gordimer, the Nobel Prize winner for Literature and a fellow South African, actually answered the telephone herself! And she said *yes*!

Mymoena's younger sister, Zaida, cheers Mymoena on. Soon Mymoena's confidence starts to grow. Today there were five more e-mail replies from Nobel Laureates saying yes, in response to her phone calls. Zaida beams proudly at her older sister.

It is the day before she is scheduled to fly to Dublin, and Mymoena has two very important things to do. First, she is heading to a mosque in town to offer up prayers for the success of her journey. And what a mosque it is. Here, women and men are allowed to worship side by side, and the service is being led by a visiting religious leader of the Muslim faith from abroad—and she is a woman! Mymoena sees it as a sign of hope, that her efforts are on the right track and that it is indeed possible that, one day, equal rights for women and girls can become the norm throughout our world.

Then she rushes home to finish preparing her gift for the women of the "One Million Signatures" campaign. She has created a beautiful scrapbook to capture the tremendous wisdom she has gained from her interviews with Muslim women who worked for equal rights in South Africa over the past thirty years. She has photos of the community activist who joined a group called the Spirit of Faith when she was only nineteen. This was a group of Muslim women who were united with the leaders of the antiapartheid movement in South Africa, but who were also laying the groundwork for securing their own rights. There is the information provided by the female Muslim lawyer who set decades of precedent using Sharia law in the courts of South Africa, clarifying case law to make it clear that equal rights for women and Sharia can coexist. And finally, she has photos and bios from the Web site of the Nobel Foundation for each of the Nobel Laureates she has convinced to sign on. In the end she was able to get eighteen of them!

The "One Million Signatures" Campaign

Mymoena is staring out of one of the windows as the airplane begins its initial descent into Dublin. She's heard all the stories, myths, and legends about Ireland, and she's thinking of these now. She isn't surprised at what she sees; rather, she's quite charmed.

Dublin is a thoroughly modern *and* ancient city. Its cobblestone streets, perhaps hundreds of years old, lay at the feet of slick glass-and-steel high-rise office buildings. The city's modern highway systems lead from a shimmering, glimmering downtown rife with workaday life into the green outlying districts, where stone farmhouses built in the sixteenth century tremble when jets pass overhead. Ireland, and Dublin in particular, embraces its past and its future.

After adjusting to the contradictory scenery, it begins to sink in that Mymoena is about to meet with the leaders of the "One Million Signatures" campaign. She doesn't know what to expect. Everything she has read suggests that standing up to the Iranian government will bring only beatings, torture, imprisonment, and death. She finds herself wondering if these women are brave, incredibly determined, or just plain crazy for speaking out in public in Iran.

Mymoena pulls up to the hotel in an old black taxi, and the leaders are waiting for her in the lobby. One by one she meets the women. Shaking their hands, she gazes into their eyes, hoping to catch a hint of what it is that motivates them. What she discovers are strong, committed, and intelligent women who have deep purpose in their lives. Mymoena finds herself smiling as she listens to them banter with one another, tease one another, and then in turn become serious as they hone in on the issues. Looking at them, all she sees are ordinary people—no superheroines, but rather mothers and working people (a pregnant lawyer stands out among the group); they're all just salt of the earth. Mymoena is deeply impressed.

"I'm a member of the 'One Million Signatures' campaign," says Parvin, a young activist from Tehran. "After the revolution most of the laws about women and equality for women changed. Since that time, we have tried to bring back equal rights.

"About two years ago we had a big demonstration against discrimination of women and violence against women. The demonstration took place on June 12, 2005, and we decided to make that a day of action for women against inequality in law. We wanted to have one day for ourselves to show that we are against the law and we're against inequality.

"In 2006, we had another demonstration against violence in civil law—about divorce, about inheritance, about polygamy. This demonstration was stopped by the police, and more than seventy women were arrested. They sent us to court and jail. After that, we decided to examine other ways of having a greater impact.

"We decided to gather one million signatures from men and women in Iran to show support for changing the laws. Soon we were trying not only to gather signatures, but to increase the consciousness that women are people. We wanted to push the government to change the law.

"Now, not only are we working in Tehran gathering signatures, but we're also gathering signatures in many other cities in Iran. Some people who would never do anything like this before are now a member of a women's movement."

Mymoena finds herself in awe of these courageous women. They face the possibility of prison, beatings, and death every day.

"We are talking about our lives," they tell her, trying to explain.

It is clear from the look of concern on Mymoena's face that she has found some sisters in arms, and she fully accepts the challenges they bring to the table. Mymoena could not possibly say no to these new friends.

A Final Blast of Inspiration

Then the guest of honor, Shirin Ebadi, arrives. Everyone calls out in greeting, and Shirin is welcomed warmly by each woman in the room. Shirin stops in front of Mymoena, grabs her hands, and smiles.

"As I explained to you before, the government is really trying to stop these women from continuing their efforts on the 'One Million Signatures' campaign. One of the women who was detained went to trial; she had to stay in prison for six months.

"There are other people who are actively participating in this campaign who are not able to join us here in Dublin," Shirin continues. "One of them is a young lady named Dlarlam who was sentenced to two years in prison. She is a young girl, only twenty-three years old, and just recently she finished her studies in university. Last year she participated in a peaceful gathering of women's activists and, without the knowledge of the people gathered there, the police came into the meeting and started brutally beating the women. The police broke her hand. I filed a complaint against the police for her. We had many witnesses; we had the medical report to confirm that her hand was broken because the police had beaten her up. But none of this was taken into consideration. For no other reason but the fact that she participated in that meeting, the revolutionary court started watching over her and controlling all of her movements.

"I was the lawyer for this case, and the court said she was guilty for two reasons—for threatening national security and for participating and propagating principles that are against the Islamic revolution's principles. She was sentenced to two years and six months in prison.

Dlarlam said, 'I will go and hand in myself because I want the police to know that prison is not something that will stop me from continuing my efforts to search for equality and have equality in my country.'"

The government will not stop these women from continuing their efforts in helping feminism find its way into the country. They accept the possibility of persecution—they take it as the price to pay to be able to create a better life for their own children.

Later on, we sit in a cozy tea shop in Dublin, listening to Mymoena as she tries to put words to all of the intense emotions fluttering inside her right now.

"It was very nice meeting those women from Iran because they're quiet, strong people, and they believe in what they're doing," Mymoena says. "They weren't scared and were enthusiastic; it doesn't seem like they were about to go to jail or on trial or anything.

"At first," she goes on, "I was a bit nervous about presenting my project to these women, but afterward I felt more relaxed because they started asking questions about South Africa and I am from South Africa, so it felt easier. I could talk more about that. They were quite interested in South Africa, and Sharia law in my country, because it is much different than the Sharia law that they follow. They said that they were hopeful because of what's happened in South Africa.

"I think I learned quite a lot from the experience. It was quite amazing meeting so many strong women. The women seemed so full of life. They are incredible role models for younger girls. These women stand up for their rights.

"And it was so very good to see Shirin again," Mymoena adds. "She asked me very difficult questions about my project, and she was really happy that so many new Nobel Laureates are now signed on to the cause."

Mymoena smiles happily as she sips her Irish breakfast tea. Her dream? "Well, one day, thanks to the efforts of the incredible women of Iran, I really dream that I will be able to visit Shirin in her home country."

We also want to be with Mymoena and Shirin on that happy day. We hope that it will come very soon.

aureate
Shirin Ebadi

Shirin Ebadi was born in northwest Iran in 1947, in the city of Hamedan. She has two sisters and a brother, all of whom are highly educated. When she was one year old, her family moved to Tehran, the capital of Iran. On warm summer evenings, Shirin and her siblings moved their beds outside to take in the sweet-smelling air and the clear night sky. Growing up, Shirin and her siblings were treated as equals by their parents. She did not realize that her female friends, like most Iranian girls, were treated much differently than their brothers at home. In Iran, most boys received more attention from their fathers. They were disciplined less frequently

and enjoyed more affection from aunts and female relatives.

Shirin attended Firuzkuhi primary school and went on to Anoshiravn Dadgar and Reza Shah Kabir secondary schools. She received her law degree in three and a half years, then took the entrance exams for the Department of Justice. After a six-month apprenticeship in adjudication, Shirin started serving officially as a judge in March 1969. She was only twenty-two years old, and she was the first woman in the history of Iran to serve as a judge. While serving as a judge, Shirin continued her education and received a doctorate in law from Tehran University in 1971.

In the 1970s, Iran was in a state of unrest. People were growing increasingly upset with the monarchy, specifically the practices of the shah. In 1978 a revolution began. In 1979, the shah was overthrown and the Ayatollah (a title given to high-ranking religious leaders) Khomeini came into power as the new ruler of the country. Unfortunately, many of the Iranian people did not foresee that the ayatollah and his ruling party would take away most of the rights of women and other minority groups in Iran. In 1979, the new leadership declared that it was no longer legal for women to serve as judges. All female judges were dismissed from their posts and given clerical jobs. Dr. Ebadi, outraged by the situation, requested early retirement. For several years she stayed at home taking care of her two daughters, writing books, and working to get her job back.

After many years of trying to return to the bench as a judge, in 1992 she succeeded in obtaining a lawyer's license and set up her own practice. As a lawyer, Shirin took cases that involved the unfair treatment of women and children because the conservative leadership had stripped so many rights from these specific groups. Dr. Ebadi has defended many high-profile cases, which included serving as a pro bono lawyer representing the family of Dariush and Parvaneh Forouhar—a husband and wife who were found stabbed to death as a result of speaking out against the oppressive government in Iran. Similar murders terrorized Iran's intellectual community in 1998. Shirin has also taken a number of pro bono cases representing children, and drafted the first child protection legislation in Iran.

"From childhood, I fell in love with a phenomenon I later learned was justice. When I was a child and saw other children fighting, I would go aid the underdog, without even knowing what they were fighting about, which would also cause me to get in the middle and get beaten. That is why I later became a student of law. And later, because of this feeling, I became a judge, as I thought I could help execute and bring about justice. When the Islamic revolution came about and said a woman could no longer be a judge, I changed my job and became a lawyer. It was the same feeling that encouraged me to become active in defending human rights."

Several years ago, Dr. Ebadi began to receive threats of incarceration and even death from the Iranian government. Regardless, she continued her work in human rights and challenged the unjust treatment of people in Iran, stating that "Human rights is a universal standard. It is a component of every religion and every civilization."

In 2003, Shirin Ebadi was awarded the Nobel Peace Prize for her efforts for peace and women's rights in Iran and across the Middle East. She continues to live in Iran, working to defend the human rights of all people.

In 2006, fellow women's rights activist Parvin Ardalan organized a rally to demand equal rights for women in Iran. Soon thereafter, Ardalan, Shirin Ebadi, and other women launched the "One Million Signatures" campaign. Together with many other women, they have spearheaded the campaign aimed at collecting signatures to change the laws in Iran in a way that would establish equal rights for women.

In 2007, Parvin Ardalan was awarded the prestigious Olof Palme Prize "for her success in making the demand for equal rights for men and women a central part of the struggle for democracy in Iran."

Shirin Ebadi remains dedicated to creating a better future for the people of Iran, and the people of the world. "My words may appear as a dream to you in the turmoil of the world today, but I do have a dream. I dream about a world that does not have poverty, prejudice, ignorance, or oppression in it. In this dream, I see the globalization in the hearts of people—a globalization in which everyone can feel compassion for the pain of others."

voices of peace

WHY CAN'T I STAND UP ALONE?

Shirin Ebadi

"Not only is a woman a citizen, but she is also a mother who nurtures future generations. Therefore, if women are educated to their potential, they will have the ability to affect the future not only for themselves but for everyone."

Rigoberta Menchú Tum

"I believe that participation is very important. If there is a woman sitting at home lamenting what is going on out in the streets, she is surely not going to be contributing anything. But if there is a woman who gets together with others and tries to struggle alongside them, she can make an impact."

Máiread Corrigan Maguire

"In the world of today, women have a tremendous opportunity and tremendous responsibility to help change the world by allowing the feminine side of their nature out and encouraging the feminine side of the male nature by being more loving, more gentle, and by being kinder and more able to show our emotions. When a man and woman bring a child into the world they need to nurture that child—to teach it kindness and compassion—to teach it to respect human life, to teach it to respect the environment and beautiful creation."

Desmond Tutu

"Some of the most celebrated people today, some of the people who are the most admired are not macho. You can say a lot of things about Mother Teresa, but macho is not one of them. Yet, almost universally, she is held in the highest regard. And yet she wasn't powerful. I don't even think she was successful. But people were aware of this minute woman who had poured out her life on behalf of the poor."

Ten Things You Can Do to Help

Work for the Rights of Women and Children

(1) Provide Access to Education

Education is a human right, and it is crucial to overcoming global poverty. More than 90 million children (a majority of whom are girls) around the world do not have the opportunity to attend school. You can help promote universal education, by raising funds for school building, holding a school supply drive, and educating others about the need for universal education.

(2) Denounce Physical and Sexual Abuse

Women and children both routinely face physical and sexual abuse around the world. Work to raise awareness about the issue of abuse, and work to get rid of the taboo about speaking out about it. Hold a community forum to foster open and honest discussion about the problem, and encourage others to continue speaking out against it.

(3) Promote Equal Access to Jobs and Equal Pay

Women all over the world face discrimination in the workplace. There are many places where it is very difficult for women to gain employment, especially in certain fields. Even when women are allowed into the workforce, there is often a noticeable discrepancy in the pay men and women receive for the same jobs. Work with your government to pass equal-rights legislation to allow women to work in the fields they wish, and to ensure that they receive equal pay.

(4) Explore Positions of Leadership/Leadership Development

Women and children are often told that they should not or cannot be effective leaders. You can change this! Harness your own power as a leader—accept responsibilities in an organization or your community. Use these skills to mentor others as you encourage them to become leaders in their families, schools, communities, and governments.

(5) Champion Children's Rights

The rights of children need to be specially protected, as the young are often unable to protect themselves from abuses. The United Nations created the Convention of the Rights of the Child (CRC), which entered into force in September 1990. All countries in the world except two (the United States and Somalia) have ratified the CRC. Pressure the governments of the United States and Somalia to ratify it. Contact the governments of other countries to stress the importance of continuing to strengthen their enforcement of the rights outlined in the CRC.

(6) End the Use of Children as Soldiers

Thousands and thousands of children are forced to be child soldiers around the world. Many of them are kidnapped from their homes and tortured as they are trained to be soldiers, then are injured or killed during combat. Learn about the places and situations in which children are forced or otherwise enticed to be soldiers, and pressure your government to do something to stop this practice.

(7) Speak Out Against Human Trafficking

Trafficking is when people, who have often been bought and sold, are transported from one place to another, and are forced into various situations, including labor, prostitution, and, in the case of children, adoption. This problem affects women and children disproportionately; up to 80 percent of all people trafficked are women and girls, and around 50 percent are minors. Work to enact local, national, and international legislation outlawing human trafficking, and to raise awareness of this issue.

(8) Provide Immunizations and Health Care

Three million child deaths a year could be prevented if all children in the world had access to existing vaccines. Talk with local health care organizations to sponsor workshops for communities in need, and work with organizations to help provide health care and immunizations to all who need them. Organize a health fair where people can come for immunizations and basic checkups, and give the people who come to the health fair some information about health issues.

(9) Boycott Forced Labor

The ability to work is a right when it is voluntary; it is a human-rights violation when the workers are forced to do the labor. Both women and children are victims of forced labor. Even when women and children are paid for working in awful conditions—such as in a sweatshop—they can still be forced to be there, through debt bondage or other illegal means. Research various companies, and ensure that you buy from companies that use fair labor practices. Encourage those you know to do the same, and you will increase your impact!

(10) Support Laws Protecting Women and Children

There are international conventions that are designed to protect both women and children. However, there are also various governments that have not signed on to these conventions. Find out your government's policies regarding the protection of women and children, and work to make these policies stronger and more comprehensive. If your government does not have laws protecting women and children, pressure them to adopt such laws. Organize others to do the same, and present a powerful, clear voice to your government.

CHAPTER 9

How Can I Help My Family?

Adolfo Pérez Esquivel & Fito—Breaking the Cycle of Violence

As people, we have to build bridges amongst ourselves—we have to build bridges of humanity and peace in order to confront the conflicts and the war, the violence that we see and that we experience throughout our world.
—Adolfo Pérez Esquivel

The Bounty of Argentina

Argentina is a vast country sprawling north to south, almost one third the size of the continental United States. It's the land of the tango, and gauchos, and it's sometimes referred to as the Texas of South America, because everything is bigger here. A steak, for example. When you order the smallest cut at a restaurant in Buenos Aires, the steak still hangs over your ten-inch dinner plate by a good two inches, at least. The bountiful platter of potatoes and vegetables that accompanies your night's repast makes you wonder if Argentina alone could solve world hunger.

And you can't help but be charmed by Buenos Aires's grand beauty, the salty smell of the harbor air, the aroma of grilled meat assaulting your senses, or the absolute savoir faire of the city's fashionistas as you step out of the taxicab that has transported you from the Buenos Aires airport to your hotel.

It's all there in Buenos Aires—fashion, food, music, culture. All you have to do is step outside your hotel door and turn either way to find yourself face-first in the thick of the lightning-paced action

Argentina has to offer. It's like a New York City with loads of European charm. It's a place of dreams, art, fashion, and history.

But not all of the history is pleasant. Stop by the Escuela de Mecanica de la Armada, one of the 340 torture centers that were spread across the country during Argentina's "Dirty War" in the late '70s and early '80s, for a quick lesson in remorse. The Escuela de Mecanica de la Armada is but two stories tall—you can hardly imagine that anything of importance went on inside these walls. But then you see something— many things—hanging from the bars of the cast-iron fence that surrounds it.

The things you are squinting at seem to be human figures. You step closer to get a better view and see a cutout of a bluish-gray figure, rendered from a sheet of steel. It's a naive figure of a man, face turned skyward in a silent scream. You walk over to the next figure—his hands tied behind his back, one leg cut off midthigh, the other just above the ankle. The mute agony, his faceless anonymity hits you in the solar plexus. The next is a black silhouette of a very pregnant woman, the names of people—perhaps sons and daughters, husband, friends, and relatives scrawled across her in red and white. This is a monument in honor of the women who were tortured. Art has thrust the dead in your face, and you're gasping for air now. Who could do this to another human being? you wonder.

You walk in a daze from figure to figure. The moral outrage in you responds. Then you head back to your hotel, taking in the life now on the streets of the city, the beauty and grandeur. You wonder how the torture and disappearance of innocent people could have happened in such a magnificent place.

Meet Adolfo

Just ask Adolfo Pérez Esquivel, the Nobel Peace Laureate from Buenos Aires. An artist and a professor, he eloquently spoke out against Argentina's "Dirty War"—during which the military used harsh illegal measures to repress opposition—and, as a result, was almost tortured to death at places like Escuela de Mecanica de la Armada.

In 1976, the army took over the country of Argentina in a military coup that lasted seven years. Anyone with protest in his or her voice was whisked away during the middle of the night, taken to an undisclosed location, tortured, and often killed. Tens of thousands of teachers, writers, artists, activists, community leaders, and students were "disappeared," never to be seen again. The mothers and sisters and husbands and daughters of the *desaparecidos* (the "disappeared ones") were distraught, as the military denied any knowledge of their where-abouts. Desperate themselves, they began to walk in front of the military offices at May Square, in the heart of Buenos Aires, with white scarves wrapped around their heads and handmade signs in their hands. Each sign held the black-and-white photo of a loved one who had been "disappeared," with the haunting words: HAVE YOU SEEN HIM? HAVE YOU SEEN HER?

As a fellow artist and activist, Adolfo Pérez Esquivel decided to speak out, to try to tell the world what was going on. Before long, Adolfo too was "disappeared." But this time, the world *did* notice. Amnesty International declared him their number-one prisoner of conscience, and a tremendous letter-writing campaign began throughout the world—eventually putting enough pressure on the Argentine military that Adolfo was released. He was placed under house arrest, but he would not let his voice be silenced, and he was awarded the Nobel Peace Prize for his incredible leadership and courage.

"We reap what we sow," Adolfo says. "If we plant seeds of hope, we can harvest them later. If we plant violence, we harvest more violence. This is why it is so important for us to preserve our history. We need to be very clear that what we sow, we will later reap."

The trauma caused by years of military dictatorship has had a profound effect on life in Argentina, especially in economic terms. From the beginning of the military dictatorship in 1976 until today, people's living conditions have declined dramatically.

"Argentina lived through more than ten years of extraordinarily violent repression—organized state terror," Adolfo explains. "So there's a tremendous legacy. If we look at the kids who are on the street, kids who don't have access to education, don't have access to health care, we have to understand that as part of the legacy of the military dictatorship. The children who die every year in Argentina because they don't have food in this country that could produce enough food to feed the entire world—this is part of the legacy, as well. Poor street kids in Argentina today face a violent society that excludes, marginalizes, and punishes them. Poverty is punished in the same way that delinquency is punished. This is wrong, and this is something that we must work to change."

Ten years ago, Adolfo began to create that change in a very concrete and innovative way.

Adolfo's Peace Villages

After more than thirty years of working with the poor throughout Latin America, Adolfo had seen far too many young people give in, give up, and succumb to the powerful magnet of poverty and violence. He felt compelled to do something more.

Then it struck him like a divine thunderbolt: a way to reach out to these street kids, teach them things they would be able to use in daily life, train them with job skills that would allow them to survive. He would create a series of *Aldeas Jóvenes para la Paz*, or "Youth Villages for Peace."

"The idea is that these villages would serve as a center for life, communion, participation, spirituality, and resistance against oppression," Adolfo explains. "In our society, a young person who is poor is often thought of as a delinquent. What we are trying to do is raise awareness, values, and self-esteem. The idea of the villages emerges as a necessity: a need to create a space of freedom where we embrace critical awareness and values in young people, and it is precisely in these villages where life, uncertainties, hopes, pain, and grief can be shared."

At the *aldea*, young people would learn trades like poultry raising, beekeeping, rabbit ranching, bakery skills, dairy production, sheet metal work, carpentry, plumbing and electricity basics, leather working, and organic farming. They would also get remedial classes in reading, writing, and math, as well as an opportunity to sing and dance, to play music, to draw and to dream.

It was a beautiful vision. Could one man conceptualize, finance, construct—in essence *will* these villages of peace into existence? Or was this an impossible quest? For many years, hundreds of people said no to Adolfo's requests for land, for buildings, for equipment, for teachers, yet he marched on. And that perseverance paid off—his first *Aldea Jóvenes para la Paz* opened its doors ten years ago, and the young people began pouring in.

"Why do we do this?" He smiles. "Because we believe in the strength of people, in the energy of our people, to change and transform society. But we can only do this if we first make a commitment, if we develop a critical consciousness. This is the first step in every path to freedom, and to freedom from the cycle of violence, as well."

Meet Fito

Today we are going out of town to meet Fito, a young man who has taken advantage of the *aldeas* to learn and grow and has decided to use the skills he has learned to help break the cycle of violence in his own community.

As you head out of the city, the huge multiplex cinemas, gigantic shopping centers, and subdivisions thin out, and a brand-new sight startles you. Right there on your left, penned off between the railroad tracks and the highway, is a cobbled-together, forlorn-looking area of shacks that can be described only as a slum. The structures are made of old bricks, sheet metal, cardboard, and plastic, and you wonder what life must be like for these poor souls who are surrounded by the city's wealth and beauty.

About thirty minutes later, exiting off the highway, you peer out the taxi's windows and notice that the side roads are made of a rich, rusty-red dirt that's tamped down. Turning down yet another side road, you head toward Adolfo Pérez Esquivel's first *Aldea Jóvenes para la Paz.*

Fito is standing right in front of the village, waiting for you amid a large group of students. The first things you notice about Fito are his eyes. They are fiery, mischievous. He bounces from group to group, rocking on his heels with an infectious energy. As he talks with his friends, they burst out in gales of laughter, the camaraderie genuine and warm.

"*Buen dia,*" Fito greets you, and before you know it, he's taking you on a tour of the *aldea.* Wandering among the various buildings and sheds, you peer into a room where metalworking is taught. Arcs of sparks fly around the young welders, and the din of the sound of hammer on metal echoes against the sheet-metal walls. You amble across the lawn to another building, equipped with the same electronic milking machines used commercially, and watch in amazement as some students, giggling and laughing with pride, begin to milk the *aldea's* fine-looking cows. Energetic activity is a key phrase in describing day-to-day learning at the *aldea*—in this building, you can actually learn the craft of beekeeping, and the young people won't leave you alone until they show you everything they've learned, and their beehive, too! You follow your nose into yet another building to discover a bevy of students kneading dough, mixing flour and other ingredients to prepare the dishes that will be served to all the youth for lunch. (A hearty meal made from organic foodstuffs grown or raised at the *aldea* is served to the students before classes start each afternoon—for some it will be their only meal of the day.)

With a crooked grin, Fito takes a roll from the table and bites in. "This is like home to me," he says. "I have been coming to the *aldea* since I was twelve years old."

But later that afternoon, when you get the opportunity to talk to Fito alone, the laughter and the jokes are gone.

"I like the *aldea* because, the way I see it, everyone is a good person," Fito says. "People are only different in the ways that they think about things. And I like that, that one is able to speak up."

"There was a time when drugs provided a means of expression for me," Fito says quietly. "But this did not help anything at all. On the contrary, I lost a lot.

"I cannot talk to my father today. My father is someone who started taking drugs very early in life, and he now wonders what he is going to do with his life. It has been months since I last saw him," Fito tells us. "I love him very much, although I do not forgive him for everything.

"Drugs are a form of violence. One sometimes does not realize how drugs can consume you, and yet, at the same time, it was as if drugs were the only thing my father knew about. At one time, all I heard about was drugs . . . to me, it is violence. And I am not interested in them anymore," Fito says with resolve.

"And my mother—my mother is my life." The glint of a tear appears in Fito's eye. "She had to face life on her own, with nine children. She had to face going to jail, and she had to go to jail to visit one of her sons. But she always tried to give us everything. My mother had a good job, but she lost the job because of problems with my older brothers. But regardless of what we did, she was always there.

"I used to become very angry. But I have learned a lot. Now, my brother makes fun of me because I am such a pacifist. If there is a fight, it is me who says no, no . . . and then there's a hug. When I go to parties or dances, I never go with the idea in mind to hurt anyone or to hurt myself, but rather with the intention of having fun, because that is what parties are for. Not everyone thinks the same way. But I am a peacemaker, and I stay relaxed. It is a good thing for me, to be able to get up the next day and be whole, whereas others who drink too much and get too excited—they wake up with a broken arm or in the hospital. No, I have always tried to avoid those problems," Fito says, and that mischievous, playful smile is back on his face.

You are awed by his incredible honesty, his calm resolve, his clear and steady gaze. You wonder at how self-aware Fito is—at some moment in his life, he must have taken a cold, hard look in the mirror, with drugs and prison tearing his family apart, and, with a brave heart, decided to do something about it. Maybe it was the loving support of the teachers at the *aldea* that kept that little spark alive until, finally, a sturdy little flame was glowing.

Fito's Project Begins

The next day, you return to the *aldea*, where Fito is going to explain his project idea to Adolfo Pérez Esquivel.

Fito ambles up to Adolfo in the front office of the *aldea*, and Adolfo greets him with a kiss on each cheek. Adolfo is in his mid-seventies now, but he is so full of life that he seems at least twenty years younger.

Fito fidgets nervously with the baseball cap in his hands, but then he cuts right to it. "I have attended many workshops here. They say you only pass through them, that we're only passing by, but one does take a lot along the way.

"For my project, I want to work with some of my friends here, and take what we have learned at the *aldea*, and use those things to make life better for our families."

Adolfo leans forward and smiles, nodding his head. "And how would you do that?" he asks. "We can make our houses better. We can put in some plumbing and some electricity and

maybe even a toilet, a sink. We can patch the roof and put in better doors, better windows. We can plant herbs and fruit and vegetables, and maybe we can even have rabbits—you can make a lot of money by raising rabbits, and you would always have something to eat."

Adolfo beams. "We all need to educate one another—parents, teachers, and students. This is a very good idea. There needs to be a dynamic relationship in our communities, because this is what provides a true sense of community."

Fito looks up at Adolfo, hopefully.

"As the indigenous people of Cauca have said, 'You have to make words walk.' Talk on its own is meaningless; words without action are empty," Adolfo says, standing. "So I think that they would very much like your project idea, too."

Fito jumps up and says, "Do you want to see the rabbits?" Tugging Adolfo along, Fito leads the way to the rabbit hatchery, a simple building that has but two brick walls supporting a corrugated tin roof. There are three cages, each approximately a hundred feet long and seven feet wide. Made of mesh wire wrapped around iron rebar, each set of cages holds a great number of rabbits. Fito and his friends at the school are learning to build these cages, and they're learning to care for the animals as well.

As you walk into the rabbit *ranchero*, you can see that they're rather hearty and healthy. When you get up close, you notice that they're not only hearty-looking, they're huge!

"They're *super* rabbits!" Fito says, hefting one of the burly beasts from its cage, the bundle of fur squirming all over the place. "When I graduate, I'll raise my own," he adds. "I can get twenty pesos at the market for a guy this size."

Fito holds up his rabbit proudly, and Adolfo laughs, shaking his head.

We Need to Help Our Families

You climb into a taxi, and Fito is your guide once again. As you're ferried over the bumpy red-dirt roads, he tells you all about the area and his community. The tiny, one- or two-room homes along these roads are simple structures, quite humble, made of brick or wood. Alejandro, one of Fito's friends from the *aldea*, lives with his family in one of the modest bungalows you've seen. A rickety wood gate opens to a dirt front that is covered with a few children's toys, a rusted bicycle, a small pigeon coop, and other odds and ends. Fito and Alejandro lead you around the side and point to the area where they'll cultivate the soil, turning it into a high-yield vegetable garden, which will in turn provide food and money for Alejandro's family.

Over there, point the boys, is where they'll build a rabbit *ranchero*. They go on to talk about the violence and the crime in their neighborhood, and how most of it comes from need, from the lack of a viable personal economy. Once you can take care of your own basic needs, they say, only then can you start to think of somebody else. It makes sense, and it is a real evolution of thinking for Fito and his friends. Fito and Alejandro are rightfully proud and hopeful about their brand-new undertaking.

Three months go by. We return to Alejandro's house, where half a dozen students who are part of the working crew for Fito's project have gathered. This time we are here with Adolfo Pérez Esquivel and three of the teachers from the *Aldea Jóvenes para la Paz*.

Inspired, the teachers from the *aldea* have decided to pitch in and help. The teachers at *aldea* are a mostly volunteer force—locals who know what bad alternatives the streets in their neighborhoods can offer these young people if they aren't educated or given skills with which to earn a living. They themselves have seen it all; they have seen the unemployment, poverty, and violence that have beaten down Argentina's masses. Experience is a great, if unforgiving teacher.

The students race up to their maestros and hug and kiss them on either cheek. They greet one another as friends because they know they're in this together—*this* is the chance to lift themselves from poverty, gangs, violence and death. Then Fito and his friends take us on a tour of the homes where they are working, each young person standing proudly in front of his or her own abode, pointing out the improvements that have already been made and talking vibrantly about all the plans that they have for the months to come.

Altogether, twenty-two homes are being improved over the course of twelve months through the efforts of these *aldea* work teams. Their heartfelt efforts will increase the quality of life and improve the food security for more than a hundred people in this one small neighborhood alone.

Hope

We walk down the street with Fito, and he is lost in memories. "My mother always told me that she was proud of me. When she left jail, the first thing she did was come see me. We were practicing as a band. I did not even know what a bass or a guitar was, but through observation and asking a lot of questions, I learned about music. And today, I have a band. Sometimes

we get work, sometimes not, but there's always another opportunity." Fito grins.

"And this is what surrounds me. There's Ariel, who plays keyboards. He is the one who faces things head-on. He is someone who really works for the band, and his family supports him in this as well . . . his mother, father, stepfather, and brother, too—they all support him.

"And there's Nicolas, my brother, and another guy whose name is also Nicolas. Then there's Pitu, and Johnny, who plays the guitar. We sometimes have problems as a group, but, as in any other band, we always try to 'row in the same direction,' which is essential."

"What is the name of your band?" you ask.

"Vagancia de Barrio, that is our name. Some of our themes relate to protest. Argentine *cumbia*—South American dance music—often contains themes about violence and crime. We try to use the same music style, but our themes are different; they are more about the current reality. We try to give people information, because sometimes that is what is lacking in music. Sometimes you listen to songs that contain a lot of poetry but say nothing. We want to convey a message, convey something that moves us forward a bit."

Now it is night in rural Argentina, and Fito and his band have set up their equipment in a garage behind Ariel's house. "Modest" doesn't quite describe their keyboards, guitars, and amplifiers—it's all in such poor condition that most of it is held together with duct tape and wires, and the electricity powering it all is a complete mess of tangled cords. But you like garage band music, and you know that this jury-rigging is all part of the game.

Fito sits hunched over the bass guitar on his lap, his slight yet powerful body rocking gently as he twists the tuning pegs to the desired, proper pitch. The rest of the band loosens up, improvising a few riffs.

Then, beauty springs forth as the outfit launches into—quite surprisingly—Beethoven's *Für Elise*. It's not what you expected, that's for sure. But the drummer rolls into a rhythmic salsa-esque beat, transforming it into a danceable delight.

The music filters down the street, and, as the band plays on, neighbors and family clutching cups of *limonada* materialize out of the humid night, tapping their feet and dancing to the beat. In this little corner of the universe, happiness is found in a ramshackle garage where music is being made on ramshackle instruments by talented young men who live on the harsh edge of despair—with a bright, steady flame of hope in their hearts.

Later on, Adolfo puts his arm across Fito's shoulders and shares an old secret. "I once had a philosophy professor who used to tell me, it is more difficult to be a person than to be a doctor. That is, it is more difficult to be oneself, Fito, than to be that image which we want to portray to others. Do we become persons, or do we continue to act out characters—that is the great dilemma in life." Adolfo's green eyes are twinkling, and then he laughs, and Fito looks up at him and smiles.

"In our society today, many people continue to wear masks; they are afraid to recognize themselves in one another. I believe that you, Fito, you now have the capacity and the courage to recognize yourself in others, rather than to hide behind a mask from the past." Fito's smile gets wider, and as you watch the two walk down the barrio road together, your own heart begins to fill with hope once again.

laureate

Adolfo Pérez Esquivel

Adolfo Pérez Esquivel was born in Buenos Aires, Argentina, on November 26, 1931. Adolfo's father was a fisherman in Spain before moving to Argentina, but after the move he held various odd jobs that paid very little to support his family. When he was young, Adolfo sold newspapers and worked as a gardener to help contribute to the family income. Adolfo's mother died when he was three years old, and he was raised largely by his grandmother, who instilled in him many indigenous beliefs, including a love of the earth and respect for nature.

He was an artist and grew up to become a famous muralist and sculptor. His large-scale works can be viewed in countless parks and museums across Europe and Latin America. Adolfo's faith in humankind is bottomless, as is his belief in God, and this is clearly reflected in his paintings, drawings, and sculptures. His unique spiritual perspective has continued to influence him throughout his life.

Argentina's political history is one of great turmoil. Between 1930 and 1973, the country was in an almost constant state of instability. In 1976, a military dictatorship was installed that carried out Argentina's Dirty War, cracking down on "opinion leaders"—artists, professors, schoolteachers, journalists, activists, and intellectuals. Censorship was strictly enforced, and people who spoke out or were suspected of "subversive" behavior were put in jail. Sometimes arrests were made in the middle of the night, and the friends and families of those detained would never hear from them again. The people who were taken this way are known as the "disappeared."

As an adult, Adolfo Pérez Esquivel trained as an architect and sculptor. In 1974, after becoming very concerned about the human-rights abuses of local leaders who had been working for peace and democracy, he gave up teaching and devoted his time to nonviolence movements in Latin America. That same year, he was named secretary-general of the newly formed *Servicio Paz y Justicia* (Peace and Justice Service, or SERPAJ), which coordinates nonviolent activities in the region.

Also that year, Adolfo Pérez Esquivel began a campaign for solidarity with indigenous people in Ecuador. While there, he had a vivid dream in which he saw the crucified Christ wearing an indigenous poncho

It was this religious experience that inspired his book, *Christ in a Poncho*, first published in French in 1981, and later, in English, in 1983. The book documents stories of nonviolent actions by the disenfranchised and downtrodden groups he supported in Latin America.

In 1977, Adolfo himself was "disappeared" and tortured by the Argentinean military for fourteen months. He was released after being named Amnesty International's Political Prisoner of the Year, which led to thousands of letters being written to the Argentinean government demanding his release. Upon that release, Adolfo continued his work leading Servicio Paz y Justicia.

Adolfo Pérez Esquivel was awarded the Nobel Peace Prize in 1980 for his leadership for human rights and true democracy for the people of Latin America.

In his Nobel Prize acceptance speech, Adolfo Pérez Esquivel declared, "we believe in the vocation and participation of our people, who day to day are awakened to their political conscience and express their desire for change and the complete democratization of society. A change based on justice, built with love, and which will bring us the most anxiously desired fruit of peace."

In the Nobel Prize presentation speech, it was noted that, "for Esquivel, as for Gandhi, nonviolence involved much more than a mere passive acceptance of the world as it is. It is a strategy in a struggle to change the world, using means that will not stifle the good intentions and the result one aims to achieve." This statement remains true today with the current work undertaken by this powerful leader.

In the late 1990s, debt relief became a primary focus for Adolfo Pérez Esquivel and he supported the Jubilee Campaign, an international campaign that called for the cancellation of all third world debt by the year 2000. Adolfo came out strongly, stating that enforcing the repayment of third world debt is "a massive and systematic violation of human rights." Debt cancellation has remained one of the foremost issues for his foundation.

The work of SERPAJ also continues to grow and meet the needs of the people of Argentina. Since its inception, SERPAJ has worked tirelessly to support Latin American peoples in their struggle and to promote the construction of inclusive social models based on full protection of the basic rights of men, women, and children. Recently, the organization has launched a program specifically aimed at helping the country's youth. Under Adolfo's guidance, SERPAJ has launched two "Peace Villages" that provide education for homeless and orphaned children. Within these villages, youth are immersed in productive skill-building activities and training workshops that aim to encourage the young people's sense of autonomy, build the sense of value in their work, and empower them to be responsible and engaged citizens. The program centers on the ideas of youth respecting and valuing their own cultures and includes exploration of issues such as health, violence, addiction, and crime.

He also works with the "Mothers" and "Grandmothers of May Square," groups of women working to bring about truth and justice with respect to the crimes of the dictatorship and to locate the children of the "disappeared" and reunite them with their biological families.

voices of peace

HOW CAN I HELP MY FAMILY?

Adolfo Pérez Esquivel

"As people, we have to build bridges amongst ourselves—we have to build bridges of humanity and peace in order to confront conflicts and war, the violence that we see and that we experience throughout our world. Violence is not just the physical aggression. Sometimes violence is not the barrel of a gun, but rather it is in the thinking and attitudes of people. It is when people lose respect for other people."

Máiread Corrigan Maguire

"I think if we can begin to teach non-violence in our homes (where we solve our problems through loving one another), if we teach it in our schools, if we teach it in our communities, and if everybody did that around the world, we could very quickly shift from a violent, militaristic, unjust, cruel world to a loving, forgiving, caring world."

Shirin Ebadi

"When there is injustice to one people and there is no way of receiving justice and when several generations live under the poverty line and there is no hope for the improvement of their lives, they may forget their sanity because of hopelessness. And thus they may resort to violence."

Oscar Arias Sánchez

"Wherever violence continues, everyone is the loser. It takes very little to turn the peace of one day into a violence of the next. The strength of forgiveness and dialogue can silence the guns and put everyone to work for real solutions. It is our responsibility to create a different future. Understand that by fighting for the impossible; one begins to make it possible. In that way, no matter how difficult the task is, one will never give up."

Ten Things You Can Do to Help

Break the Cycle of Violence

(1) End Violence Against Women

The cycle of violence often begins with violence toward women. These widespread problems include physical, sexual, and emotional violence. Ending violence toward women is an imperative first step to ending violence as a whole. Work with local groups that support women who have been victims of violence and raise awareness of the issue by hosting assemblies or public events in your community.

(2) End Violence Against Children

Children are the most precious and vulnerable population on the planet. Protecting the right of all children to have a childhood free from violence is a crucial step in ending the cycle of violence. Set up a safe zone in your school or community where children can go to receive help if they are victims of violence. Go to local organizations that specialize in working with parents and families and work with them to create a space in the community for parents to learn ways to eliminate violence from their homes.

(3) Address Violence in the Media

It is virtually impossible to get away from the waves of violence that are constantly flooding our senses from television, newspapers, the radio, and the Internet. Do research on how witnessing violence affects brain activity and development in young people. Create a presentation for your community and hold a violent-media trade where families can exchange violent movies, video games, toys, books, etc., for ones that do not glorify or promote violence.

(4) Take a Pledge of Nonviolence

It is not always possible to control the actions of others, but you can control yourself. World leaders in nonviolence such as Martin Luther King Jr. and Gandhi stressed the importance of taking a personal pledge to lead a life of nonviolence. Develop your own pledge for nonviolence and ask those in your community or school to sign the pledge themselves.

(5) Meet Basic Human Needs

In order to survive, there are some basic things that every human needs. Shelter, food, water, and a level of safety are motivating factors in every person's life. One of the primary causes of violence is often the fact that human needs are not being met. Gather a group and create a survey for your community to find out what impact violence has on their everyday lives. Ask what it is that people would need to eliminate violence from their lives completely. Work with your local government to ensure that basic needs of people are being met or to find ways that resources can be allocated equally.

⑥ Create an Alternative

Because we are all products of a global cycle of violence, we often don't feel like we have choices as to whether or not to interact in emotionally or physically violent ways. It is important that we take it upon ourselves to learn and teach alternatives to violence in our communities. Create a program for elementary school students to teach ways they can solve conflict without violence.

⑦ Get Connected

Studies have shown that it is easier to be violent toward a stranger than a friend. Building bridges between people is a way to connect via our shared humanity, and can prevent the escalation to violence in a conflict situation between acquaintances as well as random acts of violence based on hate.

⑧ Look Behind the Scenes

Many types of violence, such as domestic violence, remain hidden from view and are often taboo subjects for discussion. Making people aware of violence and its effects on your community can motivate people to get involved. Engage the media, community members, and educators in a campaign to get the message out about hidden forms of violence. Create community partnerships to ensure that services are available to those who seek help.

⑨ Play Together

Professional sports and sports figures often fuel the fire of violence on the field. Create a sports program that values nonviolence for youth in your community. Bring in coaches who are committed to nonviolence and train them in violence prevention. Work to strengthen the policies of school and recreational sports programs. Find local prominent athletic figures who are dedicated to nonviolence and ask them to speak to your program about nonviolence and the promotion of good sports etiquette.

⑩ Find Role Models

How can youth be nonviolent when they are constantly bombarded with violence? Promote healthy relationships by creating mentoring programs with mentors who understand and value nonviolence. Encourage adults within schools and families to be trained in nonviolent strategies so that they can incorporate nonviolence into their personal practices and be role models for youth. Find local community leaders who can be recognized for their nonviolent leadership by honoring them at a community award ceremony.

CHAPTER 10

How Should We Invest for the Future?

Jody Williams and Jessica—Creating Human Security

If we meet the basic needs of everyone on the planet (more or less), if we address the basic environmental threats against the planet, we're increasing security for everybody.
—Jody Williams

Show Me Missouri

We're heading to St. Louis, Missouri, to meet with a college student named Jessica, who wants to shift her state's investments out of the Sudan and to bring those dollars back home. We are eager to hear what she has to say.

As we cruise past St. Louis' iconic Gateway Arch, we learn about the city and the state that it calls home. St. Louis has long been called the "Gateway City," as it marked the first leg of the Oregon Trail which so many traveled as they settled across the United States. St. Louis hosted the World's Fair back in 1904, and it hosted the Olympics in that very same year! It was the St. Louis Chamber of Commerce that funded Charles Lindbergh's historic flight across the Atlantic Ocean in 1927.

This is Middle America, folks—this is where you come to discover the soul of our country. You can tell by the view from a coffee shop on the corner in downtown St. Louis. What do you see? The everyday, regular person in America who goes to work each morning and pays taxes—a person who lives modestly. The average person who goes to church on Sunday, then watches the football game later in the afternoon. The regular Joe who volunteers each week at the homeless shelter. These people are the backbone of the United States, the unheralded heroes of the working class. They come in all shapes and sizes,

every color of the rainbow. These people are what the real America is all about. Jessica is one of these people.

Being Jessica

It's a very bright, beautiful day in St. Louis. Jessica is wearing a white pullover hooded sweatshirt with SAVE DARFUR across the front. She's blond, athletic, funny, and she is also on fire. Why? Because she heard Nobel Peace Laureate Jody Williams talk about the situation in Darfur at her college, and she wants to learn more.

Jessica drives with both hands, rapping and tapping her fingers on the steering wheel as she sings along to a pop music tune. She is taking us to a university that has created a Camp Darfur event, because Jody Williams is going to be there. As you ride along with her, she rolls out her story.

"When I was five years old," she says, "I was just happy. I loved to do everything—be with my family, play outside, be creative. We'd play school. And I did all kinds of sports. I was an athletic kid.

"Volleyball was my thing." As she peers at the road in front of her, she explains, "I played for my high school, and for a traveling team.

"I like to laugh—that's one of my favorite things to do," she continues. "I'm known for telling really bad jokes, but that is just a way not to have everything be so serious. Life is funny, and we have to be able to laugh when funny things happen."

And tells us she is a klutz. "Maybe I just don't pay enough attention—tripping over things, running over things. Without my contacts I'm legally blind, so if I'm trying to find them, I'm knocking everything over. Yeah, I'm just one big klutz."

What's her favorite thing about her university, William Woods? "Well, there are two things, really," she says. "Once I got there, I found the program that I'm majoring in, American Sign Language and Interpreting. It seemed like fate—I love every minute of it."

And then there is her sorority. "At home, I have my mom and two sisters, who mean everything to me. They're my best friends, my role models. I think I need some people to be sisters while I'm at college. That's what my sorority sisters were from the first second, and probably for the rest of my life."

Jessica is just so unexpected—a volleyball-playing sorority girl klutz who's a whiz at sign language and tells bad jokes, the daughter of a cable repairman and a distant relative of Jesse James, and now she is driving long miles across the state of Missouri because she wants to save Darfur. It's hard not to fall under her funny, enthusiastic spell.

Jessica and Jody Williams

Nobel Peace Laureate Jody Williams is an American everyone can be proud of. She's from a state in the country—Vermont—which she laughingly tells you had a larger population of cows than people when she was growing up. She is an American right down to her Motown music-loving core. She is also a human-rights activist to the nth degree, a fearless leader and advocate of the downtrodden and abused.

Jody will often tell the story of how she became personally involved in activism. When she explains that she was merely exiting a subway station in Washington, D.C., when someone handed her a flyer for a lecture about the war in Central America, you're stunned. That's all it took to get this colossus of a woman up and fighting the good fight? Well, like Jessica, she's the type of American too few people get a glimpse of. They're both women with a fierce sense of right and wrong. Their moral compasses point toward a just society for all.

Jody won the 1997 Nobel Peace Prize for her work with the International Campaign to Ban Landmines. This well-documented international effort has saved hundreds of thousands of lives. Hard-charging Jody has also campaigned tirelessly on behalf of her imprisoned fellow Nobel Peace Laureate Aung San Suu Kyi, and she now leads the Nobel Women's Initiative, which has brought all the living women Nobel Peace Laureates together as a unified force.

Jody has already started speaking to the crowd when Jessica slips into the back of the room. "I was at the World Social Forum in Nairobi, Kenya, in January of last year," she says, "and I was asked if I would lead a U.N. mission on Darfur. So I did it, and it was a horrific experience. We flew over Chad to get to the camps near the border. When we were flying, we got a real sense of the villages. Some of the villages were only two or three huts, some as big as thirty. From up in the sky you can see that the villages are separated by two or three miles, which is a long way to go if you don't have vehicles."

Jody continued before the hushed auditorium full of students. "I had no trouble imagining the Janjaweed militia allied with the Sudanese military attacking those villages. They wait until almost dawn so it's still dark. They come on camels—sometimes supported by aircraft dropping bombs and the army in mechanized vehicles—and surround the villages, and then, with great screeching whoops, drive into the village. They just randomly shoot whoever comes out as they try to run and hide, often isolating the women and then raping them. Rape is used as a weapon of war in Darfur, as a plan to destroy the people of Darfur and the fabric of their communities."

Jody shakes her head in disgust, then goes on. "At the last refugee camp we visited in Chad, I asked to meet with a group of women. I had a woman translator, and a woman security guard, and I met with about thirty women. I heard the stories of women raped by the Janjaweed or Sudanese military. One of the women had been raped outside the refugee camp by four Chadian men when she'd gone to get water for her family. One woman had gone with a couple of other women back to their village to see if there was anything left. On the way she was taken by militia and raped for several days. When she got back to the refugee camp, her husband divorced her on the spot. Now she struggles to manage alone with their eight children. I asked these women about their hopes for the future. They had *none*. They did not believe they had a future. They did not believe they would ever know security.

"So we gathered all of their information and returned to Geneva to write our report for the Human Rights Council," Jody continues, "and we decided to write the report in a different framework than most of their reports are written—we wrote it analyzing the situation in the context of the 'Responsibility to Protect.' The Responsibility to Protect means that the primary responsibility to protect citizens from war crimes, crimes against humanity, ethnic cleansing, and genocide falls to the government of the country first. And when that government cannot or will not protect the people, it becomes the responsibility of the international community—through the U.N. Security Council—to protect them. Many people at the U.N. hated the fact that we wrote it in that format because we didn't just condemn Khartoum, we condemned every government in the world."

Jody looked up at the young people crowded into the hall. "I have a lot of respect for the people who keep trying to force the unresponsive governments of the world to do something to protect the people of Darfur. It's ordinary people like you and me standing up to take action to make the world a better place. And it *does* make a difference."

Jessica is riveted to her chair, struck by the power of Jody's speech and the raw truth of her emotion. She rushes up to the stage the second Jody concludes, and blurts out, "I want to do something to help the people of Darfur."

At Camp Darfur

Jody turns around and says, "Hello!"

"My name is Jessica Gabrian," Jessica says breathlessly.

"Hi, Jessica. How are you?"

"I'm doing great." Jessica smiles. "I really just wanted to let you know that I thought your speech was phenomenal. The part that really got to me was how people complain, but if all they do is complain it doesn't really do any good."

Jody laughs. "Yes, inspiration is good, but it must be followed up with action. Inspiration without action is a waste of time. Are you going over to the Darfur Camp they have set up?"

Jessica nods her head enthusiastically, and they head out into the darkening night.

Jessica gathers up her courage and launches in. "I came here today because I want to do a Global Call to Action project for Darfur. I want to focus on divestment from Sudan. From the information I read, Sudan has a lot of oil, and 70 percent of the money that Sudan receives from oil goes straight to the military, which is supporting terrible things in Darfur. For me, it's just overwhelmingly wrong."

Many countries, including the United States, have investments in Sudan's oil industry. Divesting would take these funds out of the area and prevent them from being used to perpetuate the genocide.

Jessica goes on. "Some critics argue that divestment will, in fact, make life worse for the citizens of Sudan," she says. "So what will happen if the divestment is successful in stopping the atrocities going on there? Will Sudan be able to flourish economically after that, or will it be going backward from then on?"

"Well," Jody replies, taking a deep breath, "I think about what happened in South Africa under the apartheid regime. It was one of the most brutal, racist countries in the world, and what made that government change was total isolation in the world. It was that pressure combined with internal pressure that brought about change in South Africa.

"Having just met with people from Darfur, their lives can't get any worse," Jody continues. "There are already 230,000 in refugee camps in Chad, two and a half *million* displaced inside their own country. How can divestment make their lives worse? If we can stop Khartoum from murdering them and burning down their villages, that will make their lives better. I fully support divestment and total isolation of the regime."

"Okay, great! Now, is there any way that we can make sure that this money is invested instead in some of our big needs here at home, things like education? Is there any way to control that?"

"There are some movements for socially responsible investing," explains Jody, "which means just exactly what it says: people who—with their retirement money, their IRAs, their investment money—tell the investing company that they want their money to go only to companies doing

X, Y, or Z; they can even pick the terms. It really is the responsibility of citizens to see where their money goes and pay attention—if it's invested in companies they don't believe in, then they move it! We can check on that, too. That'll be one of your missions."

"One of *mine*? Jessica asks, laughing.

"We'll divide responsibilities," Jody offers.

"I'm from Missouri," Jessica says, "so I'm thinking I'd like to do something with divesting in Missouri. Do you have any advice? Can we work together?"

"Sure we can work together!" Jody smiles. "I'm not certain of the position of the state of Missouri on divestment or the universities there. I think we should check out what Missouri's doing—"

"So you think we should start with universities?" Jessica asks.

"I think we should see what's going on there—where there's been movement, where there hasn't been movement," Jody replies.

"Great!" says Jessica, her inner fire building. "It's already in action then, I guess."

Jessica and Jody finally reach the entrance to Camp Darfur, and they kneel and place their candles in holders set up on the ground. Groups of students can be seen gathered together writing letters or just conversing. One of the camp organizers, a student named Paul, welcomes Jody and then asks, "What do you think the value is of talking to college students about what's happening in Darfur? Why is this important?"

Jessica is listening intently to what Jody has to say.

"It's part of a process of learning about activism, right?" Jody answers as she slips a donation into a cardboard box labeled FUNDS FOR DARFUR. "And learning that it's really not that miraculous—it's taking the first step, and every time you do something and you have a little bit of positive response from taking action, you understand it does make a difference. You're doing it because it's the right thing to do and not because you want recognition or anything—you do it because you're part of the global community."

"So character matters?" Paul asks, surprised.

"Character *really* matters," Jody replies. "It is the only thing that matters. My dad taught me that the best thing you can do in the world is to do the right thing when nobody else is looking. It's really easy to do the right thing when people are looking, but when nobody's looking . . ."

"That's wise, that's very wise." Paul says.

"Yup, Dad was a cool dude," Jody concludes, smiling up at Jessica. Jessica is beaming back at her, all fired up and ready to go.

Jessica Goes into Action

It's summer, and Jessica has just graduated from college and moved back into her family's modest, suburban home outside of St. Louis. But she is busier than ever, working a summer job while she launches her divestment campaign for Missouri. Today, she is traveling halfway across her state to meet with Mark Mathers, the director of investment for the state of Missouri.

Jessica is totally focused as she walks up the steps of the state capitol building, down the long corridor to the Missouri state treasurer's office.

Mark seems happy to meet with the sincere young student. He tells her that he manages only a portion of the investments for Missouri—but that, "in the state of Missouri, when we looked at public pension money, we estimated that roughly $1 to 2 billion were invested in companies operating in Sudan, and also in Syria, North Korea, Cuba, and Iran. That is just in *one state*. You multiply that by forty-nine other states, and you can see the magnitude of the problem."

Jessica leaves feeling stronger than ever about her divestment campaign. At least the state is aware of the problem, and it is screening those portfolios over which it has some control.

But that is only a tiny percentage of all of the investment funds in Missouri.

Jessica drives back to St. Louis—a friend of hers is a teacher, and she has invited Jessica to attend a conference on Education in Missouri, a subject very close to her heart. As she drives, she explains.

"If we can get these Missouri funds out of Sudan," she says, "I want to see them help the people here at home. How many schools in Missouri are falling apart? How many thousands of children don't have health insurance? Why not invest in our own education, our own infrastructure, our own state?"

Ray Wilson, a parent and educator whom Jessica meets at the St. Louis conference, strongly agrees. "Funding is the biggest thing. Achieving the goals of the No Child Left Behind Act is very doable, but unless you are willing to fund it fully, you're not going to get much more than a cliché. I like the cliché, but I don't think it's funded right. I don't feel that our country really deals with education the way that it possibly could.

"Let me give you an example. I was part of a school that was number fifty-two out of fifty-two elementary schools. But when I walked into that school, I found teachers who wanted to teach. I found administrators who were all about being administrators. But they needed funding and support. We were given the funds for a program to assist kids and rally the parents. The school went from number fifty-two to the top ten, and it stays there to this day."

Jessica is learning, and she is learning fast. Next, she heads to Kansas City, where she settles in for a long conversation with the superintendent of schools, Anthony Amato.

"What is the biggest issue facing education in Missouri today?" she queries.

"Our hopelessness."

"What do you mean?" Jessica asks.

"The culture in our city is one in which we really have had a very difficult time believing in ourselves, and therefore believing in our children and believing we can make a difference. When you get year after year of scores that indicate that you are not moving ahead, year after year of incidents throughout the system, year after year of difficulty attracting good teachers—people start believing that the system cannot be fixed. That feeling of despair permeates every nook and cranny, so you really *have* to do everything that needs to be done to counteract that. Lack of systems and despair go almost hand in hand, and those are two of the biggest obstacles I see."

Jessica leaves in a hurry—she has succeeded in securing a meeting with the state treasurer of Missouri herself, Sarah Steelman, and she is extremely excited.

"Is there a problem with any of the international investments that are held by the state of Missouri right now?" Jessica asks.

"We started looking at the companies that the state pension plans were investing in," Sarah says, "because I was worried that they were investing in companies that had been tied to terrorism."

"Were any of those companies tied to the country of Sudan specifically?" Jessica says, honing in like a laser beam.

"Some of them are tied to Sudan," Sarah admits, "so we implemented a screening process where those companies are identified if they have ties to Sudan, North Korea, or Syria. If they do, our divestment policy kicks in on the pension plan, and we have to divest those companies from our holdings."

"Has there been talk of taking that money out of Sudan and investing it locally?" asks Jessica.

"That's a good question," the state treasurer says. "One of my goals has been to invest more money back into Missouri, and we're actually in the process of doing that. It's good for our economy, it creates jobs, it creates revenue—it helps everybody. It's something we all should be looking at."

Jessica leaves the state capitol with a very clear-cut plan of action in mind. She e-mails Jody Williams and sets up a time to talk to her by phone that very same day.

Dollars and Divestiture

"Jody, I have done the research on Missouri—I know what is happening here now, and I know what it is that I need to do," Jessica says, feeling upbeat and strong.

"Whoa," Jody says. "How did you get to meet with all of these people?"

"Well," Jessica admits, "that's one of the best things I learned from playing volleyball—never give up. I must have made about a million phone calls."

Jody laughs long and hard. Then Jessica outlines her plan for action. First, she is going to educate people in Missouri about the problem and tell them how they can get their own dollars taken out of investments that are supporting the situation in Darfur. Second, she is going to work with a local restaurant to create a Dining for Darfur event, with 15 percent of the money spent in the café that night donated to a school for women in Darfur, plus a letter-writing campaign and information booth to get the word out about the issue, too.

One week later, Jessica is back on the road, crisscrossing the state again. In Fulton, she reaches out to some firefighters. On the University of Missouri campus, she sets up an information booth, and almost a hundred students stop by. She makes arrangements for a Dining for Darfur event. And then she sets up a meeting with a group of Missouri schoolteachers.

"Everybody ready?" Jessica asks. The teachers nod. They don't know exactly where she's taking them, but they're all ears.

"Seventy percent of Sudan's oil revenues go to military funding which is helping to support the Janjaweed militia that's going into villages," Jessica says, "burning them to the ground and killing the people there. Divestment has been the big campaign all across the country and all across the globe to try to help stop this situation. The state of California has completely divested, and many other states and universities are taking their investment dollars out of Sudan.

"I got the chance to interview the Missouri state treasurer, Sarah Steelman," Jessica says. "She told me that Missouri teachers' pension plans have money invested in Sudan. I was surprised, and I figured there was a probability that the teachers in Missouri don't even know this."

By the looks of frozen horror on the teachers' faces, you know that this is true.

The room erupts into noisy discussion until finally someone asks, "Just who controls our retirement money?"

Another teacher speaks out. "There are several companies that manage the state teacher retirement funds. They have such a diverse lot of investments that it's very easy for a trickle of it to get over to a place like Sudan, and you don't even notice it."

A third teacher interjects, "But I think if you raised awareness, then people would begin to question it."

Jessica smiles. "I have the draft of a letter about this that you can use," she says sincerely. "If you guys would like to take one home, I have addresses; I have some copies you can take to school, too, to give to friends."

"I have a friend who couldn't be here tonight, and I definitely want to give her a copy," one of the teachers says.

"Perfect," Jessica reponds. "I can also send it to you in e-mail format so you can send it out to more teachers statewide, as well."

And just like that, a grass-roots teacher education effort for Missouri begins.

Taking the Campaign on the Road

The next time we see Jessica, she is at the Busboys and Poets restaurant in Washington, D.C., holding her second Dining for Darfur event. She is attending a master's program in American Sign Language at Gallaudet University here now, but that has not stopped her campaign for divestiture from Sudan at all.

Jessica is excited; she has raised almost $1,000 already to give Jody Williams to help the women at the Darfur refugee camps, and she has just received some more great news. Last week, President Bush signed legislation into law that allows states and local governments to cut investment ties with Sudan because of the violence in Darfur. The bill permits state, county, and municipal officials to adopt measures to withdraw investments from companies involved in the four sectors that provide vital funding for Sudan's government—oil, power production, military equipment, and mining. "This will make it much easier to get taxpayer dollars completely out of any companies that are operating in Sudan right now," she says enthusiastically.

"Of course, I'm continuing my efforts to get the word out in Missouri," she states, "but now that I'm lucky enough to be going to grad school here in D.C., I decided to take my Darfur campaign on the road with me."

Jessica laughs, then looks up at us shyly. "This is just exactly the kind of thing that I love to do—it just makes me so happy to be able to get out and do something like this," she says quietly.

Lucky Jessica. Lucky you. Lucky world.

laureate
Jody Williams

Jody Williams was born in Vermont in 1950. She learned to abhor injustice at an early age after observing fellow schoolchildren ruthlessly picking on her brother who was deaf and suffered from schizophrenia.

After attending the University of Vermont in Burlington, Williams returned to Brattleboro, where she earned a master's degree in teaching Spanish and English as a Second Language from the School of International Training in 1976. She then taught ESL in Mexico for two years. Teaching in Mexico was Jody's first exposure to extreme poverty. From Mexico, she moved to Washington, D.C. There, she worked two

jobs and attended the School of Advanced International Studies at the Johns Hopkins University.

Concerned by a leaflet she received on the street one day, Williams attended a meeting to learn more about U.S. involvement in a civil war in El Salvador. Because it seemed to her another misguided U.S. intervention, she became immediately and passionately involved in work to stop this intervention. Transforming that passion into a career, she worked for two years leading delegations to Central America as coordinator of the Nicaragua-Honduras Education Project. She also served as the deputy director of the organization Medical Aid for El Salvador, developing humanitarian relief projects.

In late 1991, Bobby Muller, president of the Vietnam Veterans of America Foundation, called Williams to see if she was interested in coordinating a new initiative to ban landmines worldwide. After years of building awareness about U.S. policy toward Central America, Williams leaped at the opportunity to mobilize nongovernmental organizations (NGOs) around the world to press their governments in a common and worthwhile cause.

In October 1992, the International Campaign to Ban Landmines (ICBL) was formally launched. The steering committee issued a "Joint Call to Ban Anti-Personnel Landmines" that included putting an end to their use, production, trade, and stockpiling.

As the campaign's chief strategist, Williams wrote and spoke extensively on the landmine problem and the need for a total ban. Her audiences included the United

Nations, the European Parliament, and the Organization of African Unity.

Together with Shawn Roberts, she coauthored *After the Guns Fall Silent: The Enduring Legacy of Landmines* (VVAF, 1995). Their book detailed the more hidden consequences of landmine use, such as the socioeconomic effects on people in mine-contaminated countries. Besides the exorbitant medical costs of treating landmine victims, the long-term consequences to a community include reduced employment opportunities and lost access to land for agriculture, grazing, and trading.

Working without an office or staff, Williams ultimately convinced more than a thousand NGOs from sixty-plus countries to support the campaign. The ICBL gained tremendous visibility when Princess Diana became a vocal landmine critic and visited landmine victims in Angola and Bosnia—two of the most heavily mined countries in the world.

In little more than five years, Jody Williams and the ICBL achieved their goal of raising public awareness about landmines and effecting a landmine ban. In recognition for their efforts, the Norwegian Nobel Committee named Williams and the ICBL as corecipients of the 1997 Nobel Peace Prize.

In conferring the award, Francis Sejersted, chairman of the Nobel Committee, said, "There are those among us who are unswerving in their faith that things can be done to make our world a better, safer, and more humane place, and who also, even when the tasks appear overwhelming, have the courage to tackle them. . . .

You have helped to rouse public opinion all over the world against the use of an arms technology that strikes quite randomly at the most innocent and most defenseless."

To date, more than 156 countries have signed the Landmine Ban Treaty. For her role in helping make this happen, Williams also received the 1998 Distinguished Peace Leadership Award from the Nuclear Age Peace Foundation and the Fiat Lux Award from Clark University. She has been named a 1997 Woman of the Year by *Ms.*, *Glamour*, and *Vanity Fair* magazines, and has received honorary doctorate degrees from numerous universities.

While she no longer serves as the coordinator of the ICBL, Williams serves as its international ambassador. Recently, she has supported the ICBL's efforts for a new Cluster Munitions Treaty by participating in diplomatic negotiating rounds. The Oslo process is on track to produce a signed international treaty banning cluster munitions before the end of 2008.

Jody is also spearheading the Nobel Women's Initiative, which was established in 2006 by her and sister Nobel Peace Laureates Shirin Ebadi, Wangari Maathai, Rigoberta Menchú Tum, Betty Williams, and Máiread Corrigan Maguire. These six women—representing North and South America, Europe, the Middle East, and Africa—have decided to bring together their extraordinary experiences in a united effort for peace with justice and equality.

voices of peace

HOW SHOULD WE INVEST FOR THE FUTURE?

Oscar Arias Sánchez

"Any definition of security that deals only with human enemies, guns, and bombs is far too narrow. We also must talk about human security—security against disease, security against hunger, security against the future impoverished. As scary as terrorism is, there are far scarier threats to our human security that receive only a fraction of the attention."

Jody Williams

"We have to think in terms of human security for our common global security. If we meet the basic needs of the majority of people on the planet, if we address the basic environment threats of the planet, we are increasing security for everyone. That's a huge psychological shift, particularly for governments and militaries, but I think it's one of the consequences of the globalized world."

Aung San Suu Kyi

"The greatest threats to global security today came not from economic deficiencies of the poorest nations but from religious, racial (or tribal), and political dissensions raging in those regions where principles and practices that could reconcile the diverse instincts and aspirations of mankind have been ignored, repressed, or distorted."

Betty Williams

"When the peace movement first started, the chief constable in Northern Ireland came to my home, and he said to me, We're going to put in barbed-wire security and cameras. And I said No, no, no, no, you're not. My best security will be having none. If you do that and have men with guns at my house, then men with guns are going to come and attack them. The best security is *no* security."

Ten Things You Can Do to Help
Create True Human Security

(1) Educate Yourself About Current Affairs

Genocide is a horrific violation of human security. Learn about the history of genocide, and examine the factors that led to widespread insecurity and eventual genocide within the regions where this atrocity has occurred. As you are learning, educate others. Then, take action that will address genocide, such as a divestment campaign, which takes money out of the hands of the governments supporting and perpetrating these abuses.

(2) Determine What We Need

The basic needs of human beings include food and water as well as a sense of safety and belonging. What happens when people's basic needs are not met? What type of instability does that create? Learn about these various needs, and educate others about them. Then, create a project that addresses basic human needs that may not be met in your community, or the communities of others.

(3) Define Security

The world has a long history of military conflict. What has military conflict done for humankind? Has it provided safety and security? Does it help meet the basic needs of humanity? Host a public gathering or event to bring people together to discuss how to build true security.

(4) Say "I've Got Your Back"

People are social creatures and depend on one another in order to survive. Ensure that your relationships with others are positive and help provide for their security and well-being, instead of engaging in relationship behaviors such as teasing or gossip. Encourage others to make their relationships better, as well. Furthermore, get connected! Join a community organization to forge relationships with the people around you. Work on the specific goals of that organization as part of addressing the needs of your community.

(5) Protect Our Environment

If human security is tied directly to human needs, and human needs are tied directly to resources, and resources come from our environment, then protecting the environment is essential to human security. Take on an environmental project and find the ties to human security. Chances are, they're there!

⑥ Promote Symbols of Security

Many people have held a specific symbol of security at one time or another in their lives. Children may hold a blanket, a stuffed animal, or other toy when they feel they need a greater sense of security. Ask people around you to submit their symbols of security, and then create a community art project that can be displayed in a public place. This art project can serve as a reminder to the community to continue discussing and working for true security.

⑦ Tell Your Leaders What Security Means to You

Many governments spend large portions of their budget on military costs; often this exceeds the amount spent on programs that enhance human security, such as education, foreign aid, infrastructure building and maintenance, health care, and even disarmament. Let your government know that you want these priorities to change, and work for a reduction in the gap between military spending and spending on those programs that help promote true security.

⑧ Take a Can-Do Approach!

According to the United Nations, "Human security means protecting vital freedoms; protecting people from critical and pervasive threats and situations, building on their strengths and aspirations." It also means creating systems that give people the building blocks of survival, dignity, and livelihood. Work to develop your skills in nonviolent conflict resolution, deliberation, dialogue, debate, democratic process, negotiation, diplomacy, and community organizing. Help others to develop these skills and find the power in their ideas, their actions, and their voices.

⑨ Know Our Rights . . . and Defend Them

Human rights span the civil, social, cultural, and economic spectra and include such things as the right to life, liberty, freedom of expression, equality before the law, participation in culture, to work, and to education. When these rights are not recognized or are taken away, instability occurs. Let your elected officials know what your values are concerning human rights, and take action when you see human rights being violated or ignored.

⑩ Defeat Fear

People do things when in a state of fear that they would never imagine doing otherwise, and the more potent the fear, the less rational the actions. Evaluate and interpret your fears carefully and try to understand the ways you and others act when in a state of fear. Dig down to the roots of what it is that is truly making you fearful and determine whether your actions and beliefs are in line with your core values, or are simply a reaction to the fear that you are feeling. Become a master of your own personal fear and then examine fear as it relates to human security on a global scale.

CHAPTER 11

The Courage to Act

Aung San Suu Kyi & Charm Tong— The Struggle for Freedom in Burma

I've always thought that the best solution for those who feel helpless is for them to help others. I think then they will start feeling less helpless themselves.
—Aung San Suu Kyi

Arriving in Burma

The monsoon rains are lashing down on the airplane as you arrive in Rangoon, Burma, in 1995. Gazing out of the plane's window, you see dark gray skies, and the wind is violently whipping the palm trees and other tropical vegetation. You hustle into the dreary, in-need-of-update airport terminal that is dimly lit by flickering fluorescent lightbulbs only to see that there are more soldiers with machine guns than passengers here. The scowling Burmese soldiers appear to be only too willing to open fire for any reason, bad or good.

After collecting your luggage in the sickly yellow-walled baggage area, you head toward the exit and feel the burning stares of the soldiers boring through your back. You find it hard to breathe—as if you are unconsciously holding your breath to avoid drawing any further attention.

As you walk toward the taxi stand, you notice that while the soldiers are keeping a sharp eye on

you, the taxi drivers do all they can to pretend that you're just a mirage. Finally one cabbie waves you over as the rain pounds harder, and you throw your bags into the filthy, cluttered

trunk. You give the driver the name of the hotel, and it is only when he stares into his rearview mirror that you realize that this is the first time you've made eye contact with a Burmese civilian since arriving.

As the taxi winds its way through the gloomy and depressed streets of Rangoon, you read the body language of the city's denizens. They move slowly through the sweltering downpour, only too aware of the heat the countless soldiers loitering in doorways and under the eaves can bring. One move in the wrong direction, a "wrong" look, any perceived transgression of whatever the soldiers decide today is "the Law" could find these oppressed people imprisoned or, worse, tortured and murdered. This is what Burma is today, this is the condition of life here in a country run by one of the most universally condemned regimes in the world, and despite the temperature you feel a cold chill creep up your stiffened spine.

An Oppressive Regime Takes Control

For decades the news emanating from this oppressed Asian country has left you bewildered. This country—roughly the size of Western Europe—has been subjugated by a brutal, illegal ruling military junta called, oddly enough, the State Peace and Development Council (SPDC), which continues to enslave its own people, arresting anyone voicing opposition to virtually any of its policies. The ruling regime gets its funding from the opium it sells into Southeast Asia, the rubies mined by its broken-backed citizens, the forests that are clear-cut for timber exports, the natural gas reserves that allow these military leaders to snub their noses at the rest of the world. How did the country of Burma ever reach this depressing state of affairs?

The United Kingdom spent two-thirds of a century, from 1824 to 1886, colonizing this country, which sits nestled between Thailand, India, China, Laos, and Bangladesh. Burma was then treated for years as a province of neighboring India until 1937, when it became a self-governing colony. From 1948 until 1962, Burma's new constitution and the effects thereof were disputed, and the country struggled for unity. General Ne Win led a coup in 1962, installing a xenophobic rule along with a military dictatorship, which began the country's long fall into the brutal abyss. He installed economic policies that were devastating, crushing the free market mentality that the people of Burma thought they'd chosen, and then to top his own act, abolished the new constitution and renamed the country "Myanmar."

The downward spiral in Burma continued through the 1980s when, finally, young Burmese students, fed up with their government's antics, bravely staged demonstrations and other acts of defiance. Countless thousands of beleaguered Burmese joined in the protests with the students, and the country found itself at a violent crossroads on August 8, 1988, when the military were ordered into the streets and towns, killing thousands. Weeks later, Aung San Suu Kyi gave her first speech as a leader of the democracy movement. The people had found their hero, their champion, in this slight daughter of one of the original Burmese founding fathers, General Aung San, who helped negotiate their nation's independence from Great Britain back in 1947.

Then the military leaders of Burma, calling themselves the State Law and Order Restoration Council (SLORC), seized power in a violent coup and installed martial law. In the next election, Daw Suu ("The Lady" as Aung San Suu Kyi is often referred to) and her National League for Democracy (NLD) defeated SLORC overwhelmingly, winning 392 of the available 485 seats—despite the fact that she was already under house arrest at the time. SLORC flatly refused to turn over the power to Aung San Suu Kyi and the NLD, then went on to arrest and imprison countless party members. And that was the situation: utter chaos, violence, and insanity. Could it get any worse?

Yes, it could and did get worse. SLORC renamed itself the State Peace and Development Council, and continued to hound and harass the people of Burma, rounding them up and detaining them for years on end, burning down villages across the country, a genuine reign of terror.

The Courage of Aung San Suu Kyi

Burma's most famous dissident, Aung San Suu Kyi (pronounced "Ong San Sue Chee"), is a woman of no uncertain charm and delicate beauty. She couldn't weigh more than ninety-five pounds soaking wet. It is this tiny woman the military junta are most afraid of. For the better part of two decades Daw Suu has remained under strict house arrest and is generally not allowed to see anyone at all, with the occasional exception of a doctor when her health is seriously at risk.

She was conferred the Nobel Peace Prize for her courage and leadership of the democracy movement in Burma in 1991. Winning the Nobel Peace Prize means that in order to accept it, the recipient must journey to Oslo, Norway. But Daw Suu knew that if she left her homeland, SLORC would never allow her to return. So she did not go to Norway. She chose to remain in Burma in order to remain visible to her people, to remain a beacon of light and a shining hope to all.

In August 1995, we had the extraordinarily rare opportunity to meet with Daw Suu in her lakeside home/prison in Rangoon, Burma. Her charm, wit, and her deep Buddhist training and belief—not to mention her incredible and unshakeable courage—were evident as we discussed with her the topic of hate.

"I think that those who abhor one another are basically those who feel insecure," she says, adjusting the yellow flowers in her shiny, jet-black hair. "They feel threatened by what is different, whether it's a different color, or a different religion, or a different belief. So, one would say that they have no inner confidence, no inner serenity.

"It's a lack of spiritual development," she adds. "People who are spiritually developed do not think of others in terms of their differences, but in terms of what they have in common. That is why a spiritually developed person is full of compassion: because he can think of every other human being as the same sort of person as he is, basically, with hopes and fears. He can feel a lot of compassion for others."

Daw Suu is deeply philosophical in her answers. Through experience, through study, she understands that the tools of diplomacy and nonviolence are the best ones to use in order to help her people, and she continues, "It would help if people were frank about their inner feelings, but only in a positive way. I do not think it does any good for people to go around saying how much they hate others . . . some people like to pride themselves on their frankness and openness, but, in fact, they are just hurting other people. Using the excuse of frankness, they hurt other people, insult other people. I do not think that helps."

You're amazed at her composure, her passion, and her compassion. You're genuinely impressed at her lack of fear for herself. When asked how she'd approach her jailers, she says, "I think that first of all, you must listen to that person. You've got to try to ask him to explain why he feels the way he feels. It's not enough to say, 'I hate this,' or, 'I hate that.' You have to ask, 'Why do you hate that?' or, 'Why do you think a certain belief is bad?'

"Then, I think," she says, "you would have to carry on from there, because if you want to create understanding between two people, each side must learn to listen to the other—both sides, to a certain extent, must be frank about their fears. Quite a lot of people do not like to admit their weaknesses to others, and they hide these weaknesses. In doing so, they create a barrier."

"The first step is confidence building," she concludes. "If the two sides can start having confidence in the other's goodwill, then you can carry on from there, and I think they will be much more honest and not just talk about what they hate, but what they fear. Hate and fear are the opposite sides of the same coin. It's the same thing. You don't hate unless you fear, basically."

We raise the question of evil.

"Well," she says, warming up to an immense topic, "I once listened to a radio program about Karl Popper and he was asked the question, 'Do you believe in evil?' He said, 'No, but I believe in stupidity.'" She smiles. "And I agree very much with him there. I don't think that there is such a thing as evil, but I think there is such a thing as ignorance and the root of all evil is ignorance. The more you understand, the broader your vision, and the broader your understanding is of the world around you, the less room there is for evil.

"I suppose you could call it a lack of empathy," she explains. "If you could feel for others as you would feel for yourself, then there's very little room for evil, because mostly, evil is what you do to others. I do not think there is a word for evil in Buddhism. We speak of ill will, we speak of ignorance, we speak of greed, but we don't speak of evil as such. There is no evil, just stupidity."

You are simultaneously so thrilled and surprised by her lionhearted courage that it literally takes your breath away. You ponder her life, her situation, and ask what has surprised *her* the most.

"It's just *people* that surprised me both negatively and positively—the depths to which they can sink as well as the heights to which they can rise. The most surprising thing in the world is that although death is all around all the time, most people act as though they'll never die. They just act as though they can do what they like and get away with it and not think of the consequences. They create so much misery for others in order to make money and have power. People behave badly because they have only a very short-term vision of life. They think of it in a very narrow sense. If they had a broader and longer-term vision of life, they would probably be less inclined to go around creating as much misery as they possibly can."

Meet Charm Tong

You meet Charm Tong, and, as you listen to this twenty-six-year-old Burmese activist speak, you think that she would be one in a long list of people whom Aung San Suu Kyi would be surprised about—in a very good way.

Charm Tong (her name translates as "silver flower") hails from the Shan state, which is located in the northeast section of Burma. She has known nothing but turmoil and tragedy all her life as a result of the brutality of the SPDC, but she will tell you that she's a lucky one—many of the people she knew and held dear have been killed. When she was only six years old, her family escaped from the Burmese military as it came to burn down her village. She spent her first ten years in an orphanage on the Thailand/Burma border. She then spent many years in Thailand. "There are many refugees in Thailand, and I am just one of them," Charm Tong says with quiet confidence.

"Aung San Suu Kyi means a lot to me and also to the people of Burma," Charm Tong says, smiling now. "Her courage, standing up and sacrificing everything, sacrificing her life and everything in her life for the freedom of our people. Given all her pressure, she still stands. For many young people, she's our role model."

And she is one of the reasons why Charm Tong volunteered to help out at a local newspaper when she was only sixteen years old, learning to take the testimony of the thousands of Burmese refugees who were flooding over the Thai/Burma border.

Charm Tong almost always dresses in red and black, "They are my favorite colors!" she says. And she crisscrosses the Thai/Burma border on a motorcycle.

"I have my motorbike so we can go anywhere in the area," Charm Tong laughs.

"Do you wear a helmet?" we ask.

"Yes," she replies, "I wear my helmet all the time. The last one was stolen, but now I have a new one—a black one. My motorcycle is red."

You begin forming the image in your mind of Charm Tong zipping around the border towns on a motorbike, decked out in all red and black. You can't help but find her to be the epitome of cool—Burmese activist cool.

And Charm Tong is also cool enough to tell this joke:

The people of Burma speak many different languages. So the Burmese army came to a Karen village and they found a group of Karen friends hiding from them in the jungle. So the Burmese army asked them in Burmese, "Where are you going?" And they answered in Karen—"We do not understand the Burmese language."

Then the soldiers asked them again, "Where are you going?" and they replied, "We do not understand." The soldiers asked, "Where are you from?" and they replied, "We do not understand." Finally the Burmese army said, in Burmese, "Okay, now you can go." And the Karen friends left. So the Burmese soldiers shouted out, "Come back, come back—that means you understood everything!"

To remain calm, poised, charming, and courageous, when a murderous military junta has their guns pointed at you and your fellow citizens, is something more than you can grasp. Aung San Suu Kyi has been able to manage this. And somehow, so has Charm Tong.

For the past few years, Charm Tong and some of her friends have been running a school for refugee youth from Burma, a kind of leadership-training camp. Her generosity of spirit shines through as she explains, "After the intensive nine-month class, they can work more effectively and they can speak about Burma. They can do human-rights documentation. They bring medicine and food relief into Burma, crossing the borders for people who are hiding in the jungles. We are planting the seeds in our people, especially in young people. They are now working in various community organizations, working on environmental issues. Some of my former students are working to raise awareness on HIV/AIDS. Some of them became teachers and medics and some of them became community radio broadcasters doing programs to help promote education and health education for the border migrants."

She leans forward and says, "I think this is a sign of hope, a sign that more and more people in the community are working for human rights and democracy. I think this will increase. I think the Burmese military may have guns, but they are weak compared to our people, who have so much knowledge and so much skill and such a willingness to promote freedom and the human rights of others. I think we have more strength than they do."

Charm Tong's poise and quiet strength stun you. You dig deeper, and ask her if she ever really experiences total despair. Everyone has a bad day now and then. What does she do to lift her spirits and reinvigorate her resolve?

"For me," she says, taking a deep breath, "I just take a moment to be quiet and also to look into what just happened—why did it happen like that? I will also just look at my breathing, follow my breath, and I feel better each time I do that; I think its a form of meditation. And I can talk to my friends and colleagues, who also share the same pressure and stress that I have each day, every day."

The Saffron Revolution

We have been fortunate enough to meet Charm Tong at a very crucial moment in the life of the Burmese Democracy movement.

On August 15, 2007, a sudden surge in fuel prices sparked a mass movement against the decades of military repression and economic hardship in Burma. It was led, miraculously, by Buddhist monks in their saffron-colored robes, walking peacefully and reciting *metta* (loving-kindness) through the streets of Rangoon, Mandalay, and many other Burmese cities and towns. At first they asked the people of Burma not to join in; "We monks will do this, please don't join us," one courageous young monk said at the beginning of September. Another stated, "As monks, we see everything. We see how the rich live and the poor . . . we see how everything is getting worse and worse." They were standing up for the people of Burma, and they were saying, Enough is enough!

Day by day, the support for their nonviolent moral protest grew. One day, they were able to walk directly past the house where Aung San Suu Kyi was being held under house arrest, and Daw Suu was able to say a few words of loving-kindness to them, tears running down her face, before the military moved in and barricaded her street, shuttling her away. She, more than anyone else, would know the incredible danger they all now faced as a result of their incredibly courageous action on behalf of the poor and suffering people of Burma. By the end of September 2007, there were ten thousand monks leading more than one hundred thousand Burmese citizens through the streets of Rangoon. It was the biggest challenge to Burma's ruling military regime in nearly twenty years.

And then the brutal, vicious crackdown began. A sixty-day curfew was declared in Rangoon, and soldiers began to raid the monasteries of Burma. Hundreds of monks were imprisoned, many were killed, and several have been charged with treason. Witnesses have reported seeing the dead bodies of monks floating down a river in Rangoon, and many other atrocities have been reported to the human rights activists who have been desperately trying to reach them. Except for the Thai-Burma border, all other borders have been effectively shut down, making it almost impossible to escape from Burma. The military regime has its soldiers and civilian militia going door to door and arresting anyone who was photographed or filmed showing any kind of support for the mass protests at all—along with their families, their friends, and anyone else who tried to stand in their way.

The world has expressed outrage at these actions, and Burma has become front-page news around the globe, with Burmese-rights activists worldwide working around the clock to push for a concerted international effort to deal with this brutal military regime. On November 18, 2007, the All-Burmese Monk's Alliance released a statement saying that the Saffron Revolution would go on and that they would continue to boycott the military regime, and urging the public to join them in continued protest against the junta.

The Courage to Act

We first connected with Charm Tong by e-mail in September 2007. She had heard about the Global Call to Action through her network of friends in the human-rights field, and she said yes to joining the call on behalf of the people of Burma. On November 11, 2007, only a few short weeks after the Saffron Revolution began, she boarded an airplane and flew to London, England, in order to bear public witness to the suffering of her people. Charm Tong, frequently vilified by the state-controlled press in Burma, has no qualms about appearing again on the regime's surveillance screens. "I know that they already have a photo of me . . . so what difference does it make if they end up with a couple more?" she says, with appropriate gallows humor, and the heart of a champion.

She has an impressive schedule set up for her by the Burma Campaign UK—a meeting with a humanitarian-aid organization, where she says, "We are very concerned about the current situation, and as long as the State Peace and Development Council keeps burning houses, pushing people off their land in order to build dams or natural gas pipelines, I think the problems of the internally displaced people and refugees and migrant workers will only continue to increase."

She meets with a leading member of Parliament at the House of Commons, where she tells about a young monk, who was arrested during the protests and ultimately had to disrobe and flee to Thailand.

She tells the Conservative Party Human Rights Commission that rape is being used as a weapon of control by the military government despite efforts to raise awareness of this atrocity.

She returns to the House of Commons and meets with the shadow secretary of state for international development, where she tells how doctors are being discouraged from bearing witness for victims of rape. "We can see that in Burma the military regime controls every level of the life of the people," she says. "Even those who should be able to be the witness and to strongly speak out—they cannot."

She gives a public talk before a huge crowd at the London School of Economics, organized by their Amnesty International club, where she speaks about the plight of the hundreds of thousands of Burmese refugees, saying, "They are not recognized as refugees by the U.N. High Commission for Refugees; therefore they receive hardly any aid at all."

And she does an interview with BBC World Service, where she states, "I think all of us in

the international community can do so much to help, to bring about change—we can make the dream of these brave people come true. We have to continue to tell the story, to do what we do at all levels. The people of Burma do not want much. They just wish that there could be a change and that they could sleep without fear of somebody knocking on the door and taking them away from their home at any time. It has been happening for so long, and I think that it is time; I think that all of this violence should finally stop."

It is a whirlwind schedule, but Charm Tong seems so very happy to be here, to be able to bear witness for her people, to be able tell the world what is really going on in the land of her heart.

Somewhere deep inside yourself, you wonder if you would ever have the courage to continue on with a life similar to Charm Tong's. You marvel at her and all of the other Burmese activists, and then you ask her where it all comes from.

"Each time we work and we see our people and their suffering and their hope and what they've told us and the way that they don't give up—there are so many problems that they are facing every day and they are still trying to struggle—and this is what makes me continue to want to work. Each time we meet, I think there is strength in that, and the support makes me want to continue to do what we believe is right. It makes me believe that there will be change.

"I think that all the support from different networks in the international community is a sign of solidarity, that the world has not forgotten all of our hope and our struggle. I think that is what keeps us working and that is why we will not give up.

"My parents and their generation have been involved in this struggle for almost half a century. We really wish to see things change in our generation, to see a peaceful Burma in our lifetime. I think we still have to keep that hope."

Charm Tong's sense of resolve is truly inspiring. We are so very sad to have to say good-bye.

One week later, the Burma Campaign UK welcomes a series of tough new European Union sanctions on Burma—a ban on imports of Burmese gems, timber, and metals, and a ban on investment in these sectors. And it urges the European Union to do even more.

Charm Tong's voice is simply one of the many thousands that are now being raised on behalf of the people of Burma. But in your heart you believe that her voice is actually being heard, that policy makers and governments are finally listening, and that her incredible courage, the courage to act, truly does have a chance of making a difference in the lives of the people of Burma, whom she so dearly loves.

This is the Global Call to Action, folks—pick your issue, roll up your shirtsleeves, and get to work. It is as simple as the shining courage of the people of Burma, who risk their lives to help each other, and live in hope of a friendly assist from someone just like you.

laureate
Aung San Suu Kyi

The youngest of three children, Aung San Suu Kyi was born in Rangoon, Burma, on June 19, 1945. She was named "Aung San" after her father, "Suu" after her grandmother, and "Kyi" after her mother. In Burmese her name means "a bright collection of strange victories." Her father was a general in the army and spent the majority of his life leading the struggle for Burma's independence. Her mother was a nurse and met her father while caring for him in the hospital after he had received wounds in armed conflict against Britain. Following her father's assassination, Suu Kyi's mother was appointed ambassador of Burma and continued to work for freedom and peace in her country.

In 1962, General Ne Win led a coup on the Burmese government and revoked the constitution, enacting a military dictatorship that led the country into unending turmoil. In August 1988, thousands of people—primarily students and monks—came together to peacefully protest the military regime. They wanted democracy, peace, and an end to the oppressive rule they had endured for so long. In response to the protestors, the government created the State Law and Order Restoration Council (SLORC), and martial law was declared. SLORC Soldiers were ordered to meet the crowd at city hall and shoot them. The soldiers killed more than two thousand people. Aung San Suu Kyi, who had returned to Burma to care for her sick mother, was enraged by the slaughtering of so many citizens. She decided to work for a democracy in Burma, just as her father had done until the day he died.

Aung San Suu Kyi began to speak out about the people of Burma, standing up and organizing nonviolently to bring peace and democracy to the country. Her supporters, under her leadership, started a new political party called the National League for Democracy (NLD). She and her party became very popular among the Burmese. In 1990, the regime agreed to hold elections in Burma. The NLD and Aung San Suu Kyi won the elections in a landslide —a victory that was actively ignored by the military regime.

Aung San Suu Kyi was put under house arrest before the elections took place. The regime completely cut her off from the outside world; although groceries were brought to her, all visitors were strictly forbidden. Though she was regularly encouraged to leave Burma to visit her family, she refused, knowing that once she left, she would never be able to return to Burma. In 1991, Aung San Suu Kyi was awarded the Nobel Peace Prize for her nonviolent struggle for democracy and human rights while noting that ". . . Suu Kyi's struggle is one of the most extraordinary examples of civil courage in Asia in recent decades. She has become an important symbol in the struggle against oppression." Still under house arrest, her sons accepted the prize in her honor at the Nobel ceremony in Oslo, Norway.

In 1995 Suu Kyi received a brief reprieve and was released from house arrest; however, she was still told that if she were to leave the country, she would not be allowed to return.

In 1999, Suu Kyi's husband, whom she had not seen in many years, was suffering from prostate cancer. He petitioned the Burmese government to be able to travel to Burma to visit Aung San Suu Kyi one last time. The regime would not grant the visit, hoping that this would force Aung San Suu Kyi to leave the country to be at his side. She did not leave, and her husband died in England before he and Suu Kyi had a chance to see each other again. In 2000, Aung San Suu Kyi was restricted and again put under house arrest. She was briefly released two years later and allowed to travel inside Burma, but in May 2003, after an assassination attempt in Depayin, she was arrested again, and this time she was put in prison for four months. She remains under house arrest to this day, yet she does not give up hope that someday Burma will be free.

During the month of September in 2007, thousands of monks marched in protest of the oppressive regime in Burma. Extreme censorship was enforced by the government—restricting Internet and media access for weeks. These pro- tests, later named the Saffron Revolution, drew the attention and the support of the world. Pressure for the regime to begin genuine and substantial talks and negotiations with Aung San Suu Kyi came from the United Nations and other world leaders, including Nobel Peace laureates. To date, these meetings have not materialized, but the world has not given up hope that Aung San Suu Kyi, and the Burmese people, will be free.

In support of the Saffron Revolution, nine Nobel Peace Prize winners, including Desmond Tutu, Jody Williams, Shirin Ebadi, Betty Williams, Adolfo Pérez Esquivel, Máiread Corrigan Maguire, and Rigoberta Menchú Tum, released a statement on February 19, 2008. The statement called for the rulers of Burma to "create the necessary conditions for a genuine dialogue with Daw Aung San Suu Kyi and all concerned parties and ethnic groups in order to achieve an inclusive national reconciliation with the direct support of the United Nations."

On May 6, 2008, U.S. President George W. Bush presented Aung San Suu Kyi with the Congressional Medal of Honor, stating that the medal would be "a fitting tribute to a courageous woman who speaks for freedom for all the people of Burma." The same day, Canada conferred honorary citizenship to Suu Kyi while pressuring the military regime in Burma for her release. "We once again call upon the regime to release Aung San Suu Kyi and all other political prisoners, and to respect the human rights and fundamental free- doms of all the people of Burma," said Canadian Foreign Affairs Minister Maxime Bernier. "We stand alongside those who, like Aung San Suu Kyi, share our commitment to freedom, de- mocracy, human rights, and the rule of law."

voices of peace

THE COURAGE TO ACT

Oscar Arias Sánchez

"The truth is that nearly the entire world agreed to impose sanctions on the white regime in South Africa, and those sanctions paid off. I think the same can and should be done with respect to Myanmar. This is a woman with a great courage, with an immense dedication to fight alone for democratic ideals which she has defended, and the world somehow has forsaken her; and this isn't just."

José Ramos-Horta

"Some of the greatest moments in my lifetime that I have observed that really gave me hope were when the Berlin Wall collapsed, when the Soviet empire imploded, when apartheid ended, and Mandela was freed. That gave me hope that humanity can free itself from a past of oppression and violence, that anything is possible if you strive for it."

Jody Williams

"It's really hard to be Aung San Suu Kyi. That woman stands before the full might of that evil dictatorship with just her moral authority, fighting for the rights of her people for a different future, a future of democracy. She doesn't want a country ruined by war and civil war and fighting; she wants a negotiated solution to the problem. THAT is bravery; THAT is bravery."

Aung San Suu Kyi

"The quintessential revolution is that of the spirit, born of an intellectual conviction of the need for change. Without a revolution of the spirit, the forces which produced the iniquities of the old order would continue to be operative, posing constant threat to the process of reform. There has to be a united determination to persevere in the struggle, to make sacrifices in the name of enduring truths, to resist the corrupting influences of desire, ill will, ignorance, and fear."

Ten Things You Can Do to Help

The Struggle for Freedom in Burma

1) **Embrace Knowledge as Power**

Take some time to review facts and figures on Burma's history, and read speeches by Aung San Suu Kyi. Check out books, Web sites, newsletters, local media, and articles about the history and current situation in Burma. Use your knowledge to call for the unconditional and irreversible release of Aung San Suu Kyi and other political prisoners.

2) **Embrace Language as Power**

The military regime in Burma officially changed the name of the country to Myanmar in 1989. Those who support the struggle for peace and democracy in the country still refer to it as Burma. Tell classmates and teachers about this. If you are looking at maps in geography class, try to use the name Burma when referring to the country.

3) **Make Money Talk**

Money is a powerful tool, and the removal of monetary support speaks volumes to governments. In some cases, it has worked to even change the regime in a country! Get your local university, businesses, government, or school districts to take their investments out of companies that support the military regime in Burma. Call for the implementation of banking sanctions that specifically target the regime. For further information on how these sanctions work visit the Human Rights Watch Web site.

4) **Contact the United Nations**

Create a petition to send to the U.N. secretary general Ban Ki-moon urging him to make Burma a priority under his "good offices." The secretary general and his special envoy to Burma, Ibrahim Gambari, must press the regime to bring about national reconciliation. In 2007 Aung San Suu Kyi stated this must be effectuated in a timely and meaningful manner. An international arms embargo, under the auspices of the United Nations would be a major step toward restoring peace and democracy in the country. If you are a student, set up a table on campus and ask students and faculty to sign. Go out into your community and others as well. Hand out information sheets about Burma and encourage those you meet to get more involved seeking an arms embargo against this regime. Partner with Amnesty International and Human Rights Watch; both organizations have called for an arms embargo.

5) **Use the Local Media**

Your local newspaper or television station has a broad reach, but it may not always pay attention to issues like Burma. Write a letter to the editor of your local newspaper expressing your opinion about the situation in Burma. Create a calling campaign with people who agree to call your local news station and demand that they cover what is happening in Burma on the local news.

⑥ Raise Your Voice Through Silence

Symbolic gestures can be very powerful to get a message across. Hold a silent demonstration at your school, in front of your capitol building, or in a heavily trafficked public area to raise awareness of the silencing of the Burmese people. Advertise ahead of time and get others to join you. Ask your faith groups to sponsor interfaith services, to join in vigils, and to remind their congregations that Burma's struggle is nonviolent and led by the world's only imprisoned Nobel Peace Laureate.

⑦ Use Your Internet Connections

One out of every four people who use the Internet reads blogs—so blog often about Burma! Create a short video clip to post online using YouTube or another video platform, create an audio podcast that people can download, post pictures and writings on your personal Web page, and ask friends to link to sites about Burma. Get your message out there every way you can!

⑧ Treat the Symptoms

Ending the brutal military rule in Burma is important, but in the meantime, there are thousands and thousands of people who need your help. There are a number of organizations such as the Shan Women's Action Network, the Thailand Burma Border Consortium, and the Mae Tao Clinic that help provide safe haven, food, education, and medical relief to Burmese who have fled persecution in Burma. Use the Internet to connect with these organizations to see what you can do to help.

⑨ Support Women—Demand an End to Rape

Women and girls in Burma have been made victims of rape as a weapon of war. Educate yourself on the issue of rape as a weapon of war and then do something about it. For example, hold an awareness event and fund-raiser in your community and send the funds to an organization that supports Burmese victims of rape.

⑩ Talk to Their Neighbors

Countries directly neighboring Burma have the power to do a lot to address the situation there. Thailand could recognize the Burmese refugees and support them, as well as put economic pressure on Burma. China is directly supporting the military government in Burma through trade, investments, and loans. India could express support for Burma's democracy movement. Write letters to these governments and put pressure on them to do more to end the suffering of the Burmese people.

CHAPTER

12

More About PeaceJam

PeaceJam provides year-long, ongoing educational programs for youth from kindergarten through college. The participating Nobel Peace Laureates are directly involved in developing the curriculum and the program itself.

PeaceJam Programs

PeaceJam Juniors

The PeaceJam Juniors Program is a standards-based curriculum for ages 5-11 that explores the childhood stories of 12 Nobel Peace Laureates and the character traits they embody. Students study the personal experiences of these amazing world leaders and then engage in service-learning projects that address needs in their local community. As a result, students gain academic and social skills, including leadership, conflict resolution, problem solving, and character development.

PeaceJam Leaders

The PeaceJam Leaders Program is a new standards-based curriculum for young people between the ages of 11 and 14. It explores the adolescent stories of 12 Nobel Peace Laureates and the strategies they used to overcome problems in their lives and their communities. Through this age-appropriate curriculum, youth explore their own identities and reexamine the choices they make, including their role models and the peer groups to which they belong. Youth also develop leadership and problem-solving skills while engaging in service-learning activities that address local needs.

PeaceJam Ambassadors

The PeaceJam Ambassadors Program is designed for youth ages 14-19 and explores issues related to peace, violence, social justice, and oppression. Youth study the lives and work of 12

Nobel Peace Laureates and the strategies they use to address pressing global issues. Participating youth create and implement their own Global Call to Action Projects, becoming creative leaders who are committed to solving the most difficult problems facing our world. The program also includes an annual PeaceJam Youth Conference where youth spend a weekend with a Nobel Peace Laureate, giving them an unprecedented opportunity to share with, learn from, and be inspired by a world leader for peace.

PeaceJam Juvenile Justice

The PeaceJam Juvenile Justice Program is designed for incarcerated youth and youth recently released from the juvenile justice system. This curriculum addresses issues of gangs, drugs and alcohol, domestic violence, property theft, and other risky behaviors. Participants develop skills in the areas of civic responsibility, reconciliation, and leadership while being challenged to rewrite their life stories, reevaluate their role models, and learn the power of peace.

PeaceJam Scholars

The PeaceJam Scholars Program is a college-level program where college students serve as mentors for participants at PeaceJam Youth Conferences, support local PeaceJam groups, and study international issues connected to the work of the Nobel Peace Laureates, with opportunities to engage in service and research that extends that work into the community.

VISIT OUR WEB SITE TO FIND A PEACEJAM OFFICE NEAR YOU!

CHANGE STARTS HERE

www.PeaceJam.org

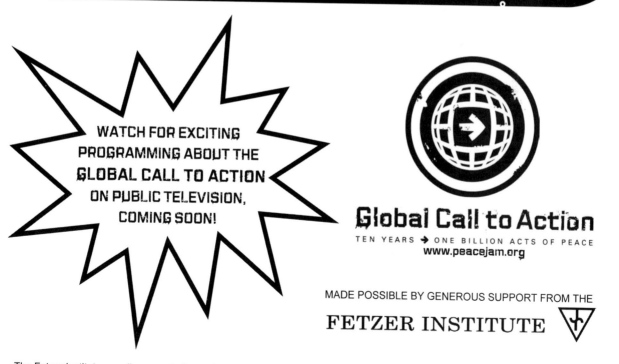

Global Call to Action Challenge

The Global Call to Action depends on your voice. Make yours heard in the Global Call to Action Challenge, a video-making and sharing program for young advocates from around the world.

Find out more at www.GCAchallenge.org

WATCH FOR EXCITING PROGRAMMING ABOUT THE GLOBAL CALL TO ACTION ON PUBLIC TELEVISION, COMING SOON!

Global Call to Action

TEN YEARS → ONE BILLION ACTS OF PEACE
www.peacejam.org

MADE POSSIBLE BY GENEROUS SUPPORT FROM THE

FETZER INSTITUTE

The Fetzer Institute proudly supports PeaceJam in its efforts to inspire one billion acts of service and peace by the year 2018 as an important part of our effort to bring love and forgiveness to the center of individual, community, and organizational life. Learn more at www.fetzer.org.

Acknowledgments

First, last, and most important, we want to thank all of the members of our family. Their deep love and loyal support make this book, and all of our work in the world, possible.

Second, we have to thank everyone who worked so very hard on this project. To all of the Nobel Peace Laureates featured in this book, we owe you our undying gratitude for your tremendous compassion, leadership, and inspiration. To each and every Nobel staff member who helped us along the way, we salute you for your incredible heart, deep patience, and for your faith in the young people of the world. And to all of the young people featured in this book and DVD, we pledge our everlasting friendship and support as you continue to struggle to transform your little corner of the world—you are amazing and you are beautiful, and we believe in each and every one of you.

Finally, we need to thank a huge host of others—there would be no book without the efforts of this tremendous and tenacious crew: Jes Ward, who acted as Editorial Assistant for this book, and who did so very much more; our extraordinary film and photo team—Dave Wruck, Stuart Alden, Adrian Milne, Penpa Dolma, Brett Engle, Laurel Harris, Giacomo Buonafina, and Gary Blackwell; our tremendous PeaceJam staff who provided assistance and support in so many different ways—Kate Cumbo, Ryan Hanschen, Rudy Balles, Joanna Rau, Leroy Lemos (and a big thanks also to Pani and Jaala and Darcy Gifford); our fantastic book agent, Lynn Franklin, and to Deb Kovacs and Alan Schwartz and Jim Christian, who introduced us to the Penguin Group; and to the extraordinary team of passionate professionals at Penguin—especially to Douglas Whiteman, for his strong support, to Eileen Kreit, for her amazing vision and leadership, and to Kristin Gilson, for her incredibly talented editing—thank you so much for your deep understanding of what this book could truly become. We also want to thank Debra Kagan and the Pearson Foundation for their wise and essential support. Finally, we have to thank those who were there at the very beginning: Mike and Brett and Adam Engle, and the Mind and Life Institute, and Barry and Connie Hershey, and The Fetzer Institute, especially Arthur Zajonc and Tom Callanan who created the process that gave birth to the Global Call to Action—plus hundreds of other friends and key supporters who helped us to come this far—there is not enough room to thank them all. For the tremendous photos found throughout this book and in the DVD, deep thanks and respect go to Ivan Suvanjieff, Stuart Alden, Dave Wruck, Penpa Dolma, Brett Engle, Steve Floyd, Zoriah, Alan Schwartz, Mandana Beigi, Stock.xchng and Shutterstock. Hats off in salute to the stars of the DVD—Brittany Williams, Deon Buca, Orlinda Ramirez, Jason Perez, Warren Swiney, Jaala L. Hemingway, Tsering Yangkyi, Rudy Balles, Pantea Beigi, Ryan Hanschen, and Penpa Dolma. And to the artists who have lent their music to this project, our gratitude is impossible to measure; a giant thank-you to The Go, The Arctic Monkeys (and Pete Smith), The White Stripes, The Muldoons, Beth Neilson Chapman, Flobots, and everyone else involved. A million apologies to anyone whose name belongs here and was missed somehow; you know who you are, and you have our eternal gratitude as well, you know you do!

resources

The following is a list of resources to start you on your way in gaining the knowledge necessary to create your Global Call to Action project. PeaceJam firmly supports the building of critical thinking skills, which includes obtaining information from a variety of sources. We strongly suggest that PeaceJam participants explore information on all sides of an issue and create independent, thoughtful, and informed opinions. The resources listed below are not necessarily endorsed by PeaceJam but are intended to provide a starting point for research.

CHAPTER 1: Equal Access to Water

Web Sites

- Centers for Disease Control and Prevention: Center for Infectious Disease. http://www.cdc.gov/ncidod/diseases/water/index.htm.
- Ecological Footprint Quiz. http://www.myfootprint.org/.
- Energy Information Center. http://www.worldenergy.org/.
- Home Energy Saver. http://hes.lbl.gov/.
- World Water Council. http://www.worldwatercouncil.org/.

Books and Articles

Australian National University, "New Filter Promises Clean Water for Millions," news release, January 19, 2005. http://info.anu.edu.au/ovc/Media/Media_Releases/_2005/_January/_190105filters.asp.

———, "Step by Step Guide to Making Water Filters," news release, 2005. http://info.anu.edu.au/mac/Media/_pdf/ClayPotFilter_final_web.pdf.

Environmental Protection Agency, "Fifteen Things You Can Do to Make a Difference in Your Watershed." http://www.epa.gov/adopt/earthday/.

———, "Lead in Drinking Water: What You Should Know to Protect Children in Your School or Child Care Facility," fact sheet, December 2005. http://www.epa.gov/safewater/schools/pdfs/lead/toolkit_leadschools_3ts_training_factsheet.pdf.

Godoy, Julio, "French Firms Spearhead Water Privatization," CorpWatch India, March 22, 2002. http://www.waternunc.com/gb/CorpWatchIndia02_2002.htm.

Public Citizen, "Water Privatization: Issues & Debates." http://www.citizen.org/cmep/Water/articles.cfm?ID=10842.

Shiva, Vandana, *Water Wars: Privatization, Pollution, and Profit.* Cambridge, MA: South End Press, 2002.

Srivastava, A., "Communities Reject Coca-Cola in India," CorpWatch, July 10, 2003. http://www.corpwatch.org/article.php?id=7508.

Swisher, M. E., James Sterns, and Jennifer Gove, "Starting a Farmers' Market," University of Florida, August 1, 2003, revised July 26, 2006. http://edis.ifas.ufl.edu/FY639.

Movies and Videos

Diary of Jay-Z in Africa: Water for Life (2006). United Nations & MTV. http://www.mtv.com/overdrive/?id=1545981&vid=120275.

Safer Water Worldwide: Industrial Toxicologists Develop Cost-Effective, Life-Saving Disinfection (2006). American Institute of Physics. http://www.sciencedaily.com/videos/2006/1206-safer_water_worldwide.htm.

Troubled Waters (2006). United Church of Christ & Church World Service. www.troubledwatersdoc.com.

Events

- World Water Monitoring Day: An annual event between September 18 and October 18 that gets students and teachers, families, and others involved in local watershed activities. To order a monitoring kit, register your site, and report your data, visit http://www.worldwatermonitoringday.org.

CHAPTER 2: The Spread of Global Disease
Web Sites

- Centers for Disease Control. http://www.cdc.gov/.
- Centers for Disease Control and Prevention: Division of Tuberculosis Elimination. http://www.cdc.gov/tb/faqs/.
- Centers for Disease Control and Prevention: National Center for HIV/AIDS, Viral Hepatitis, STD, and TB. http://www.cdc.gov/nchhstp/.
- Doctors Without Borders. http://www.doctorswithoutborders.org.
- European Center for Disease Control. http://ecdc.europa.eu.int/.
- Global Campaign for Microbicides. http://www.global-campaign.org/.
- Global Tuberculosis Institute. http://www.umdnj.edu/globaltb/.
- Human Rights Watch: HIV/AIDS and Human Rights. http://hrw.org/doc/?t=hivaids&document_limit=0,2.
- Malaria Foundation International. http://www.malaria.org/.
- National Foundation for Infectious Disease. http://www.nfid.org.
- National Institute of Cholera. http://www.icmr.nic.in/niced.htm.
- Project Hope. http://www.projecthope.org.
- UNICEF: Children and HIV and AIDS. http://www.unicef.org/aids/.
- United Nations Development Programme: HIV/AIDS. http://www.undp.org/hiv/.
- Waterborne Disease Center. http://www.waterbornediseases.org/.
- World Health Organization. http://www.who.int/en/.
- World Health Organization: Communicable Diseases. http://www.who.int/infectious-disease-news/.

Books and Articles

Abeku, Tarekegn A., "Response to Malaria Epidemics in Africa," *Emerging Infectious Diseases* 13, no. 5 (May 2007).
Carmichael, Mary, "The Unholy Trinity of World Health," *Newsweek*, July 2, 2007.
Hunter, Susan, *Black Death: AIDS in Africa*. New York: Palgrave Macmillan, 2004.
Stine, Gerald J., *AIDS Update 2007*. New York: McGraw-Hill, 2007.

Movies and Videos

Frontline: The Age of AIDS (1983). PBS Home Video.
Malaria: Fever Wars (2006). PBS Home Video.
Pandemic: Facing AIDS (2003). HBO Documentary Films.

Events

- AIDS Walk: A fund-raiser for AIDS research. Check Web site for dates. http://www.aidswalk.net/.
- World AIDS Day (December 1): Promoting awareness of the AIDS pandemic and encouraging projects to address the issue.

CHAPTER 3: Human Rights for All
Web Sites

- Afghanistan Independent: Human Rights Commission. http://www.aihrc.org.af/.
- Amnesty International. http://www.amnesty.org.
- Center for Economic and Social Rights. http://www.cesr.org/.
- Global Issues. http://www.globalissues.org/HumanRights/.

- Human Rights & Equal Opportunity Commission. http://www.hreoc.gov.au/.
- Human Rights Education Associates. http://www.hrea.org/.
- Human Rights Foundation. http://www.humanrights.co.nz/.
- Human Rights in China. http://www.hrichina.org/.
- Human Rights Watch. http://www.hrw.org/.
- Human Rights Web. http://www.hrweb.org/.
- Idealist: Action Without Borders. http://www.idealist.org/index.html.
- The Peace People: http://www.peacepeople.org/.
- Social Justice: A Journal of Crime, Conflict, & World Order. http://www.socialjusticejournal.org/.
- United Nations Human Rights. http://www.ohchr.org/.
- United Nations: Universal Declaration of Human Rights. http://www.unhchr.ch/udhr/index.htm.
- United Nations: World Conference Against Racism. http://www.un.org/WCAR/e-kit/minority.htm.
- Universal Rights Network. http://www.universalrights.net/.
- Youth for Human Rights International. http://www.youthforhumanrights.org/introduction/index.html.

Books and Articles

Barry, Brian, *Why Social Justice Matters*. Malden, MA: Polity, 2005.

Corrigan Maguire, Máiread, *Visions of Peace: Faith and Hope in Northern Ireland*. Maryknoll, NY: Orbis Publishing, 1999.

Gearon, Liam, *Freedom of Expression and Human Rights: Historical, Literary and Political Contexts*. Portland, OR: Sussex Academic, 2006.

Hunt, Lynn, *Inventing Human Rights: A History*. New York: W. W. Norton, 2007.

Reichert, Elisabeth, *Social Work and Human Rights: A Foundation for Policy and Practice*. New York: Columbia University Press, 2003.

Movies and Videos

Black Gold (2006). Fulcrum Productions.

God Sleeps in Rwanda (2005). Women Make Movies.

Memoria del Saqueo (*Memory of the Looting, a Social Genocide*) (2004). ADR Productions.

World According to Sesame Street, The (2006). International Street Productions.

Events

- Amnesty International Film Festival: A film festival dedicated to showcasing films related to human rights. http://www.amnestyusa.org/filmfest/.
- International Human Rights Day (December 10): A day to honor the adoption of the Universal Declaration of Human Rights. It's celebrated to promote human rights for all people. http://www.ohchr.org/EN/UDHR/Pages/60UDHRIntroduction.aspx.

CHAPTER 4: The Challenge of Extreme Poverty
Web Sites

- African Green Revolution: African Poverty—A Common Challenge. http://www.africangreenrevolution.com/.
- Amnesty International USA: Economic, Social, and Cultural Rights. http://www.amnestyusa.org/Economic_Social_Cultural_Rights/Poverty_and_Human_Rights/page.do?id=1102186&n1=3&n2=29&n3=230.
- Care: How Care Is Fighting Poverty. http://www.care.org/campaigns/poverty.asp.
- Earth Institute: Extreme Poverty—A Global Emergency. http://www.earth.columbia.edu/articles/view/1780.
- Franciscans International: Human Rights and Extreme Poverty. http://www.franciscansinternational.org/docs/statement.php?id=488.
- Global Issues: Causes of Poverty. http://www.globalissues.org/TradeRelated/Facts.asp.

- Global Poverty Forum: Links and Resources—Poverty and Development. http://globalpolicy.igc.org/socecon/develop/indexlinks.htm.
- Grameen Bank: Breaking the Vicious Cycle of Poverty Through Microcredit. http://www.grameen-info.org/bank/bcycle.html.
- Millennium Project: Fast Facts—The Faces of Poverty. http://www.unmillenniumproject.org/documents/3-MP-PovertyFacts-E.pdf.
- Millennium Villages. http://www.millenniumvillages.org/.
- NetAid: Global Poverty. http://www.netaid.org/global_poverty/global-poverty/.
- New Global Citizens: Global Challenge—Extreme Poverty. http://www.newglobalcitizens.org/extreme-poverty.html.
- Poverty.com. http://www.poverty.com/index.html.
- UNICEF: Millennium Development Goals. http://www.unicef.org/.
- United Nations Development Programme: Millennium Development Goals. http://www.undp.org/.
- United Nations Human Rights. http://www.ohchr.org/EN/Pages/.
- UNITeS. http://www.unites.org.

Books and Articles

Benn, Hillary, "Ending Extreme Poverty: A Challenge for Our Generation," June 28, 2006. http://www.csis.org/media/csis/events/060628-benn-remarks.pdf.

Collier, Paul, *The Bottom Billion: Why the Poorest Countries Are Failing and What Can Be Done About It.* New York: Oxford University Press, 2007.

International Food Policy Research Institute, "Economic Growth and the Challenge of Reducing Poverty and Undernutrition in Africa," April 2, 2004. http://www.ifpri.org/2020africaconference/program/day2summaries/ndulu.pdf.

Osava, Mario, "The Root Cause of Poverty in Latin America," September 12, 2005, Global Poverty Forum. http://globalpolicy.igc.org/socecon/inequal/income/2005/0912redis.htm.

Sachs, Jeffrey, *The End of Poverty: Economic Possibilities for Our Time.* New York: Penguin Books, 2005.

Yunus, Muhammad, *Banker to the Poor: Micro-Lending and the Battle Against World Poverty*, 2nd edition, New York: Public Affairs, 2003.

Movies and Videos

How Is Global Justice Possible? Thomas Pogge (2006). Chautauqua Lecture Series. http://www.chautauqua.eku.edu/video-archive/videos0506.php.

Journey to Planet Earth: Land of Plenty, Land of Want (2003). Public Television Series.

World on Fire (2004). Sarah McLachlan. http://www.worldonfire.ca/.

Events
- International Day for the Eradication of Poverty (October 17): Promoting awareness of global poverty and encouraging actions to work toward its eradication.

CHAPTER 5: The International Arms Trade
Web Sites
- Amnesty International USA: International Trade in Arms and Military Training. http://www.amnestyusa.org/Our_Issues/Arms_Trade/page.do?id=1011003&n1=3&n2=24.
- Arms Control Association. http://www.armscontrol.org/.
- BBC News: At-a-Glance—The International Arms Trade. http://news.bbc.co.uk/2/shared/spl/hi/pop_ups/03/world_the_international_arms_trade/html/1.stm.
- Campaign Against Arms Trade. http://www.caat.org.uk/.

- Carnegie Endowment for International Peace: Nonproliferation. http://www.carnegieendowment.org/npp/.
- Control Arms. http://www.controlarms.org/.
- Federation of American Scientists. http://fas.org/asmp/.
- Human Rights Watch: Arms. http://hrw.org/doc/?t=arms.
- International Action Network on Small Arms. http://www.iansa.org.
- International Campaign to Ban Landmines. http://www.icbl.org.
- Monterey Institute of International Studies: James Martin Center for Nonproliferation Studies. http://cns.miis.edu/.
- New American Foundation: American Strategy Program. http://www.newamerica.net/programs/american_strategy/arms_security.
- NGO Committee on Disarmament, Peace and Security: Disarmament Times. http://www.disarmtimes.org/.
- Pugwash. http://www.pugwash.org.
- Saferworld. http://www.saferworld.org.uk/.
- Stockholm International Peace Research Institute. http://www.sipri.org/.
- United Nations Office for Disarmament Affairs: Peace and Security Through Disarmament. http://disarmament.un.org/.

Books and Articles

Berrigan, Frida, "America—The World's Arms Pusher," *Los Angeles Times*, May 21, 2007. http://www.latimes.com/news/opinion/commentary/la-oe-berrigan21may21,1,2465404.story?ctrack=1&cset=true.

Berrigan, Frida, William D. Hartung, and Leslie Heffel, "Weapons at War 2005: Promoting Freedom or Fueling Conflict?," World Policy Institute Special Report, June 2005. http://www.worldpolicy.org/projects/arms/reports/wawjune2005.html.

Inbar, Efraim, and Benzion Zilberfarb, *The Politics and Economics of Defence Industries.* Portland, OR: Frank Cass, 1998.

Mother Jones, "U.S. Arms Sale: Arms Around the World." http://www.motherjones.com/news/special_reports/arms/.

Ohlson, Thomas, ed., *Arms Transfer Limitations and Third World Security.* New York: Oxford University Press, 1988.

Rotblat, Joseph, ed., *Scientists, the Arms Race, and Disarmament: A UNESCO/Pugwash Symposium.* London: Unipub, 1982.

United Nations General Assembly, "Arms Trade Treaty, 'Nuclear-Weapon-Free World,' Outer Space Arms Race Among Issues, as General Assembly Adopts 54 First Committee Texts," news release, December 6, 2006. http://www.un.org/News/Press/docs/2006/ga10547.doc.htm.

Movies and Videos

Atomic Café, The (1982). The Archives Project.
Do It for Uncle Graham (2004). Just Us Productions.
Lord of War (2005). Entertainment Manufacturing Company.
Making a Killing: Inside the International Arms Trade (2006). The DVD Group Inc.

Events

- Disarmament Week (October 24–30): A week to promote awareness of the need to recognize disarmament as a crucial component to the creation of a more peaceful and stable world.
- No Nukes Day (August 6): Held on the anniversary of the atomic bomb attack on Hiroshima, it is a day to raise awareness about the extreme danger of nuclear weapons.

CHAPTER 6: The Problem of Racism

Web Sites
- American Psychological Association Public Interest Directorate: Racism . . . and Psychology. http://www.apa.org/pi/oema/racism/.
- Anti-Defamation League: Rasicm. http://www.adl.org/hate-patrol/racism.asp.

- Chronology on the History of Slavery and Racism. http://innercity.org/holt/slavechron.html.
- Civil Rights Coalition for the 21st Century. http://www.civilrights.org/issues/hate/.
- Human Rights Watch: Racism & Human Rights. http://www.hrw.org/campaigns/race/.
- Irish Famine: Racism. http://www.nde.state.ne.us/SS/irish/unit_2.html.
- National Organization for Women: NOW and Racial and Ethnic Diversity. http://www.now.org/issues/diverse/.
- Race, Racism and the Law: Speaking Truth to Power!—Race, Racism and the Law. http://academic.udayton.edu/race/.
- Southern Poverty Law Center: http://www.splcenter.org/.
- United Nations World Conference Against Racism: http://www.un.org/WCAR.
- World Against Racism Foundation. http://www.endracism.org/.

Books and Articles

Altschiller, Donald, *Hate Crimes: A Reference Handbook*. Santa Barbara, CA: ABC-Clio, 1999.

Barnes, Annie S., *Everyday Racism: A Book for All Americans*. Naperville, IL: Sourcebooks, 2000.

Bonilla-Silva, Eduardo, *Racism Without Racists: Color-Blind Racism and the Persistence of Racial Inequality in the United States*, 2nd edition. Lanham: Rowman & Littlefield, 2006.

Frank, Anne, *The Diary of a Young Girl*. New York: Bantam, 1993.

Gould, Stephen Jay, *The Mismeasure of Man*. New York: W. W. Norton, 1996.

Lee, Martin A., *The Beast Reawakens: Fascism's Resurgence from Hitler's Spymasters to Today's Neo-Nazi Groups and Right-Wing Extremists*. New York: Routledge, 2000.

Movies and Videos

Ali (2001). Columbia Pictures Corporation.

American History X (1998). New Line Cinema.

Children of the Camps (1999). PBS Home Video.

Frontline: A Class Divided (1985). PBS Online. http://www.pbs.org/wgbh/pages/frontline/shows/divided/etc/view.html.

Remember the Titans (2000). Jerry Bruckheimer Productions.

Schindler's List (1993). Amblin Entertainment.

Triumph des Willens (*Triumph of the Will*) (1935). Leni Riefenstahl-Produktion.

Events
- International Day for the Elimination of Racism (March 21): A day to recall the dire consequences of racism, as well as to recall our obligation to work to end racial discrimination.

CHAPTER 7: The Crisis of the Environment
Web Sites
- AOL: Research & Learn—Earth Focus on Global Warming. http://reference.aol.com/planet-earth/global-warming.
- Care2. http://www.care2.com.
- EcoEarth.Info. http://www.ecoearth.info/.
- EnviroLink. http://www.envirolink.org/.
- Environment Directory. http://www.webdirectory.com/.
- Friends of the Earth International. http://www.foei.org/.
- Greenpeace. http://www.greenpeace.org/international/.
- National Center for Atmospheric Research. http://ncar.ucar.edu/.
- National Renewable Energy Laboratory. http://nrel.gov/.
- National Resources Defense Council. http://www.nrdc.org/.
- Nature Conservancy. http://www.nature.org/.
- Partner Regions. http://www.partnerregions.org/environmental-issues.html.

- Sierra Club. http://www.sierraclub.org/.
- TalkClimateChange. http://www.talkclimatechange.com/?gclid=CI-F6I6pgI8CFRuNYAod7gQEnw.
- Truthout: Environment. http://www.truthout.org/.
- U.S. Department of State: Environment and Conservation. http://www.state.gov/g/oes/env/.
- WWF for a Living Planet. http://www.panda.org/.

Books and Articles

Cairns, John Jr., "Scientists, Time Management, and the Global Environmental Crisis," Virginia Polytechnic Institute and State University, December 2005. http://johncairns.net/Papers/cairnsscientists.pdf.

Carson, Rachel, *Silent Spring*, 104th edition. Boston: Houghton Mifflin, 2002.

CBS News, "Global Warming May Spread Disease," June 20, 2002. http://www.cbsnews.com/stories/2002/06/20/tech/main512920.shtml.

Dumanoski, Dianne, "A Humanity Crisis," Global Environmental Action Conference, Summary of Remarks, October 12, 2002. http://www.ourstolenfuture.org/Commentary/DD/2001-1012DDhumanitycrisis.htm.

Gore, Al, *Earth in the Balance: Ecology and the Human Spirit*. New York: Rodale, 2006.

Lynas, Mark, *High Tide: The Truth About Our Climate Crisis*. New York: Picador, 2004.

Speth, James Gustave, *Red Sky at Morning: America and the Crisis of the Global Environment*, 2nd edition. New Haven: Yale University Press, 2005.

Tolba, Mostafa Kamal, *Saving Our Planet: Challenges and Hopes*. New York: Chapman & Hall, 1992.

Movies and Videos

China Syndrome, The: Creating a Controversy (2004). Columbia TriStar Home Entertainment.

Fire Down Below (1997). Seagal / Nasso Productions.

Inconvenient Truth, An (2006). Lawrence Bender Productions.

Events

- Earth Day (April 22): http://www.earthday.org/default.aspx.
- World Environment Day (June 5): A day to promote awareness of the environment and to focus on political action and attention. http://www.unep.org/wed/2007/english/.

CHAPTER 8: Equal Rights for Women

Web Sites

- Amnesty International USA: Children's Rights. http://www.amnestyusa.org/Our_Issues/Children/page.do?id=1011016&n1=3&n2=78.
- Amnesty International USA: Women's Human Rights. http://www.amnestyusa.org/Our_Issues/Womens_Human_Rights/page.do?id=1011012&n1=3&n2=39.
- Balkansnet.org. http://balkansnet.org/women1.html.
- Child Rights Information Network. http://www.crin.org/.
- Children's Rights: Children's Rights Today. http://www.childrensrights.org/.
- Conner Prairie: Women's Roles in the Late Nineteen Century. http://www.connerprairie.org/HistoryOnline/1880wom.html.
- Feminist.com: http://www.feminist.com/.
- Human Rights Education Associates: Children & Youth. http://www.hrea.org/learn/guides/children.html.
- Human Rights Watch: Children's Rights. http://hrw.org/doc/?t=children.
- Human Rights Watch: Women's Human Rights. http://hrw.org/wr2k1/women/women7.html.
- Human Rights Watch: Women's Rights. http://hrw.org/women/.
- National Organization for Women. http://www.now.org/.

- Public Broadcasting System: Global Connections. http://www.pbs.org/wgbh/globalconnections/mideast/questions/women/.
- Rights of Women. http://www.rightsofwomen.org.uk/.
- UNICEF. http://www.unicef.org/index.php.
- United Nations: Convention on the Rights of the Child. http://www.unhchr.ch/html/menu3/b/k2crc.htm.
- United Nations: Women Watch. http://www.un.org/womenwatch/.
- Unrepresented Nations and Peoples Organization. http://www.unpo.org/.
- V-Day. http://www.vday.org.

Books and Articles

Barlas, Asma. "Women's Rights and Role in Islam," paper presented at DePaul Law School, March 7, 2005. http://www.asmabarlas.com/TALKS/20050307_DePaul.pdf.

Baumgardner, Jennifer, and Amy Richards, *Manifesta: Young Women, Feminism, and the Future.* New York: Farrar, Straus, and Giroux, 2000.

hooks, bell, *Ain't I a Woman: Black Women and Feminism.* Cambridge, MA:South End Press, 1999.

Pardeck, John T., *Children's Rights: Policy and Practice*, 2nd edition. New York: Routledge, 2006.

Peters, Julie, and Andrea Wolper, eds., *Women's Rights, Human Rights: International Feminist Perspectives.* New York: Routledge, 1994.

UNICEF, *Children's Rights Bibliography.* New York: United Nations Publications, 2000.

Walker, Alice, *The Color Purple.* New York: Pocket Books, 1990.

Wollstonecraft, Mary, *A Vindication of the Rights of Woman.* New York: Penguin Classics, 2004.

Movies and Videos

Flying: Confessions of a Free Woman (2006). Zohe Film Production.

Iron Jawed Angels (2004). HBO.

Norma Rae (1979). Twentieth Century-Fox Film Corporation.

Real Women Have Curves (2002). HBO Independent Productions.

Wide Angle: Growing up Global (2002). PBS Home Video.

Events

- International Women's Day (March 8): A day to celebrate the collective power of women—past, present, and future.
- Universal Children's Day (November 20): A day of worldwide understanding between children, and a recognition of the day on which the Declaration of the Rights of the Child was adopted in 1959 and on which the Convention of the Rights of the Child was adopted in 1989.
- V-Day: A collection of various activities and performances focused on stopping violence against women and girls, held in the spring of every year. http://www.vday.org.

CHAPTER 9: Breaking the Cycle of Violence

Web Sites

- The Conflict Center: http://www.conflictcenter.org/.
- Institute for Peace and Justice: Five Steps to Break the Cycle of Violence. http://ipj-ppj.org/Reflections%20-%20Advocacy%20Suggestions%20-%20Lesson%20Plans/five_steps_to_break_the_cycle_of.htm.
- National Institute of Justice: An Update on the "Cycle of Violence." http://www.ncjrs.gov/pdffiles1/nij/184894.pdf.
- PeaceCenter: http://1.salsa.net/peace/.
- Project Pave: http://www.projectpave.org/.
- U.S. Department of Justice: Break the Cycle of Violence by Addressing Youth Victimization, Abuse, and Neglect. http://ojjdp.ncjrs.org/action/sec5.htm.

- U.S. Department of Justice: Breaking the Cycle of Violence. http://www.ojp.usdoj.gov/ovc/publications/factshts/pdftxt/monograph.pdf.
- USAID: Women Court Workers Breaking Cycle of Violence in South Africa. http://www.usaid.gov/sa/success1.9.html.
- Women's Aid: "The Cycle of Violence." http://www.womensaid.org.uk/page.asp?section=0001000100050014&itemTitle=Cycle+of+violence.

Books and Articles

Biggar, Nigel, *Burying the Past: Making Peace and Doing Justice After Civil Conflict*. Washington, D.C.: Georgetown University Press, 2003.

Bostic, Patrina A., "Taking Steps to Break the Cycle of Violence," *Herald-Tribune* (Sarasota, FL), October 8, 2007. http://www.heraldtribune.com/article/20071008/NEWS/710080342/-1/RSS01.

Bransten, Jeremy, "Russia: Military Conscripts Caught in Deadly 'Cycle of Violence,'" Radio Free Europe, October 21, 2004. http://www.rferl.org/featuresarticle/2004/10/BB73A9D2-32EE-4CD1-9D36-58C442E34A9E.html.

Grossman, Dave, and Gloria Degaetano, *Stop Teaching Our Kids to Kill: A Call to Action Against TV, Movie, and Video Game Violence*. New York: Crown, 1999.

Hazler, Richard J., *Breaking the Cycle of Violence: Interventions for Bullying and Victimization*. London: Taylor & Francis, 1996.

Hernandez, Arturo, *Peace in the Streets: Breaking the Cycle of Gang Violence*. Washington, D.C.: CWLA, 1998.

McDonald, Steven, "Breaking the Cycle of Violence: Why I Forgave My Assailant," 2004. http://www.primalspirit.com/ps3_2mcdonald_cycle_forgiveness.htm.

Minow, Martha, *Breaking the Cycles of Hatred: Memory, Law, and Repair*. Princeton, NJ: Princeton University Press, 2003.

Steinmetz, Suzanne K., *Cycle of Violence: Assertive, Aggressive, and Abusive Family Interactions*. New York: Praeger, 1977.

Movies and Videos

Hip-Hop: Beyond Beats and Rhymes. http://www.bhurt.com/beyondBeatsAndRhymes.php/.

The Shawshank Redemption (1994). Castle Rock Entertainment.

Events

- Stop the Violence Day (November 22): A day calling for an end to violence of all kinds.

CHAPTER 10: Creating Human Security

Web Sites

- Brookings Institution: Human Security and the Global Challenge of Internal Displacement. http://www.brookings.edu/views/speeches/deng/20000511.htm.
- Center for Unconventional Security Affairs: Coalition Advocating Human Security. http://www.cusa.uci.edu/cahs.htm.
- Center for Unconventional Security Affairs: Human Security. http://www.cusa.uci.edu/human_security.htm.
- Commission on Human Security. http://www.humansecurity-chs.org/.
- Human Security Centre: The Human Security Report 2005. http://www.humansecurityreport.info/.
- Human Security Network. http://www.humansecuritynetwork.org/links-e.php.
- Human Security Report Project. http://www.hsrgroup.org/index.php?option=com_frontpage&Itemid=1.
- Human Security Review: http://humansecurityreview.com/human-security-101/.
- International Atomic Energy Agency: Human Security and the Quest for Peace in the Middle East. http://www.iaea.org/NewsCenter/Statements/2006/ebsp2006n019.html.
- Nobel Women's Initiative. http://www.nobelwomensinitiative.org/.

- Project Ploughshares: The True Measure of Security. http://www.ploughshares.ca/libraries/Reduce/securityBWpdf.pdf.
- Social Science Research Council: Afghanistan and Threats to Human Security. http://www.ssrc.org/sept11/essays/rubin.htm.
- United Nations Institute for Disarmament Research: Human Security. http://www.unidir.org/html/en/human_security.html.
- United Nations Trust Fund for Human Security. http://ochaonline.un.org/humansecurity/QA/tabid/2188/Default.aspx.
- WomenWarPeace. http://womenwarpeace.org/.

Books and Articles

Berrigan, Frida, "Seeking True Security," *In These Times,* August 9, 2004. http://www.inthesetimes.com/article/904/.

Buttedahl, Paz, "Viewpoint: True Measures of Human Security," International Development Research Centre, December 12, 1997. http://archive.idrc.ca/books/reports/V223/view.html.

Dodds, Felix, Tim Pippard, and Mikhail Gorbachev, *Human and Environmental Security: An Agenda for Change.* Sterling, VA: Earthscan, 2005.

Henk, Dan, "Human Security: Relevance and Implications." *Parameters*, Summer 2005. http://www.carlisle.army.mil/usawc/Parameters/05summer/henk.pdf.

Human Security Centre, *Human Security Report: War and Peace in the 21st Century.* New York: Oxford University Press, 2005.

Nef, Jorge, *Human Security and Mutual Vulnerability: The Global Political Economy of Development and Underdevelopment*, 2nd edition. Ottawa: International Development Research Centre, November 1999.

Newman, Edward, and Oliver P. Richmond, *The United Nations and Human Security.* New York: Palgrave, 2001.

United Nations Office of the Special Adviser on Africa, "Human Security in Africa," December 2005. http://www.un.org/africa/osaa/reports/Human%20Security%20in%20Africa%20FINAL.pdf.

Movies and Videos

Chasing Freedom (2004). Blueprint Entertainment.

Life and Debt (2001). Tuff Gong Pictures.

Lost Children (2005). Dreamer Joint Venture Filmproduction.

Take, The (2004). Barna-Alper Production.

Events

- Human Rights Day (December 10): A day to promote freedom, security, and peace in all nations.
- International Human Solidarity Day (November 10): A day to recognize the connectedness between all human beings, and to work to improve all people's situations.

CHAPTER 11: The Struggle for Freedom in Burma

Web Sites

- Altsean Burma. http://www.altsean.org/.
- Amnesty International. http://www.amnesty.org.
- BBC: Asia–Pacific. http://news.bbc.co.uk/2/hi/asia-pacific/default.stm.
- Burma Campaign United Kingdom. http://www.burmacampaign.org.uk.
- Burma News Ladder. http://burma.newsladder.net/.
- Canadian Friends of Burma: History of Burma. http://www.cfob.org/HistoryofBurma/historyOfBurma.shtml.
- CIA: The World Factbook. http://www.cia.gov/library/publications/the-world-factbook/geos/bm.html.

- Democratic Voice of Burma. http://english.dvb.no/.
- Human Rights Watch: Asia. http://hrw.org/doc/?t=asia&c=burma.
- Irrawaddy: Covering Burma and Southeast Asia. http://www.irrawaddy.org/.
- Mae Tao Clinic. http://www.maetaoclinic.org/.
- Nobel Institute: Aung San Suu Kyi. http://nobelprize.org/nobel_prizes/peace/laureates/1991/kyi-bio.html.
- Online Burma Library. http://www.burmalibrary.org/.
- Open Society Institute. http://www.soros.org/initiatives/bpsai.
- Shan Women's Action Network. http://www.shanwomen.org.
- Thailand Burma Border Consortium. http://www.tbbc.org/.
- U.S. Campaign for Burma. http://uscampaignforburma.org/.
- WashingtonPost.com: Burma Editorials. http://pqasb.pqarchiver.com/washingtonpost/results.html?num=25& datetype=7&QryTxt=Burma%20editorials&sortby=REVERSE_CHRON.
- WashingtonPost.com: Myanmar—News Stories. http://www.washingtonpost.com/ac2/wp-dyn/NewsSearch?st=Burma&fn=&sfn=&sa=ns&cp=&hl=false&sb=-1&sd=&ed=&blt=&sdt=&x=12&y=13#.
- Yahoo! News: Myanmar—News Stories. http://news.yahoo.com/fc/World/Myanmar/news_stories/12.

Books and Articles

Aung San Suu Kyi, *Freedom from Fear*. New York: Penguin Books, 1995.

———, *Letters from Burma*. New Delhi: Irrawaddy Publications, 1997.

Aung San Suu Kyi and Alan Clements, *The Voice of Hope*. New York; Seven Stories Press, 1997.

Connolly, Karen, *Lizard Cage*. New York, Nan A. Talese, 2007.

Fink, Christina, *Living Silence: Burma Under Military Rule*. New York: Zed Books, 2001.

Larkin, Emma, *The Secret Histories: Finding George Orwell in a Burmese Teashop*. London: John Murray, 2004.

Ling, Bettina, *Aung San Suu Kyi: Standing Up for Democracy in Burma*. New York: Feminist Press at the City University of New York, 1999.

Lintner, Bertil, *Outrage: Burma's Struggle for Democracy*. London: White Lotus, 1990.

Mawdsley, James, *The Heart Must Break: The Fight for Truth and Democracy in Burma*. London: Century, 2001.

Smith Martin, *Burma: Insurgency and the Politics of Ethnicity*. New York: Zed Books, 1991.

Thwe, Pascal Khoo, *From the Land of Green Ghosts: A Burmese Odyssey*. London: HarperCollins, 2002.

Movies and Videos

Beyond Rangoon (1995). Castle Rock Entertainment.

Burma—Inside the Secret City (2006). Journeyman Pictures. http://video.google.com/videoplay?docid =7154821831490310740.

Burma's Secret War (2006). http://video.google.com/videoplay?docid=-7501284530305141078.

In Hiding: A Year of Survival Under the Burma Army 2004–2005 (2005). Front Films & Free Burma Rangers.